Welcome to

THE
EVERYTHING
PARENT'S GUIDES ®

As a parent, you're swamped with conflicting advice and parenting techniques that tell you what is best for your child. THE EVERYTHING® PARENT'S GUIDES get right to the point about specific issues. They give you the most recent, up-to-date information on parenting trends, behavior issues, and health concerns—providing you with a detailed resource to help you ease your parenting anxieties.

THE EVERYTHING® PARENT'S GUIDES are an extension of the bestselling Everything® series in the parenting category. These family-friendly books are designed to be a one-stop guide for parents. If you want authoritative information on specific topics not fully covered in other books, THE EVERYTHING® PARENT'S GUIDES are the perfect resource to ensure that you raise a healthy, confident child.

Visit the entire Everything® series at *www.everything.com*

THE
EVERYTHING®
PARENT'S GUIDE TO
Raising Siblings

Dear Reader,

In too many households, children's spats, squabbles, teasing, tattling, bickering, dickering, and arguments undermine the quality of family life. Popular wisdom has it that most sibling conflict stems from rivalry. Many people think an inborn urge to compete causes most toddler upsets, preschool children's clashes, elementary school arguments, teenage sibling fights, and adult sibling rifts. Since popular wisdom has it that sibling rivalry is innate, many parents think there isn't much they can do to shore up their children's relationships and help them get along. Many professionals urge parents to ignore as much of the unpleasantness as possible and keep a stiff upper lip amid the shrieks of "it's my turn" and "it's not fair!" But ignoring problems doesn't make them go away; they need to be addressed and solved! Research shows that parents are the key factors in how well children get along.

What unites siblings is the bond that develops as they interact and take care of one another. But little humans aren't born knowing how to serve as helpmates, much less as one another's companions and friends. Even dear friends step on one another's toes from time to time. Children must be taught to resolve their disputes without damaging their relationship. Once you know how to nurture sibling bonds and help children of all ages build and maintain positive relationships, you will be ready to tackle the project at home. It is in your power to make your one-big-happy-family dream come true!

Dr. *[signature]*

THE

EVERYTHING®

PARENT'S GUIDE TO

RAISING
SIBLINGS

Eliminate rivalry, avoid
favoritism, and keep the peace

Linda Sonna, Ph.D.

Adams Media
Avon, Massachusetts

Dedication

To my brothers, William Lee Sonna, Larry Allen Sonna, and Mark-Brian Sonna.
And to you, Mom.

• • •

Publishing Director: Gary M. Krebs
Associate Managing Editor: Laura M. Daly
Associate Copy Chief: Brett Palana-Shanahan
Acquisitions Editor: Kate Burgo
Development Editor: Katie McDonough
Associate Production Editor: Casey Ebert

Director of Manufacturing: Susan Beale
Associate Director of Production:
   Michelle Roy Kelly
Cover Design: Paul Beatrice, Erick DaCosta,
   Matt LeBlanc
Design and Layout: Colleen Cunningham,
   Holly Curtis, Sorae Lee

An Everything® Series Book.
Everything® and everything.com® are registered trademarks of F+W Publications, Inc.

Published by Adams Media, an F+W Publications Company
57 Littlefield Street, Avon, MA 02322 U.S.A.
www.adamsmedia.com

ISBN: 1-59337-537-9

Printed in the United States of America.

J I H G F E D C B A

Library of Congress Cataloging-in-Publication Data
Sonna, Linda.
The everything parent's guide to raising siblings : tips to eliminate
rivalry, avoid favoritism, and keep the peace / Linda Sonna.
   p. cm. -- (An everything series book)
ISBN 1-59337-537-9
1. Child rearing. 2. Sibling rivalry. 3. Brothers and sisters. I. Title. II. Series: Everything series.

HQ769.S5775 2006
649'.143--dc22
               2005033327

All the examples and dialogues used in this book are fictional, and have
been created by the author to illustrate disciplinary situations.

sib•ling (sĭb´lĭng)

▶ *n.* Children who spend enough time together to consider themselves to be sisters, brothers, or brothers and sisters.

Acknowledgments

Special thanks is given to research specialist David Donaldson for his invaluable assistance, to Lyn Bleiler for her contributions to the chapters on only children and multiples, to Michele Potter for her research on superstar siblings, and to Carol Parker for her contributions to the chapters on adopted siblings and sibling loss. Thanks is also given to Lois Mark for her extensive editorial help throughout, as well as to Beverly Stough, Pam Paradee, Norlene Gregory, Kara Elizabeth Potter, Terry Barsano, Brinn Colenda, Mark-Brian Sonna, and Dr. Larry Sonna for reviewing individual chapters. For their suggestions, support, and stories about siblings and only children, I am grateful to Chris Robert, Denise Kunesh, Cynthia Holmire, Ken Eaves, Joel Mockovciak, Margie Henzel, Zandi Richardson, Isaiah Potter, Kyler Potter, Suzanne Pierce, Jakob Rosing, and Jack Derby. Thanks to Zion Gía, Michelle Gía, and Wesley Barnes for demonstrating that siblings need not have similar personalities or interests to be close.

• • •

Contents

Introduction xiii

CHAPTER 1: **Sibling Myths and Realities** 1
Myth 1: Siblings Need to Be Compatible to Get Along 1
Myth 2: Genes Determine How Siblings Behave 3
Myth 3: Siblings Aren't That Important 5
Myth 4: Sibling Rivalry Is Innate 8
Myth 5: Competing with Siblings Is Healthy. 9
Myth 6: Sibling Responsibilities Are Harmful. 11

CHAPTER 2: **Nurturing Sibling Relationships** 15
Parent Role Models. 15
Boosting Emotional Intelligence 17
Teaching Respect 20
Teaching Empathy. 21
Teaching Compassion 25
Random Acts of Kindness 26

CHAPTER 3: **Baby, Toddler, and Preschool Siblings** 29
The New Baby Sibling. 29
Preparing for a New Sibling 30
Toddler Jealousy 32
Big Toddler Brothers and Sisters 35
Playmates. 36
Baby, Toddler, and Preschooler Clashes 36
Toddlers and Preschoolers as Younger Siblings 38

CHAPTER 4: *Preschool, Tween, Teen, and Young Adult Siblings*. 41

Through the Years. 41

Preschool Siblings. 43

Elementary School Children 45

Young Teenage Siblings 48

Older Teenage Siblings. 49

Young Adult Siblings. 50

CHAPTER 5: *Ending Bickering and Dickering* 51

Family Meetings 51

Goals for Family Meetings 52

Scheduling Family Meetings 53

Preparing for Family Meetings. 54

Involving Children. 57

Creative Problem-Solving. 58

Family Decisions. 60

Family Fun 61

CHAPTER 6: *Controlling Competition and Rivalry* 63

Young Rivals 63

Comparing Siblings. 65

Mom's Favorite, Dad's Darling 67

Every Parent's Favorite Child 69

Fair Treatment? 70

Treating Everyone Alike 71

CHAPTER 7: *Settling Squabbles*. 73

Sibling Strife. 73

The Family Court. 74

Standard Advice for Parents 75

Producing Fair Verdicts 76

Hearing Cases 77

Making Value Judgments 78

Sibling Privileges and Responsibilities 80

Teaching New Values 82

CHAPTER 8: **Tackling Teasing and Tattling** 85

Siblings and Self-Image 85

Living Their Labels 86

Reversing Negative Dynamics 87

Joking Versus Teasing 88

Tackling Teasing 89

Time-out 89

Tackling Tattling 94

CHAPTER 9: **Uniting Siblings** 97

Forging a Bond 97

United They Stand 99

Competition Versus Cooperation 99

Competition Run Amok 100

Team-building for Siblings 102

Building Trust 104

Cooperative Games 106

CHAPTER 10: **Raising Super Siblings** 109

Finding a Niche 109

The Parent Factor 110

On the Same Path 112

Superstar Sibling Rivalry 114

In the Shadow of a Supersibling 117

Superstar Siblings 120

CHAPTER 11: **Birth Order Blues** 125

Perfectionists, Peacemakers, and Clowns 125

Personality, Birth Order, and Spacing 127

Parenting the Firstborn 128

The Firstborn Personality 129
Parenting Middle Children 130
The Dilemma for Middle Children 131
Helping Middle Children 134
Parenting the Lastborn 135
Helping Lastborns 137

CHAPTER 12: *Surrogate Siblings* 139
Lonely Onlies? 139
Onlies on the Rise 141
Myths and Misconceptions 142
Overindulgence 144
Setting Limits 145
The Burden for Onlies 147
Strengthening Social Skills 148
Foster Siblings 151
Famous Only Children 154

CHAPTER 13: *Stepsiblings* 157
Identifying Issues 157
Finishing Old Business 158
Advice and Consent? 160
Engaging Minor Children 161
Engaging Adult Children 162
A New Family Identity 163
Stepparenting Challenges 163
Solidifying Blended Family Relationships 165
The New Baby 167

CHAPTER 14: *Large Families* 169
Supersizing Benefits 169
Better by the Dozen 171
Rethinking Family Values 173
Parenting Large Families 176

Big Family Blues 177
Chaos Control 179
Taking Care of You 181

CHAPTER 15: *Twins and More* 183
Separate but Equal 183
Multiples on the Rise 185
The Biology of Multiples. 186
Preparing for Multiples. 187
Welcome Home! 189
Competition. 191
Issues in Psychological Development. 191
Identity Formation. 193
Notable Multiples 195

CHAPTER 16: *Adopted Siblings* 197
Preparing for a New Sibling 197
Changing Roles 203
Adopting a Baby 205
Adopting Sibling Groups. 206
Famous Adoptees 208

CHAPTER 17: *Losing a Sibling* 213
When a Sibling Dies 213
Grief and Mourning. 214
Stages of Grief 216
Helping Siblings Mourn 218
Sibling Suicide. 221

CHAPTER 18: *Changing Sibling Roles* 225
Entrenched Sibling Roles 225
Creating Sibling Roles. 226
Sibling Abuse. 228

Persecutors and Victims. 229

The Bad Influence. 233

Parentified Children 234

New Birth Order Roles 236

CHAPTER 19: *Special Needs Siblings* 239

Tangled Emotions 239

Life Lessons for Siblings 241

Disturbed Family Dynamics. 242

Nurturing Your Other Children 245

Information Gaps and Overloads 247

Sibling Social Relationships. 249

Expectations for Siblings 251

Help for Troubled Siblings 252

CHAPTER 20: *Healing Adult Sibling Relationships* 253

The Child Inside 253

Adult Sibling Conflicts. 255

Reliving the Past 256

Changing Family Dynamics. 258

The Family Business 260

Adult Sibling No-nos 262

Improving Adult Relationships 263

Truces and Treaties. 265

A Legacy for Adult Siblings. 266

APPENDIX A: *Resources for Parents* 269

APPENDIX B: *Organizations* 275

INDEX 277

Introduction

U ntil the first few decades of the 1900s, most brothers and
sisters enjoyed warm, loving relationships. In fact, many siblings were closer to one another than to their parents. The
downhill slide in sibling relationships began when the theories of
the father of psychiatry, Sigmund Freud, became popular. As Freud
studied adults suffering from serious mental illness, he noted that sibling rivalry was a recurring theme in their family backgrounds. Freud
maintained that every child's instinctive goal is to gain exclusive
possession of his mother. Even siblings who don't actively compete
for her attention harbor terrible desires buried deep in their unconscious to oust potential rivals from the family nest.

At first, Freud's notions struck the general public as ridiculous. It
was obvious that most siblings were protective and loving, and they
served as lifelong companions and friends. But Freud maintained
that small sibling conflicts over minor issues betrayed the dangerous
emotions swirling inside. Eventually, psychiatrists embraced Freud's
theories. As his views gained in popularity, parents became
afraid. The biblical story of Cain and Abel seemed to prove
that nasty bouts of sibling rivalry could be triggered unex-
pectedly with disastrous consequences. Small sibling
squabbles set off alarm bells in parents' minds. Parents
began protecting their children from one another and
tried to suppress conflict for fear it might turn vicious.

This weakened sibling bonds and made it harder for youngsters to settle their disputes. Sibling relationships began to deteriorate.

In the 1960s, psychologists agreed that harboring negative emotions caused lots of problems but believed that suppressing anger made matters worse. Mental health professionals used the example of a pressure cooker to explain how keeping a lid on anger could cause uncontrolled, out-of-the-blue explosions. The way to prevent them was to vent when tensions started to heat up. They viewed sibling squabbles and spats as serving as psychological safety valves. "Let it all hang out" became a popular strategy for building better relationships. When children were perturbed or irritated with one another, many parents encouraged them to say exactly what was on their minds. Professionals soon discovered that words spoken in anger were more likely to undermine relationships than improve them. Psychologists stopped recommending that people vent anger to prevent explosions. Instead, anger was likened to garbage, and people were warned about the danger of dumping it on loved ones. Behavioral psychologists discovered that rewarding good behavior and withholding rewards when children misbehaved could eliminate most problems. Parents were told to reward siblings when they got along and ignore the rest. Some children's behavior improved, but ignoring troublesome behavior doesn't necessarily make it go away and certainly doesn't teach children how to solve conflicts. Squabbles became more frequent and intense in many homes.

To explain why so many siblings who lived in luxury battled over bread crumbs, Darwin suggested that the age-old struggle for the survival of the fittest was encoded in children's genes. He maintained that the urge to outdo others was inborn, and there was no way that parents could hope to eliminate competitive struggles. Since competing at home prepared children to compete and win in the bigger game of life, siblings' determination to outdo one another might actually be beneficial. The theory made sense, and most parents came to accept a lot of conflict as normal, if very trying. Some encouraged their children to compete, hoping to prepare them for the dog-eat-dog world they would encounter as adults. But the notion that human possess an inborn urge to compete was in error. Sibling infighting does not give human families an advantage. In *The Science of Good and Evil,* author Michael Shermer points out that the time-tested strategy for survival has been for family members to cooperate and work together. In this way, they can more effectively compete with predators and other families when food and water are scarce.

Outdated psychiatric theories and misunderstandings about evolutionary theory continue to color professionals' opinions about the challenges modern families face. In *Linked for Life: How Our Siblings Affect Our Lives,* author Marvin D. Todd writes, "Sisters and brothers respond to each other with rivalry, hate, love, envy, jealousy, resentment and more." This statement would shock most parents around the globe, just as Freud's negative statements shocked parents in the early 1900s. But now that so many siblings relate more like enemies than friends, many parents consider advice from authors like Katherine Schlaerth very sensible. In her book, *Raising a Large Family,* Schlaerth states that sibling fights are to be expected and that family rules against fighting will be impossible to enforce. Like most parenting experts, Schlaerth seems to assume that because infighting among U.S. toddlers, tweens, and teens is now so common, it has always gone on everywhere. Ignorance about the past and about the current state of sibling relationships in most of the world have led many people to believe that the problems have always existed and are universal.

The first step to helping your children get along is to ignore friends and experts who say that sibling rivalry is a given and that sibling relationships are destined to be poor. The next step is to help your children bond and form strong positive attachments. Finally, you must teach siblings how to resolve their disagreements and settle their conflicts so they can sustain healthy relationships. Don't doubt your ability to help your children grow in understanding and love. Parents around the world have been succeeding since the beginning of time. So can you.

CHAPTER 1

Sibling Myths and Realities

C ontrary to what many people believe, children don't need compatible personalities or similar interests to get along. Experiences do more to shape personality than genes, and as siblings interact, they mold and shape one another. Sibling rivalry is not innate. Although sibling competition can be fun and inspires many children to improve, it can also be very negative and destructive. Children are not harmed by being actively involved in taking care of one another, as many people think. Caregiving enhances bonding.

Myth 1: Siblings Need to Be Compatible to Get Along

Many parenting books and articles say that some siblings simply cannot get along because they lack common interests and their personalities are incompatible. Millions of siblings like Rebecca and her brother prove that siblings can be as different as night and day and still enjoy one another as friends and companions.

> *There was only a two-year age difference between Henry and me. But we don't even look alike, and our personalities are totally different. As kids, Henry was a daredevil, and I didn't like to roughhouse. There wasn't anybody else near our age in our neighborhood; so, if we wanted a playmate, we had to make do with one another. When we rollerskated or rode bikes, Henry jumped curbs, raced, and did*

tricks while I coasted along. That didn't stop us from having fun. When Henry wanted to build a tree house, he had to do it on the ground because I was afraid of heights. When we finished, Henry wanted to turn it into a jail and play cops and robbers. I liked to line up my dolls and play school or house. We started off taking turns, doing things his way for awhile and then switching. Then we combined our games. I was the teacher in an old-time schoolhouse, and my dolls were my students. We pretended a robber broke in, and Henry rescued us. When I was the policeman, I put Henry in jail and sentenced him to do homework and take tests. We had a lot of fun.

Henry was kind of wild as a teenager. He dropped out of high school and worked at odd jobs before getting his GED and joining the military. I went straight to college and got a degree. We still don't really have much in common. I'm married with kids, and Henry is single. He only likes action and thriller movies, which I really can't stand. He bowls, fishes, hunts, likes football, and keeps up with the news. I could care less about those things. But I can tell him anything. When I have a problem, Henry gives me a lot of very sound, down-to-earth, brotherly advice. Often, it's me giving him sisterly advice about women. I guess our only real shared interest is each other and our parents. That seems to be enough.

Like Rebecca and Henry, all siblings have at least two common interests: their relationship and their families. Many children with other shared interests might seem to have what it takes to get along but relate like rivals, not friends. No personalities are essentially incompatible, and even children with many of the same personality traits don't get along well. Many strong-willed children with similar personalities butt heads because they try to dominate and control one another. Rather than having their parents write them off as incompatible, they need to be taught how to compromise, negotiate, and take turns making decisions. Meanwhile, mild-mannered youngsters who are as alike as two peas in a pod may invent disagreements to try to establish separate identities. Their difficulties getting along are often a reaction to all the pressure to be exactly alike.

 **Fact**

> Sibling relationships typically outlast all others, enduring longer than relationships with children, parents, and spouses. Because childhood experiences are so formative, siblings help mold and shape one another's personalities. Many siblings are deeply involved in providing end-of-life care.

Myth 2: Genes Determine How Siblings Behave

In the last few decades, news flashes from genetic researchers have given rise to the myth that heredity dictates everything from eye color to alcoholism. That should make siblings more alike than different because each youngster inherits half of his genes from his mother and half from his father. But it doesn't. Even identical twins with identical genes react differently to the very same experiences. They have different tastes in everything from clothes to hobbies to food. Many excel in different sports and academic subjects. Although you are likely to note some similarities among your children, the differences between your newborns are likely to be pronounced. You can expect them to differ even more as separate life experiences mold and shape them.

The findings that geneticists find so impressive are likely to leave the average man and woman wondering what the excitement is all about. The fact that siblings are 50 percent alike regarding a certain trait also means that they are 50 percent different. In *Separate Lives: Why Siblings Are So Different*, authors Judy Dunn and Robert Plomin point out that one of the areas of strongest similarity for siblings of the same sex is height. But even here, the similarities hardly seem meaningful. Francis Galton found that the average difference between the brothers he studied was only 1.5 inches and that between unrelated boys the difference was about 2.5 inches. So brothers are more similar. However, the author goes on to ask, "But how important is the difference between 1.5 and 2.5 inches?" Of course, these figures are merely group averages. When siblings from the same family are examined, their differences tend to be much more dramatic. The average difference in height for the brothers Galton studied was only 1.5 inches, but when individual pairs of brothers were measured, their height varied from under one-half inch to more than one foot!

Authors Dunn and Plomin also point out that 80 percent of siblings have differences in the color of their eyes that can be easily detected. For other physical features such as hair color and curliness, the detectable differences rise to 90 percent. If one sibling suffers from hay fever, there is only a 14 percent chance that a sibling will also be afflicted. Allergies are believed to be partly hereditary, but when another child is chosen at random from the general population, the chance of that child having hay fever is also 14 percent!

 ## Essential

Because siblings are different, they react differently to the very same experiences. The child-rearing methods that work for one may not work for another. You need to treat each child differently: like an individual!

Genes are not written in stone, as most high school biology students conclude when they learn how baby peas inherit traits from their parents. Genes turn on and off all the time in response to the environment. For example, too much sun exposure can turn on the genes that cause skin cancer. So even if both children inherit the skin cancer gene, parents who insist that their children slather on sunscreen can help protect them from developing what is in essence a genetic disease.

Many parents believe they can do nothing about their children's poor relationships. "They have strong-willed temperaments," parents say. "One is especially spirited. Even as a baby, he was stubborn and had a fit if he didn't get his way." "My son is a sweet, easy-going sort," other parents report. "He and the baby just took to each other right away." In the realm of behavior, siblings' degree of similarity for personality traits, mental disorders, and even IQ are so low as to be quite useless for purposes of prediction. Knowing one child's peculiarities, problems, or intellect won't help you guess whether another of your children will be similarly blessed or cursed. That even goes for schizophrenia, which strikes both members of sets of identical twins often enough for doctors to have declared it a genetic mental illness. Identical twins have all the same genes; yet in over half of the identical twin sets in which one twin has schizophrenia, the other twin does not. Chronic stress and trauma are believed to turn on the genes that cause certain mental and behavioral disorders, but the roller-coaster ride that one child considers fun may be much too scary for another. Each parenting decision must be tailor-made for each child.

Question?

My child has a genetic disorder and wants a sibling. Dare I have another?
Ask your doctor how often the disorder occurs in the general population and among siblings. Ask if there are other factors that increase the risk, such as being an older mother or having had previous pregnancies. Then ask him to help you calculate the risk.

Myth 3: Siblings Aren't That Important

When Freudian theories became popular early in the 1900s, mothers came to be viewed as critical for their children to the virtual exclusion of everyone else, including fathers. Freud regarded siblings as more of a threat than an asset. Many parents in countries where he had an influence wonder whether siblings actually benefit children. Researchers haven't provided many clear-cut answers. Following siblings across the decades to see how their personalities and relationships unfold poses daunting challenges. The results of the few research studies that have been carried out are hard to assess. Most investigations are conducted in the United States, where many children have very poor relationships. Statistical studies are in vogue, and there's no way to calculate the benefit of crawling into an older sibling's bed when the monsters living in the closet slip into a darkened bedroom or penetrate a dream. Many children make one another miserable because they fight over toys and won't share. But they share worries when their parents drink or are late getting home, and undoubtedly, that has far more value. Many children say they would rather be an only child because their sibling is so difficult. But would they feel better spending their after school hours alone in an empty house while their parents are at work or prefer to play those endless video games by themselves?

The little research that has been done shows that the effects of having siblings are mixed. Children who put one another down erode one another's self-esteem. Positive sibling relationships protect against some of the negative effects of certain childhood traumas, such as parental divorce and child maltreatment, according to a 2003 article in the *Journal of the American Academy of Child and Adolescent Psychiatry.*

Intellectual Stimulation

Later-born children learn a lot from watching and interacting with their older siblings. Younger children tend to finish potty training earlier, thanks to their sibling role models. It was long assumed that the youngest sibling in a pair reaps most of the intellectual benefits, but a 2005 study found that "First-born children seem to learn from teaching their younger siblings, contrary to the common notion that younger children benefit by learning from their elders," according to Kjell Salvanes, one of the authors of an article published in Harvard's *Quarterly Journal of Economics.* This is consistent with findings that a good way to boost academic achievement is to tutor someone else. Peer tutors typically learn about as much as they teach.

Social Stimulation

Several studies have concluded that siblings may actually play a larger role than parents in teaching important social skills. By learning to share and take turns with siblings, children learn the interpersonal skills needed to maintain good relationships with classmates and other peers. Siblings provide more compelling lessons than parents about the need to be considerate and respectful of other peoples' boundaries and personal possessions. That's because children tend to be less tolerant of misbehavior and are quicker to impose consequences than adults, who commonly back down and give in when a persistent youngster begs, wheedles, and whines. From the toddler who pushes a brother to punish him for grabbing a toy to the teen who slams his bedroom door in his sister's face to keep her out, siblings deliver messages that are hard to miss. They are more consistent about confronting misbehavior than parents, who often look the other way.

Alert!

However well or poorly siblings get along, by simply being present during one another's formative years, they serve as witnesses to what occurred and provide vital links to the past. That helps children stay connected to themselves.

Siblings can also have a decidedly negative influence on one other. A host of researchers has found that negative or coercive sibling interactions lead to problem behavior in other social settings. G. R. Patterson and L. Bank reported in *Sibling Relationships: Their Causes and Consequences* that if parents fail to monitor their children, don't discipline them to control aggressive interactions, and don't reinforce their positive attempts to relate to one another, all of the siblings tend to become increasingly aggressive and antisocial. A lot of sibling conflict during early childhood leads to increased acting out and poorer social relationships in elementary school. Negative sibling exchanges during elementary school are associated with antisocial behavior in adolescence and with criminal activity in young adult life, according to research conducted by L. Bank and B. Burraston and reported in 2001 in the *Journal of Community Psychology*. The lessons siblings teach one another about getting along with others can be very destructive. You need to be in charge to be sure that your children's lessons are good ones!

Myth 4: Sibling Rivalry Is Innate

Sociobiologists have observed that in other species sibling rivalry is often fierce from the start. Baby birds push one another aside when a parent arrives with food, caring only about their own survival. The life-and-death struggle seems heartless and brutal, but given that survival is at stake, it is understandable that the war for worms would be waged without empathy or compassion. Humans are animals, too, and it seems reasonable to assume that little Homo sapiens would also be genetically programmed to engage in a lot of no-holds-barred competition. This would certainly explain why so many U.S. siblings work overtime to land the biggest piece of cake and the first place in line at the zoo. But in most human cultures, sibling rivalry is not considered normal at all, perhaps because youngsters are not treated like peers. When they act like peers, they are helped to embrace their role as older and younger siblings by being taught how to behave toward one another. It is generally understood that siblings get upset with one another for many different reasons. Caring for one another is regarded as an important responsibility. Even two-year-olds gladly dedicate themselves to tending to the baby and are proud of their ability to help him. Older children trot off to school hand in hand and play together after school. They are friends, but there is little squabbling because older children are in charge. They have been carefully taught how to lead without bossing. Adult siblings tend to be more egalitarian; though in some cultures, the firstborn continues to take the lead in making family decisions. Adult siblings are friends and may help raise one another's children. Aging siblings take care of one another when they are ill or injured and provide one another's end-of-life care.

The biblical story of Cain and Abel describes how sibling rivalry reared its ugly head when one child's offerings were praised and accepted, while his brother's were scorned and rejected. Rivalry has long been a part of the human condition, but most cultures have many safeguards to ensure that it doesn't poison families. Many of the traditional protections have vanished in industrialized nations, where traditional sibling hierarchies have been toppled and children are commonly raised to relate to one another as peers. Nevertheless, the problem of sibling rivalry is vastly overblown, according to *The Sibling Bond.* Authors Stephen P. Bank and Michael D. Kahn state, "What used to be called sibling rivalry still does occur, but it is often due to the disorganization and fragmentation of the American family in a world of jarring and confusing change." Children growing up in chaotic homes are more likely to fight with one another, as well as with their classmates, teachers, neighbors, coaches, employers, and everyone else. Their stormy sibling relationships undoubtedly add to their turmoil, but it really doesn't make sense to attribute their sibling arguments and ill will to rivalry. But because parents are so sensitive to the problem of rivalry, many imagine it to be the cause of virtually every sibling clash.

Even in the United States, children tend to leave their childhood squabbles behind in adolescence and turn to one another as companions, confidantes, and friends. They help raise one another's children, aid one another during times of trouble, share responsibilities for aging parents, and care for one another in their own old age. They function as lifelong sources of love, nurturance, and support.

Myth 5: Competing with Siblings Is Healthy

In *Beyond Good and Evil: Why People Cheat, Gossip, Care, Share, and Follow the Golden Rule*, author Michael Shermer reviews the age-old struggle for survival of the fittest and comes up with a different conclusion. He notes that when humans first appeared on earth about

100,000 years ago, they lived in small bands of related individuals. Tribes are a relatively recent development, having appeared about 10,000 years ago. Humans didn't begin to form larger social groupings until the last 5,000 years, when they banned together in chiefdoms, states, and finally empires. Still, the family remains the basic social institution, existing in all cultures present and past. Although there have always been wars over food, land, water, and other resources that people regarded as essential, each family had a better chance of surviving if its members worked together. That meant cooperating and holding infighting to a minimum. Competition with other families and with other species aided survival. But individuals were more likely to survive if they were part of a family that could work cooperatively. It is now understood that the same holds true for many other species. Even lion cubs cuddle together for warmth and play together to practice the skills they will need to tend to families of their own. They may appear quite fierce as they stage mock battles, but they avoid using their sharp teeth and claws to hurt one another.

Alert!

The family is the most basic social institution, and it has withstood the test of time. When modern families fail, the cause is usually internal. Eliminate destructive infighting, control competition among family members, and teach siblings to cooperate.

To help ensure that individuals don't put their personal interests above the common good, families have rules, just as larger human social institutions have laws to promote harmony and lessen strife among their members. Otherwise, infighting saps too many resources, and the members split into warring factions or are defeated by outsiders. Even in the dog-eat-dog world of the modern corporation, managers now recognize that unfettered competition is destructive when it occurs in-house because individual employees or departments end up functioning like rivals. Employee softball teams provide opportunities for people to compete in ways that won't hurt the company. Sales groups may compete with other districts or regions, but competition within a team is bad for the bottom line. Productivity improves when employees who must work together to do their jobs get along. Cooperation and collaboration are rules of the modern corporate game.

Whether or not it is beneficial for families to compete in an effort to keep up with or outdo the Joneses, competition within a family is likely to do more harm than good. Children devote time and energy to trying to outdo and tear down one another instead of dedicating their efforts to improving. They are more likely to win when they work together to give one another a leg up as they try to climb to the top. Spending their time trying to pull one another down to subvert each other's progress makes it harder for them to get anywhere.

Some parents consider a certain amount of competition among siblings to be desirable. They believe that as siblings strive to outdo and outshine one another, they develop competitive skills that will serve them well in the outside world. If parents consider sibling competition to be healthy they may pit their children against one another, hold them up to one another as examples, and in other ways work to promote competition. Competition among siblings may in fact provide the motivation that spurs youngsters to try to better themselves. But for competition to be effective the children must not undermine one another or try to advance at one another's expense. Otherwise too much of their time and energy will be devoted to warding off attacks from other family members.

Myth 6: Sibling Responsibilities Are Harmful

Until just a few generations ago, siblings worked at home when they weren't in school. Parents taught older children to take care of younger ones, and older siblings related to younger ones like little parents. This pattern changed in some countries when reliable birth control reduced family size, time-saving household appliances eased mothers' workloads, and a combination of social and economic factors made child-rearing a full-time job for most women. After World War II, mothers did the housework during the day while children attended school and fathers worked. After school and on weekends, parents entertained children, or they entertained themselves with toys and television. Older siblings began relating as playmates and peers instead of as helpmates and caregivers. As traditional sibling roles dissolved, the chain of command became fuzzy. Siblings clashed more as they struggled for dominance and control, and sibling bonds weakened. Children attended school, did homework, completed a small chore which had been assigned to help them develop self-discipline, and had a lot of latitude about how to spend their leisure time. The notion of childhood as a carefree life stage came into vogue and took on a life of its own. It came to be considered a necessary ingredient for a happy childhood.

When women began entering the labor force en masse in the 1960s, parents' workloads increased dramatically. They feared that giving children more chores would ruin their chances for a happy childhood; so, parents were hesitant to put them back to work. Older siblings didn't know what to do or how to help with younger ones, and many resented having to forfeit their leisure time. Younger children resented having the siblings they had come to regard as peers take charge and tell them what to do. Older children found it hard to nurture them. When younger children were upset, they wanted Mommy or Daddy, not the child they squabbled with over toys. With the proliferation of dual-income families and single-parent households, teachers and psychologists noted that many children were more troubled. Often their problems could be traced to a single cause: The youngsters weren't getting enough time and positive attention from their busy parents. Since stormy sibling relationships were also a major source of childhood stress, professionals urged parents to set aside one-on-one time to provide individual time and attention. As parents and children retreated behind closed doors for private chats, siblings fell behind on one another's news. They lost track of what was happening in one another's lives and lost touch with one another as people.

Although families remain small, it is likely that siblings have become substantially more important in the last half-century. Family moves have reduced many children's involvement with extended family members to occasional holiday gatherings. The many single-parent households, dual-income families, and longer workweeks have further reduced parent/child contact, but many siblings spend more time together than in the past. Many toddlers and preschool children share a babysitter; elementary and high school students spend time alone together until their parents return from work.

Siblings now average more time with one another than with their parents, and their need for one another may never have been greater. But for many children, siblings are sources of considerable anxiety, frustration, and suffering. The child-rearing practices that promoted strong sibling attachments have been abandoned. Many older siblings don't know how to care for younger ones, and younger siblings resist when older children try. Many siblings relate like peers when no adult is on hand to supervise or mediate their disputes. They argue incessantly or take pains to avoid so much unpleasantness by keeping a distance, which causes them to become even more alienated. Parents who want to help their children get along face some significant challenges. The first is to find ways to nurture the sibling bond.

CHAPTER 2

Nurturing Sibling Relationships

R esearchers have turned up some startling facts about what makes for good sibling relationships. The children's personalities and interests are really not that important. Siblings who are as different as night and day—or as alike as two peas in a pod—are likely to be very close if they treat one another with respect, empathy, and compassion. But little humans aren't born knowing how to relate to others. You need to help them understand one another's feelings.

Parent Role Models

Ken isn't sure why he and his sister are so close. But like so many siblings who are dear friends, all of his family relationships are warm.

> *When you live under the same roof with another person, you are bound to rub one another the wrong way from time to time, but I don't remember having argued with my sister. Once when I was about twelve and Karen was about six, she borrowed the favorite baseball cap my grandfather had given me just before he died. It was very special to me. I kept it hanging on my bedroom wall. Karen had begged me to let her wear it, and I gave in. She lost it. Karen felt so bad that I couldn't be mad at her. In fact, I ended up comforting her. She couldn't stand for anything bad to happen to me, and I felt the same way about her. We are still that way.*

My friends didn't think girls were cool, and they teased me if I let my sister play with us. So sometimes I talked to Karen before my friends came over, explaining that we needed to be by ourselves to do guy stuff. I'd promise to do something special to make it up to her after my friends left. Usually that worked, but not always. Once she accused me of caring more about my friends than her. I explained they wouldn't play with me anymore if I let a girl play with us, which was dumb, but there was nothing I could do to change it. I felt like a heel. Sometimes when my friends wanted to play, I told them I wanted to get together but had to babysit my sister; so, I had to let her play, too. They never objected, but once a friend who came over to play asked how come I had to babysit when my mom was home. I said my mom was busy and didn't want to be disturbed too much. I was lying, but at least I was better than some of the other kids. When my best friend's little brother tried to play with us, my friend would yell at him to leave us alone and didn't care if he cried. My parents probably would have killed me for pulling a stunt like that. They're really into respecting everybody.

Research investigations have found that how well siblings get along has more to do with the kind of example their parents set than with the children's personalities and temperaments. The best way to nurture positive sibling relationships is to be a good role model. Treat your children and spouse with respect, empathy, and compassion, and your youngsters are likely to behave similarly toward one another. Are you modeling enough of these positive qualities for your children to absorb them? A good way to find out is by observing what your children say and do during creative play. While playing house with dolls and puppets and inventing stories about pretend mommies, daddies, and children, youngsters demonstrate an amazing ability to capture and reenact what transpires at home. They imitate their parents' body posture, use the same tone of voice, and even repeat some of the phrases their family members use.

Children learn more impressive lessons from watching how their parents handle their personal upsets than from being told what to do. Beware of barking commands such as "Don't talk that way to your brother!" and "Be nice to your sister!" Some parents punish a child who violates the "no hitting" rule by spanking. They grab a disputed toy away from a child to teach him not to grab. Such disciplinary methods actually teach children to bark commands at one another and to hit and grab. At best, they learn to behave in your presence and mimic you by mistreating one another behind your back.

Alert!

Is your child mimicking your harsh words, strident tones, angry threats, derogatory asides, and sarcastic comments? Stress management, parenting classes, anger management classes, and therapy can help you learn to cope so you can set a good example!

Boosting Emotional Intelligence

Psychologists now recognize that emotional intelligence (EQ) is as important as intellectual ability (IQ) for long-term success in everything from relationships to academics and employment. Schools help children develop their intellect, but the job of teaching youngsters about the world of human emotions falls to parents. No infant can identify his emotions, and all handle upsets by crying. They must be taught. Girls are generally more adept at identifying feelings—the necessary first step to being able to manage them appropriately. It is unclear whether the structure of girl's brains or the way they are raised gives them an advantage. Parents generally do a better job of recognizing and responding to their little girls' feelings than their little boys'. When a toddler girl picks up the family cat by the ears, parents are generally more able to comprehend that their daughter simply likes the kitty, wants to play with it, but doesn't know how. When the cat bites a daughter, her parents are likely to comfort her and explain that kitties don't like being picked up by the ears because it hurts them. Parents are apt to take the time to show her how to make friends by petting the cat gently so as not to scare it. The end result is that little girls learn how to get along with kitties. When a little boy picks up the family cat by the ears, parents tend to view him as being aggressive and perhaps cruel. If they simply punish him for bothering the cat and admonish him to leave it alone, the same unhappy scene is likely to be repeated the next time he tries to interact with the cat. He may behave even more aggressively toward a cat if it repays his friendly overtures by biting him and getting him into trouble. Little boys need to learn the language of feelings, too. It is important to take the time to teach them!

Feelings Children Need to Know

Abandoned	Enchanted	Mad
Adventurous	Excited	Pleased
Affectionate	Exhausted	Proud
Alarmed	Fond	Relaxed
Angry	Frustrated	Relieved
Annoyed	Furious	Sad
Anxious	Glad	Scared
Awed	Happy	Silly
Brave	Hopeful	Surprised
Confused	Impatient	Tempted
Curious	Indifferent	Terrified
Daring	Indignant	Tired
Delighted	Interested	Uncertain
Disgusted	Joyful	Vengeful
Eager	Lonely	Weary
Embarrassed	Loving	Worried

Anger is often a reaction to another emotion, such as fear, frustration, insecurity, or to stress. Unfortunately, parents tend to be overly focused on boys' aggressive outbursts. Punishing or humiliating them can quickly stop behavior problems in the short run. However, if parents are aggressive when they feel angry, children mimic them and become more aggressive over time; so they squabble more. The key to teaching children to manage anger appropriately is helping them identify, express, and resolve their underlying feelings. A child who lashes out at his sister may actually be feeling disappointed that he must wait to play with a toy until she is through. Rather than cry, he converts his disappointment into anger, pushes her down, and grabs the toy. Because girls are more able to identify and express their feelings, they are more likely to cry when they are sad. Because girls are more aware of other people's feelings, they are more able to resolve conflicts before they escalate into angry confrontations. This may explain why sisters tend to get along better than brothers. There are a number of things you can do to teach your children about feelings:

- Regularly let your children know what you are feeling. By saying, "Mommy is tired now" and "Mommy is happy," your children will learn to recognize the tone of voice, facial expressions, and body language that accompany different feelings.
- Point out your children's feelings so they can recognize the internal sensations that accompany various emotions, saying, "You look happy," "You sound disappointed," or "Is that scaring you?"
- Point out what other people and storybook characters are feeling. Make it a habit to say things such as "The baby is crying because he's hungry," "Little Red Riding Hood is worried," or "The Three Little Pigs are afraid of the Big Bad Wolf."

Trying to teach children how to get along by reprimanding and punishing them when they fight and argue is like trying to teach arithmetic by marking each error on homework assignments. A positive teaching approach is much more effective than a negative one. Children don't learn how to add and subtract by receiving a lot of negative feedback in the form of papers filled with red check marks and topped with poor grades. In the short run, such negative feedback merely points out that there is a lot they don't know and causes them to feel bad. Over time, students who receive a lot of negative feedback come to regard themselves as incompetent. Some rebel. Others stop trying.

Children need to be shown how to break hard problems into a series of simple steps. You need to walk your youngsters through each step time and again until they can proceed on their own. Just as it takes longer to teach children to solve arithmetic problems than to do them yourself, it takes much longer to teach respect, empathy, and compassion than to solve a conflict over a disputed toy by returning it to its rightful owner. The best time to begin is when your children are very young. A young toddler may not understand what you are saying, but your tone of voice can nevertheless communicate empathy, compassion, and respect. Toddlers often understand a lot even if they are not yet talking.

Teaching Respect

Deal with your children respectfully and insist that they do the same with one another. Use common courtesy expressions regularly when you communicate with your youngsters so they will mimic you, but be careful to use them properly. Don't say "please" when you mean "do it," or "please" will become a meaningless word. Say "thank you" to express appreciation. It shouldn't be used when you feel more grudging than grateful, as when you had to nag to get your child to do a chore. Similarly, don't say "excuse me" when your tone changes the meaning to "get out of my way." And don't tack on the words "I'm sorry" while blaming your child, as in "I'm sorry, but you should have done your homework if you wanted to play outside." "I'm sorry" is only a useful social lubricant when it is used to express remorse.

Teach siblings to behave courteously toward one another by insisting that they use common courtesy expressions to deter them from taking one another for granted. Words like "please," "thank you," "excuse me," and "I'm sorry" provide important acknowledgements. The command "give me a turn" implies that a sibling's feelings are irrelevant. "Please, can I have a turn?" acknowledges that a favor is being requested, which the sibling has the power to grant or deny.

Issuing stern reminders to get toddlers and preschoolers to say "please" and "thank you" may speed learning. But simply issuing a genuine "please" every time you make a request, a "thank you" every time your child extends himself or does something nice for you, "excuse me" every time you interrupt or bump your child, and "I'm sorry" every time you inadvertently hurt him may be as effective in the long run. If you do need to provide prompts, avoid engendering ill will by turning them into reprimands. Don't thank his brother yourself or growl, "Your brother agreed to take you to the park! What are you supposed to say to him?" Instead, help your child appreciate the gift and teach him how to respond correctly. To that end, you might say, "How thoughtful of your brother to take you to the park. Please thank him." Similarly, when one child bumps into another, instead of saying, "How many times do I have to tell you? Look out where you are going and apologize," consider the merits of using lines such as "Uh-oh. Did you bump into your brother on purpose? If not, don't forget to let him know it was an accident and say you're sorry." Millions of daily arguments could undoubtedly be avoided if children could simply learn to express remorse by saying "oops, sorry" when they inadvertently elbow one another in the car or at the dinner table.

 Essential

If one child approaches a sibling and demands, "give me a turn," be careful how you respond. Siding with a child who is rude and demanding encourages him to be aggressive and domineering toward his sibling. Insist that he ask politely.

Teaching Empathy

To empathize is to understand and accept someone at a deep level. Youngsters can be close and maintain rich, rewarding relationships if they empathize with one another, even though they lack common interests, have very different personalities, and were born a decade apart. A child may know intellectually that his siblings care about him.

But for a child to feel that they care, he must feel that they understand and accept him. Having empathy for a sibling strengthens bonding. Being able to empathize makes it possible for siblings to endure one another's difficult behavior without taking offense. For instance, if a sister can understand and accept that her brother makes sarcastic remarks when he is in a bad mood and does not mean what he says, she will be less inclined to perceive them as personal attacks. If a brother can understand and accept that his sister is sensitive about her weight, he is more likely to avoid making hurtful comments. If children can understand and accept that they have hurt one another's feelings, they will be more likely to apologize and try to make amends. Hence, empathy is highly effective relationship glue.

 Essential

Some children weather their siblings' bad moods and inconsiderate behavior with their easy-going natures and their "live and let live" philosophy. But most children need to be able to empathize with one another to get along.

It is not enough to feel empathetic. Siblings must communicate their understanding and acceptance of one another's feelings. Empathy does not necessarily communicate agreement. A middle-aged brother may be very unhappy that his sister isn't doing more to help their parents. But the siblings can maintain a strong relationship if the brother understands and accepts her feelings on the matter regardless of his personal opinions. The sister may maintain that she can't assist their aging parents because she has too much going on in her life and is too stressed and overwhelmed by her own problems. The brother may think that the real issue is that she is too self-centered, self-involved, and uncaring. But if he is empathetic, he can accept her feelings and communicate that he understands by saying, "I understand you feel that you have to take care of yourself right now." His take on the situation might be quite different from hers. But rather than trying to make her feel guilty or bad or trying to change her, he accepts that her feelings are real and important. Parents and children are closely bonded because parents empathize with them. Parents may be tired, but they understand and accept their infant's need for attention in the middle of the night. Their empathy causes them to get up and take care of him. Empathetic siblings are similarly moved to care for one another.

 *Fact*

There are various levels of empathy. A parent who is not very empathic may accept and respond to her infant's need for comfort even though she doesn't understand why the baby is fussing. A highly empathic parent understands why an infant is crying in addition to accepting her child's need for comfort.

Some children seem to be naturally empathetic, while others need a lot of concrete help to understand their siblings' feelings. Again, the way to begin teaching empathy is by serving as a role model. From hearing you tell the baby, "Oh, you must be crying because that loud noise scared you," children come to understand their siblings' feelings. From hearing you say, "It's OK. It was just a door slamming," siblings learn that the baby's feelings are important and need to be treated as such.

Be sure to empathize with your boys as well as with your girls. Many parents deny and reject their sons' tender emotions. They say things such as "You shouldn't be scared of that. Quit acting like a baby." Parents tend to be more responsive when little boys are angry. They say "I know you are angry, but you must not hit" when he cries because he wants his sibling's toy, completely overlooking that he is sad and disappointed. Thus, they actually encourage boys to use anger to express a range of emotions. Many boys end up confused about their own feelings, which makes it hard for them to empathize with their siblings. This may be one reason that brothers tend to fight more than sisters.

To express empathy, a child must communicate in a way that will help the sibling feel understood and accepted. To do that, the child must anticipate how his sibling might react and modify how he communicates accordingly. For instance, if a brother understands that his little sister is afraid of Big Bird, saying "I know you are scared, but it's just a man dressed up in a costume" may not help her feel understood and accepted if she is intent on acting tough and doesn't want to admit that she is afraid. The simple statement "Let's leave" might be a better way to communicate understanding and acceptance of her feelings.

 ## Essential

Angry feelings and angry actions are different. To teach empathy, accept your child's angry feelings as valid, legitimate, real, and important. To instill moral values, teach that hitting is wrong. To teach good behavior, teach your child how to express his feelings appropriately when he is angry.

Judging siblings' feelings as good or bad, right or wrong is harmful. Feelings are not something people can control. They arise as spontaneous, internal reactions. However, siblings can control their actions and need to be taught how to do so. Empathize with your child's feelings by saying, "You are upset with your brother for eating your candy." Impart moral lessons by judging your children's actions, and teach them to behave by imposing consequences. For instance, after empathizing with your child's feelings, you might say, "Although your brother ate your candy, hitting him was wrong. You need to apologize, ask him to forgive you, and give him a hug. Then we'll see what to do about your candy."

Teaching Compassion

The Encarta dictionary defines compassion as "sympathy for the suffering of others, often including a desire to help." To teach compassion, be sympathetic when your children are upset, unhappy, hurting, fearful, in pain, or sad. Comfort them when they are upset, unhappy, sad, fearful, frustrated, or angry. Be compassionate toward them even when they are treating one another with a notable lack of compassion. For instance, when a sister grabs her brother's ball and makes off with it, you can express compassion to her as you return his ball to him by saying, "I'm sorry you can't play with it now." You can be compassionate toward your son, even as you ask him to be compassionate toward his sister by saying, "I'm sorry that your sister took your ball without permission. She really wants to play with it, too." You can be compassionate toward your daughter as she continues wailing because she wants the ball you have returned to her brother by saying, "I'm sorry that your brother won't let you play with his ball now. I hope he'll finish with it soon so you can have a turn. In the meantime, what can we do to cheer you up? How about a hug or a glass of water? Would a time-out help you calm down?"

Point out when you feel compassionate toward one of your children to help his siblings identify these feelings in themselves. When the baby cries for a long time, you probably feel a mixture of irritation and compassion. Discuss your compassion for the baby with your other children, perhaps by saying, "Poor thing. I don't know what is making your sister so unhappy. I wish I could find a way to help her feel better." Involve your children in the project of cheering one another up by asking for their help and ideas. Rather than keeping your children's personal problems secret, which makes it hard for them to see one another as human beings and know how to help one another, discuss the fact that a sibling is upset because there is no money to buy her a new dress for the prom or that a brother is making poor grades.

Many authors encourage parents to keep their children's problems secret from one another, fearing that siblings will use the information as a weapon. But if they don't know about one another's personal struggles, they may inadvertently do and say hurtful things.

They may make derogatory comments about a very short peer, not knowing that their sibling is hypersensitive about his short stature. They speak critically of a "hyper" classmate not realizing that their sibling is being evaluated for hyperactivity. Siblings may be more compassionate if they are told about a brother or sister's problem and are given suggestions about how to help such as "Your brother tries very hard in school and still makes poor grades. He feels really bad about not being very smart, but he just takes longer to catch on. Some reassurance that his big brother thinks he is smart might help him. He really looks up to you."

Random Acts of Kindness

Many children say things such as "my brother is always mean to me" because they completely overlook his many acts of kindness. They only notice when he does or says something they dislike. If your children rarely have a kind word for one another and constantly argue, you may question their love for one another. In many families, siblings are so hostile and antagonistic toward one another that it is hard to perceive any warmth or caring. When there is a lot of sibling strife, it can be reassuring to receive a report that one of your children stepped in to defend a brother who was being picked on. Learning that one child heroically pulled a sister from harm's way during a moment of danger or sacrificed to do something nice for her should help you recognize that your children really do love one another.

 Essential

Avoid the parent trap: criticizing your children for being inconsiderate of one another and forgetting to mention when they have been considerate. Constantly telling a child that his sibling is behaving badly toward him won't solve their problems or improve their relationship. Watch for and point out acts of kindness.

Realistically, coming through to help a fellow human being during a moment of dire need isn't especially significant. Total strangers have been known to step in and lend assistance at such exceptional moments. Nor can a single act of kindness undo the damage of daily criticism and harassment. Nevertheless, such extraordinary moments present good opportunities to nurture the sibling bond. Be sure that the recipient of a special kindness expresses appreciation. Acknowledge the sibling who extended himself, and help him take pride in his good deed. But be sure to acknowledge the many small, daily acts of kindness your children do for one another as well: Inviting one another to play; showing a younger sibling how to tie his shoes, tell time, or make a toy work; taking turns while playing a video game; exiting the bathroom shortly after a sibling knocks on the door; remembering where a sibling left a toy he can't find; trading chores so a sibling can attend a special activity; decorating one another with decals; giving advice about hairstyles and clothing; and so forth. Remove the sting from cutting comments by helping siblings ignore contentious asides and focus on their good deeds. If a sibling says, "Here is the shoe you were looking for. Your bedroom is such a pigsty, no wonder you couldn't find it," you might say "How nice of you to help your brother find his shoe" and ignore the rest. Just as the sibling had a choice to make a hurtful comment, you have a choice about how to respond. You can focus on what your children do to hurt and alienate one another, or you can help them experience the warmth and good feelings that come from nurturing and being nurtured by one another.

CHAPTER 3

Baby, Toddler, and Preschool Siblings

I f you're worried about how your toddler will react to a new baby, a quick trip down to Mexico should prove most reassuring. There, as in most of the rest of the world, toddlers and parents are equally attached to "their" baby. The secret is to honor and nurture this special relationship by helping your children bond. Your toddler and your newborn are likely to be involved with one another for the next eighty years! They don't know how to relate as dear friends and cherished companions. Your job is to teach them.

The New Baby Sibling

Toddlers and preschoolers don't know how to interact with a new baby. Their natural inclination is to treat their little sibling like a doll. Like many parents, Roberta's mother protected the baby by reprimanding her toddler. Her daughter learned what not to do but didn't learn how to relate to him appropriately.

> *Roberta was two-and-a-half years old when I told her she would soon have a new brother. She was very excited. When I brought Wesley home from the hospital, she was eager to hold him. But as she towered over her infant brother, she looked gigantic. Alarm bells went off in my head. Toddlers are clumsy, and they don't have good judgment. I thought about the way Roberta casually dropped her doll on the floor when she was tired of playing with it. She could be very aggressive*

when frustrated. It would be so easy for her to hurt the baby.

The minute I laid Wesley in Roberta's lap she said, "Open your eyes, baby," and extended her hand toward his face. She was going to pry his eyes open as if he were a plastic doll! I barely stopped her in time. Later in the day his eyes were open, and she said, "Pretty." She reached out to touch them, and I barely pushed her hand away in time. A week later, I couldn't tell if Roberta patted, hugged, and kissed her brother so hard because she loved him so much or because she was testing me to see how much she could get away with. I was constantly telling her not to be so rough. Even when I was nursing, she had to be right there every minute. I suggested other activities, but there was no distracting her. I would have to get firm with her so I could nurse Wesley in peace. Sometimes I would send Roberta to her room for a time-out until I finished. Instead of getting better, she became more resentful of the time I spent with Wesley. I wasn't surprised when she announced that she didn't want him to live at our house any more.

 **Question?**

How can I stop my son from being rough with the baby?
Hold and guide his hand until he understands how to touch the baby gently. To teach the art of delivering gentle kisses, have him practice on your cheek. If he is aggressive, have him sit near you for a short time-out.

Preparing for a New Sibling

Parents used to wait until close to their due date to tell toddlers that a sibling was on the way. Otherwise, their initial enthusiasm waned long before the baby arrived. After fantasizing for months about having a playmate, the reality often turned out to be a disappointment for older toddlers. It is now understood that being involved in the preparations for a new baby helps children begin to bond. An attachment begins to form as they feel the baby kick and press their ear to their mother's abdomen to listen to the sounds the baby makes. As soon as the baby's movements are detectable to others, inform your toddler that a new brother or sister is on the way.

Read stories about the arrival of a new sibling. For a list of suggested books, see Appendix A: Resources for Parents. Point out infants in the grocery store to help your toddler get a more realistic idea of what a new sibling will be like. Have your toddler help decorate the nursery, choose the baby's name, and arrange the baby's clothes in the dresser. Explain how the items on the changing table will be used. Prepare an older toddler for your absence by letting him know who will care for him while the baby is being born. If he will be staying at someone else's house, have him spend the night there a few times so he has a chance to become comfortable being there. This is a good time to explain where babies come from. Peter Mayle's picture book, *Where Did I Come From?* is for children ages four to eight but may be appropriate for younger children who want to know how Daddy's seed got into Mommy's tummy. Toddlers have a hard time with change, and an infant will completely transform the household. To lessen the stress, finish major projects before the baby's due date. If your toddler will go to day care, nursery school, or a babysitter after the baby is born, see if he can attend for a few hours each week beforehand so he can get to know the program and the people. Better yet, have him attend regularly for a month so he gets into a regular routine. Similarly, if you are contemplating moving your toddler from a crib to a toddler bed or from a toddler bed to a regular bed, make the change a month or two in advance.

Alert!

Having two children in diapers is very difficult, so it will help immensely to have your toddler potty trained before the new baby arrives. *Early-Start Potty Training* presents methods for working with young toddlers and for helping older children finish learning.

Start teaching your toddler some of the skills he will need before the new baby arrives so he isn't assailed with lots of new rules at once. Play "hush, the baby is sleeping" by whispering and not making any loud noises until a timer sounds. Have your toddler sit next to you instead of on your lap when you read to him, and hold a doll or stuffed animal so your child can become accustomed to this seating arrangement. If he bumps the doll, say, "Oops! You bumped the baby! You need to say you're sorry and give him a gentle kiss!"

Toddler Jealousy

Modern ideas about toddler jealousy began with the theories of the father of psychiatry, Sigmund Freud. He theorized that all young children possess a desire to destroy other family members in order to gain exclusive possession of their mothers. As Freud's disturbing theories became popular in the West early in the 1900s, many people reinterpreted the biblical story of Cain and Abel. They took it to mean that murderous sibling jealousy had been part of the human condition since the beginning of time. The idea that toddlers might possess murderous wishes toward other family members was particularly alarming since young children tend to act out their impulses. To protect the newborn, parents strove to keep toddlers and infants apart.

 **Essential**

Biology helps mothers and infants bond. For other family members, caring for a baby seems to nurture their bonds. Discouraging toddlers from being involved with infants may deter a strong attachment. Solicit your toddler's help with the baby, and let him know that his contributions matter!

Modern parents routinely attribute their toddler's upsets after the birth of a new baby to jealousy. They assume that aggression toward the baby stems from a desire to oust their rival in order to gain exclusive possession of their parents. Some parenting authors continue to urge parents not to hold the baby when introducing him to their toddler for the first time and to try not to appear too loving. They suggest that seeing the baby cuddled on mother's lap or cradled in father's arms could trigger too much jealousy. When toddlers are crankier because of all the changes when a newborn arrives, parents commonly see the problem as stemming from jealousy. Some articles advise parents to comment to their toddler that the baby is a bother because he cries and needs so many diaper changes. Some parents put notes on the front door advising friends and relatives to be sure to pay attention to the toddler so he won't feel left out when they arrive to see the new baby. Some parents even ask visitors to bring a present for the siblings so they don't feel left out. Other parents keep gifts on hand to present to the toddler so he won't feel jealous if someone arrives with a gift for his sibling, but not him.

Simple Solutions

It makes sense to try to ensure your toddler has a positive first impression of the baby, but feigning indifference to the baby won't help! For a positive first meeting, teach your toddler how to hold the baby safely and touch him gently. Instead of saying, "No-no! Not like that," sit at his side and explain, "Do it this way," as you guide his hands. If he wants to hold the baby by himself, don't discourage him from being possessive of his new sibling! Have him sit in the middle of a large bed or on the floor so there is no risk that he will drop the baby. Sit by his side to supervise.

It is highly unlikely that a toddler will feel jealous when visitors arrive with a toy that is suitable for an infant. Instead of trying to stave off jealousy by making sure that your toddler gets a present every time the baby gets one, let your toddler participate as an older sibling. Let him help the baby by opening his gift for him and presenting it to him. Show your toddler how to shake a new rattle for the baby or brush a stuffed animal against his sibling's cheek so he can feel its softness. If your toddler wants to play with the toy, his infant sibling certainly won't mind! If the gift is an article of clothing, include your toddler in the conversation, perhaps by asking, "Won't your brother look darling in this?" Instead of warning visitors to avoid gushing over the baby and pay attention to your toddler, have your guest sit down so your toddler can participate as the visitor looks at the baby. If the visitor says, "The baby has so much hair," make eye contact with your toddler and address your toddler. For instance, you might say, "Yes. Tommy and I comb it, but it doesn't stay in place. Does it, Tommy?"

Alert!

Urging visitors to bring a toy for your toddler in an effort to reassure him that he is important and hasn't been forgotten sends an unfortunate message. Toys and material objects are poor substitutes for affection and attention. As long as you include your toddler in the conversation, he won't be ignored and forgotten.

Regression

Toddlers may want to nurse like the baby, wear a diaper like the baby, and be rocked like the baby. Many parents think fussing is a sign of jealousy. They worry that wanting to do what the baby does means that their toddler is so stressed that he is regressing. In actuality, when toddlers regress, they lose some of their skills. This is a common reaction to having to cope with so many changes when a new sibling arrives. Potty-trained children may start having accidents. Children who were making good progress using a spoon go back to using their fingers. Children who were down to one bottle at bedtime start wanting their bottle during the day. Children who were sleeping through the night start having trouble falling asleep, have nightmares, or awaken during the night. Toddlers who imitate the baby may be reacting to all the changes and feel a need for more attention; so, they try to get it the way the baby does: by fussing for a bottle. In that case, try holding your toddler on your lap and give him some attention while he drinks a glass of milk. Perhaps he simply thinks that you and the baby have a lot of fun together as you nurse and diaper and rock him and is trying to join in by mimicking the baby. In that case, you might pretend to nurse your toddler, pretend to change his diapers, or rock him. However, that encourages him to mimic the baby. You can encourage your toddler to mimic you by letting him feed the baby a bottle of water, help change the baby's diaper, or rock the baby. Hold your toddler on your lap so you can rock the baby together.

Big Toddler Brothers and Sisters

When you want time alone with the baby and a hovering toddler interferes, suggesting another activity often helps occupy your older child. Some parenting experts suggest giving a doll to a toddler and instructing him to feed "his baby" while the parent feeds the real one. But dolls are less interesting than real babies, and sending your child off can indeed trigger jealousy. The children need to bond, and it is better for toddlers to relate to a human than to a toy. Pushing your toddler away is likely to make him anxious or upset, which may translate into increased clinginess and more dramatic bids for attention. It may be more effective to let your toddler stay by your side and suggest that he stroke the baby's cheek or hand. Toddlers have very short attention spans, so chances are they will quickly tire of this pastime and move to another activity. If your toddler wants you to stop what you are doing and play with him, the answer is simple enough: You will be glad to when his brother is finished eating and other chores are completed. If your toddler proceeds to throw a tantrum, so be it. It is not uncommon for youngsters to get upset when their parents say "no" to them. If he becomes aggressive toward the baby when he is angry with you, have him sit nearby until he finishes crying and calms down. Then instruct him to apologize to the baby.

Playmates

The littlest family member will enjoy being fed, changed, and cuddled by a toddler sibling once he learns to be gentle. When toddlers or pre-schoolers and babies are bonded, babies look to them for entertainment, diversion, and comfort. Babies engage them just as they engage their parents: by making eye contact and initiating games. Toddlers and preschoolers imitate their parents and then improvise. However, young children may not notice when they are being too rough or when the baby needs a break. Point out that the baby is averting his eyes or becoming restless. Explain that babies can't say "stop" or walk away when they have had enough, so they look away. If that doesn't work, they start getting restless. If that doesn't work, they start crying. Toddlers and preschool children need to learn when to tone things down or quit. If you simply distract your older child or tell him to leave the baby alone, he won't learn how to read the baby's feelings. If your toddler is very young, he may not understand your explanations. By simply saying "the baby needs to rest" and picking him up whenever you see him averting his gaze, becoming restless, or starting to fuss, your toddler will gradually learn how to tell when it is time for a game to end. It is less time-consuming simply to tell your toddler or pre-school child to cease and desist so you can continue what you are doing and to yell at him or send him to his room if he doesn't comply. But such responses cause children to feel that their parent is mean to them and nice to their sibling. In other words, they trigger jealousy.

Baby, Toddler, and Preschooler Clashes

As soon as babies can crawl, they follow their siblings around the house. Little ones learn a lot by watching and mimicking the big people in their world, even if those people are only a year or two older. Babies also provoke their siblings, though not on purpose. Babies accidentally poke, pinch, and pull hair. When they have hold of a sibling's toy, they may not want to let go of it. An older sibling shouldn't have to put up with being abused but cannot be allowed to retaliate. You do need to intervene, but teach your child how to handle the situation when you arrive rather than simply handling it for him. Many parents find themselves being called upon to settle every sibling dispute that arises for a decade or so. If the baby has hold of a toddler or preschool child's hair, instruct him to say, "No, Baby! Let go. That hurts Tommy," while helping him pry off the baby's fingers. If your toddler can't talk yet, say the words for him so he can start to learn the correct response.

 *Question?*

My toddler hits the baby when he is mad. What should I do?
Simply admonishing him not to hit isn't enough. Hold his hands so he can't strike the baby. Teach him to say, "No, baby. I don't like that." If your toddler is not yet talking, say the words for him using the tone of voice you would want him to use.

A fifteen-month-old may seem to be purposely antagonizing an older sibling by repeatedly knocking down his tower of blocks, grinning from ear to ear while blocking a sibling's view of the television, or taking one of his toys and running off with it. Babies are still learning about cause and effect. They are amazed to discover that toppling blocks causes someone to scream and that people start yelling every time they stand in front of the television set. When they repeat the same action over and over, they are not testing limits, as some people think. They assume this is some sort of game. Of course, taking a toddler's toy and running off with it can begin a game of chase, which babies love. If you speak harshly to the baby or punish him, his sibling will do the same. To try to correct behavior he considers wrong or troublesome, he will yell at the baby or hit him. It is hard to help toddlers understand why babies behave as they do. To diffuse tensions, explain that the baby is not being mean. He is trying to play but doesn't know how.

Help your toddler or preschooler find solutions that don't involve yelling at the baby. Perhaps big brother would be willing to build a small tower for the baby to knock down or lead his sibling away from the television set and hold him on his lap. Parents tend to raise their children the way they themselves were raised, so it can be easy to slip into the pattern of taking sides or solving children's problems for them. Moving the baby away from the television because his sibling is upset and is yelling encourages the older child to yell at the baby—and to look to you to take his side against the baby. If your toddler wants your help getting the baby out of his way in order to watch television, insist that your toddler ask you in the same way that you expect him to ask for a cookie: nicely.

 **Fact**

> If the baby messes up a toddler's toys, comfort your toddler. Reassure him that you and he will teach the baby how to behave when he is old enough to learn. If your toddler doesn't want to share his toys, suggest he try to distract the baby with another toy.

Toddlers and Preschoolers as Younger Siblings

Most toddler and preschool children look up to their older siblings. They want to be with them as much as possible and do what the big kids do. If your older children are not very attached to their younger siblings, the older ones may not like having a little one follow them about like a little puppy dog, and they may be furious when their toys are touched. Young children are likely to feel very hurt if they are ousted from an older sibling's room, are not allowed to touch his toys, or are excluded when his friends come calling. In most cultures of the world, family members are considered more important than friends; so younger siblings are not excluded when older ones have friends over to play. People are considered more important than objects, so younger siblings are allowed to play with older children's toys. To keep their prized possessions from being ruined, they keep their special toys out of site. Alternatively, younger children are carefully supervised. These customs don't mesh well with typical practices in the United States, where few young siblings and older children know how to relate to one another so they can be enjoyable companions and friends. Forcing older ones to share their space, toys, and friends and telling them to be nice doesn't suggest what to do when conflicts arise. Young siblings try to relate to older children like peers but cannot. Older siblings may become bossy and punitive as they struggle to keep younger ones in line. When conflicts heat up, parents often admonish older children to "be nice." But many don't know how to protect themselves and accommodate a little one. The result is considerable frustration. It is understandable that they tend to prefer the company of classmates and neighbors and can't relax with a little sibling in the room and that forcing an older one to open his door ends up harming their relationship.

A young child is likely to feel terribly hurt when he is ousted from a sibling's room and may sob when he is prevented from returning. But this may be necessary until the older children know how to deal with a little one. Nevertheless, a youngster should not be rudely pushed out of the room or have the door slammed in his face. Little humans deserve to be treated with respect. They need to be treated respectfully so that they learn how to treat their big siblings. An older sibling should at least explain that he needs to be alone and be gentle but firm when ushering a youngster from the room. Afterward, the older child should thank his little sibling, even if he didn't absent himself voluntarily. Older children are likely to need help empathizing and behaving compassionately toward younger siblings, especially if they relate more like peers than like siblings. It may help to explain that his little brother loves him very much and wants to be with him but makes a poor companion because he is young and doesn't know how to be considerate of others. Point out that young children need to be taught, and the first step is to set a good example by being considerate when sending them away.

CHAPTER 4

Preschool, Tween, Teen, and Young Adult Siblings

Some siblings take to one another immediately and remain close for life. Others dislike one another on sight, fight during childhood, and carry their grudges to their graves. As children change, their sibling relationships need to change as well. Certain issues predictably arise at different life stages and strain siblings' relationships or create opportunities for them to get closer. By addressing developmental issues, you will be in a better position to help your children forge or maintain healthy relationships.

Through the Years

A common sibling pattern in the United States and other Western countries is for children to squabble during childhood, become close as adolescents, and solidify their relationship as young adults. This was the case for Alex.

James was six and I was three when Bethany was born. Mom says I took one look at my sister and said, "I wanted a boy—but not like James!" Growing up, James and Bethany were together on everything, and I was odd man out. I tormented Bethany mercilessly and couldn't stand my brother. In elementary school, he pushed me around. I guess I was the instigator as often as not. He was bigger and could outtalk me, but I goaded him a lot. When I was fifteen, everything changed in the space of an hour. One night James sat down and started telling me about a girl he wanted to ask out. He was shocked when he found out I had been dating on the sly. Just like that, we got to be friends. The next year he went to college, and I really missed him. We hung out together over semester break and all summer after his freshman year. The next summer, he hung out with his girlfriend. Then we were each busy doing our thing and didn't see much of each other for a couple of years. We mostly kept in touch through the family grapevine.

In my senior year in high school, my sister got invited to the senior prom. My parents said she was too young to go and then agreed to let us double-date if I kept an eye on her. She snuck some liquor into the prom, which wasn't a big deal. But we hung out together some that summer, and she was very into the party scene. I finally told my parents, and all hell broke loose. My brother wanted to move back home to help straighten her out, and I felt guilty about going to college. We stayed in touch, but things went downhill. She eloped with her boyfriend her senior year of high school and then dropped off the radar. Whenever she did call, she had big problems. I mostly listened and sometimes gave her money.

After college, I took a job in the city where my brother worked. I lived with him and his girlfriend for a couple of months until I could afford a place of my own. They later married. I always felt like part of their family. When I transferred to a job out of state, we talked every week on the phone. My sister divorced her second husband and came to stay with me to get her act together, but she met a guy and took off one month later. She married someone else and was mostly out of touch until they divorced eight years later. That was a mess because she had two kids to support. My brother took them for the summer. A couple of years later, I wrangled a transfer back to be near my brother and sister-in-law. I was married by then, and our wives became best friends. I never would have guessed that my childhood archenemy would turn out to be my lifelong buddy and friend. I don't hear much from my sister, but when I do, we pick up where we left off. It's amazing we are so close, considering how we haven't had that much contact, really.

 ***Question?***

Since going to college, my kids hardly speak. What can I do?
Unless they object, help them keep in touch by telling them what their sibling is doing. Don't hesitate to suggest they contact one another for moral support in times of trouble. Remind them about each other's birthdays and important events.

Preschool Siblings

Many children ages three to six need special help to bond with a new baby sibling. Activities designed to help them develop as spiritual beings can enhance their sibling relationships. Preschool children commonly clash with toddler siblings as they battle over toys. Older siblings object when little brothers and sisters intrude on their territory, disturb their possessions, and interrupt their private time with their friends. See Chapter 3 for ways to help preschoolers solve disputes with toddlers, as well as with older siblings.

Bonding with the Baby

The best way to forge a bond between preschoolers and a new baby is to involve them in caring for their little sibling. Most are highly motivated because helping with the baby affords more quality time with their parents. Preschoolers care for imaginary babies during games of house, and the chance to care for a live one is much more interesting. If your youngster usually resists when you invite him to help you with the baby, you may be unwittingly sapping your child's motivation. Beware of the following common errors:

- Parents often say, "Bring me a diaper so I can change the baby. Thanks. Now go pick up your toys." Many children feel hurt, angry, or jealous about being pushed aside. They may respond better when told, "Bring me a diaper, and you can help me change the baby."

- Parents often say, "You're supposed to be bringing a diaper, not watching television! All you want to do is play." Because preschool children are readily distracted, they need a lot of guidance to stay on task. They need reminders about how to do things correctly. Many preschoolers avoid situations where they have been made to feel incompetent.

- Parents often say, "What do you mean you can't remember where the clean diapers are? How many times do I have to tell you? They're where they always are: stacked on the clothes dryer." Sarcasm threatens a preschooler's fragile self-esteem. The answer to the question, "How many times do I have to tell you?" is "at least once more."

- Parents often say, "Now you can go play" after their youngster fetches a requested diaper or completes another task. To pre-school children, right is whatever pleases parents, and wrong is whatever disappoints them. If children aren't praised or reprimanded, they may believe that they are free to do as they please. In that case, having to drop what they are doing to help is an unwanted interruption that carries no reward. To stay motivated, preschool children need to be acknowledged for being good brothers and sisters.

- Parents often say, "Thanks for the diaper. You're such a good helper! Now I can change the baby." For most children, there is only one thing worse than being bad, and that is being bored. Once they have mastered a task and it no longer challenges them, praise may not be enough to motivate them. When your child can easily fetch a diaper, he is ready to tackle something new. Have him help by handing you other items and entertaining the baby while you change the diaper.

Preschool Sibling Spirituality

Children benefit from a regular spiritual practice, and the preschool years are a good time to begin. Encourage youngsters to focus on a personal goal all of the world's great religions agree is important: to love one another. Set aside time for daily prayer or contemplation. Encourage your children to ask for divine help or think of ways to promote their siblings' well-being and to be kinder and more loving toward one another. Stories have a big influence at this highly impressionable stage of life, and it is important to expose your children to positive ones. Television dramas provide thousands of examples of people using violence to avenge insults. The laugh track on comedies suggests that humiliating, sarcastic comments are funny. Many G-rated movies are not desirable for preschool viewers. Studies have demonstrated that preschool children mimic aggressive behaviors they see on television. If your children spend an hour per day learning to be violent and disrespectful, you may need to spend a lot of time trying to combat the lessons they learn from their electronic teachers. Pull the plug on unhealthy shows, and screen movies. Look for books and movies that affirm the power of love that will inspire them to try to be more compassionate and empathetic toward other children. A good place to begin is with William Bennett's character-building books, *The Children's Treasury of Virtues* and *The Children's Book of Heroes*.

Elementary School Children

Elementary school children naturally form hierarchical groups. Most siblings get along better when the pecking order is clear so that they know who is in charge when and of what and who gets to make which decisions. Otherwise, they are likely to squabble. You muddy the waters by expecting older children to be responsible without teaching them how to lead. Struggles for dominance and control can become nasty or even dangerous.

Girl Power

When a group of girls are together, the high-status girl with the best social skills usually gets to be the leader. Younger siblings naturally look up to older ones, and parents affirm older girls' status by expecting them to be more responsible and by putting them in charge from time to time. But younger siblings may try to displace an older sister if she is a poor leader. Some older sisters try to keep younger ones in line with catty comments and sarcasm or try to boss them. Older sisters may bully by threatening to spread nasty rumors or reveal shameful secrets, such as disclosing problems with bed-wetting to a sibling's friends. Some use physical force. Younger children refuse to obey her, retaliate, seek vengeance, or become alienated. In large families, some younger children ban together for protection and form a group of their own.

Alert!

A good solution for the problem of bossy big sisters is to teach them the skills they need to be good leaders. In the girl world, the leader doesn't try to force her wishes on others. She takes others feelings, wishes, and opinions into account and tries to create a consensus.

Beware of trying to shore up poor leadership skills by telling your eldest daughter, "That's not nice to say" or taking away her power by saying, "No, you went first last time. It's your sister's turn." You may resolve the dispute of the moment without producing a real cure. Effective girl leaders evade direct challenges to their authority and forge compromises in order to build a consensus, according to Deborah Tannen, author of *You Just Don't Understand*. When disputes arise, explain that by sidestepping a sibling's challenge when he demands to be first, by letting him have his way about insignificant issues, and by working for compromises when disagreements arise, older sisters are more able to get their way about issues that really matter. By saying, "You're such a baby! Just go ahead and go first. See if I care," she teaches her sibling to argue to get her way. By saying, "I really wanted to go first, but that's OK. Go ahead," big sisters build credibility while remaining in charge. If they can avoid reacting to snide comments and using negative forms of control for a week or two, they can usually solidify their position as leader.

Then younger children are more apt to go along when a big sister suddenly says, "Usually I let you go first. How about if I go first this time?" If they object, the older sister needs to try to find a compromise that will keep everyone happy. Perhaps the younger child will agree if he is offered some other favor. By being a good leader, big sisters set a good example. Younger children copy them and become less demanding and more considerate of other people's feelings, opinions, and wishes—including that of their big sister's. Through her example, a big sister helps younger children grow up.

Boy Power

According to Tannen, boys maintain their position as leader in hierarchical groups by making decisions and getting them to stick. They accomplish the latter through a combination of aggressiveness and good leadership. On the playground, boys are highly competitive. The struggle to rise to the top of the heap never ends. The youngster at the top must constantly struggle to maintain his position because those who are lower on the totem pole are struggling to displace him. Making decisions stick by being aggressive at home is unacceptable.

 *Fact*

Some parents try to channel aggression by buying their boys boxing gloves and teaching them to follow rules when they fight. But no victory is considered permanent in the boy world. An hour after a staged boxing match, the loser is likely to make another stab for the position of top dog.

Because parents are in a better position to make their own decisions stick, some try to settle every dispute. But the struggle to be first never ends; so even more disputes break out. Often boys' games sound like wars. Adults are genetically primed to respond to youngsters' distress signals. If your children sound upset as they jockey for position, you may not feel better even though they claim that they enjoy arguing. Insist that they have this kind of "fun" behind closed doors so you aren't subjected to it. You may need to assert your authority as leader and make the decision that there shall be no more arguing, and make the decision stick with firm consequences. Then teach your boys how to be good leaders, following the same methods you use for your girls.

Competitive Games

A central challenge for elementary school children is learning to follow rules and do things correctly. When they play games, they like others to follow the rules, though creative types with good negotiating skills may get siblings to change the rules to make the games more interesting. Elementary school-age boys and girls need to learn to be good sports if they are to enjoy competitive games and pastimes. The goal of a competition should be for them to grow, stretch, improve, and have fun, not to work out issues of dominance and control. Teach them that the younger or poorer player gets to decide who goes first or gets to have another handicap to level the playing field. In this way, the better player is properly challenged and doesn't get bored, and the other child doesn't get so frustrated. Teach the child who is winning to support the one who is behind by complimenting good moves ("Way to go!") and by being properly sympathetic when things aren't going well ("Too bad!"). Point out that if the child who is losing does the same, his opponent will be less inclined to show off and try to rub it in. Enforce a time-out when disputes break out. Let the siblings resume when they can agree on how to proceed. When the game ends, teach them to shake hands. Be sure that the loser congratulates the winner and that the winner doesn't gloat. Congratulate them for being good sports!

Young Teenage Siblings

Twenty-three percent of 13-year-olds responding to a 2005 *Time* poll via the Internet rated their sibling relationships as excellent. Forty-two percent said they were good, 22 percent said they were fair, and only

5 percent gave them poor marks. At this highly sensitive age when children experience so much social tension and pressure, it would be understandable for sibling conflicts to intensify. But when there is a crisis, siblings tend to turn to one another for support. Because many young adolescents consider a bad hair day to be a crisis, it's not surprising that siblings commonly find solace in one another.

On polls the majority of adolescents say they would rather discuss personal issues with their parents than peers. But they don't, fearing their parents would condemn them for considering having sex, drinking, taking drugs, or having friends who do. Teens commonly turn to their siblings for advice instead. If your teens get along with their peers but not one another, they are failing to apply their relationship skills for a reason. There may be past grudges or current issues to resolve. They may still be struggling for control like younger children. If you can't get to the bottom of the problem, find a counselor who can help you.

Older Teenage Siblings

As teens try to form a personal identity, they may experiment with different clothes, hairstyles, ideas, beliefs, peer groups, and lifestyles. This can strain relations with protective adult siblings. If an older sibling is especially conservative, he may react like an angry parent. An older sibling who threatens a teen's budding independence by trying to dictate to him is likely to alienate him. Help older siblings understand that teens don't usually argue to try to compete like an elementary school child. They are trying to become independent. To do that, they must emerge from the shadow of parents and older siblings so that they can carve out a separate identity. Help an older sibling understand that he will lose his ability to have an influence if he tries to dominate and control a teen. Teens need to be affirmed and invited into the adult world. Older siblings need to serve as advisors, mentors, and guides.

Teenagers need to understand that they can sometimes make better decisions by listening to older siblings' opinions and that doing so need not threaten their autonomy. Help your teen understand that young children are dependent because they rely on members of their family to fulfill most of their physical and emotional needs. People never stop needing guidance from loved ones. Adults rely on many different people for advice, including their siblings, but make the final decision. Once your teen understands this, he may be less likely to view advice from an older sibling as a threat to his independence.

Young Adult Siblings

The house is likely to feel empty when a sibling moves out, even if there are many children still at home. Younger children are likely to feel sad and angry. If he does not remain in touch, they may feel abandoned and doubt that he cares. In fact, he may be so caught up in his new life that he does neglect them. You can ease the transition by preparing your youngsters ahead of time. Be sure they understand where their sibling is going and why. Explain that everyone must make more of an effort to stay in touch. Encourage the siblings to call one another, send e-mail messages, chat online, or use other methods to communicate.

Siblings who mostly related by doing things together may find verbal communication unsatisfying. They may be at a loss as to what to say. You can help them by suggesting topics of conversation. Tell your older child to share news that might be of interest to his younger siblings rather than relying on you to pass the word. If younger siblings miss older ones, be sure to let them know. Pass the phone to younger brothers and sisters when an older sibling calls. Issue reminders about birthdays and emphasize the importance of calling or sending a card. You might even provide an assortment of greeting cards and some stamped envelopes so that a college student need only address, sign, and mail them. If older children don't return for important holidays, alert them that their siblings are apt to be disappointed. Rather than conveying the bad news yourself, have your older children explain it to their younger siblings. Parents aren't supposed to use guilt to try to influence their children. But if the sound of a sad little voice motivates an older child to come home for the holidays and you also reap the benefits, you're off the hook!

CHAPTER 5

Ending Bickering and Dickering

Having your children bicker over an endless array of minor issues can be draining. A lot of dickering about whose turn it is to take out the garbage and who gets to choose the television show can also take a toll. A great solution is to hold family meetings and spend them teaching your children to get along, solve problems, settle disputes, make joint decisions, and function as a team. Round out the sessions with some fun and games for some quality family time.

Family Meetings

Patrick tells how weekly meetings strengthened his family and taught him and his sister how to get along.

> *My family was close when I was young. By the time I was in fifth grade, Dad and Mom were working long hours, Tina and I were in a lot of activities, and we were lucky to have dinner together a couple of times a week. I suppose I loved Tina down deep, but mostly I thought she was a pain. I was convinced that she went out of her way just to bug me. I would go into the bathroom, and two seconds later she was pounding on the door. She would go into my room and mess with my things. When I tried to get even, she ran crying to Mom or Dad, who usually took her side. Mom and Dad were arguing a lot, too, and I was worried they might get divorced. I started getting in trouble in school, so Mom took*

me to a psychologist. He said I was depressed and wanted me to take pills, so Mom found a different doctor. The new one met with me once and said my whole family needed to come in.

After a couple of family counseling sessions, the therapist said we should continue our talks on our own by holding regular family meetings. A couple of days later, I complained to Mom about Tina going into my room without permission. Mom told me to bring it up at the family meeting. When it was time to start, I said I didn't want to attend and that I'd rather do homework even than talk about problems. Mom said we would have pizza and decide where to go on vacation, so then I got interested. It was because of those meetings that Tina and I got to be so close. We worked out a lot of stuff, like her calling me a dork in front of my friends.

Scheduling meetings was sometimes a hassle when I was in high school. But my parents laid down the law. We met every week even if it meant getting up at the crack of dawn. We actually did that a couple of times. We cooked a special breakfast for our activity, which turned out to be a lot of fun.

Alert!

Use family meetings to teach your children how to listen respectfully to one another and solve their conflicts. Once they learn to apply their new skills during their daily interactions, all of the time spent as a family can be quality time.

Goals for Family Meetings

Too often, family time that is supposed to be fun turns out to be unsatisfying or even miserable. The children argue over trifles, and parents spend most of the time struggling to get them to stop antagonizing one another. Parents commonly assume that their youngsters could get along and are simply choosing to stir up trouble. In fact, siblings may not know how to relax and enjoy one another's company.

Family meetings are designed to teach children the basics of how to take turns speaking, listen to one another, and respond respectfully so that they can function as part of a family. Once those goals are accomplished, family meetings can be used to help children to work out their differences and to help one another solve personal problems. Those are only a few of the many benefits.

Scheduling Family Meetings

The prospect of adding another commitment may seem unappealing if your schedule is already bursting at the seams. But family meetings can be real time- and energy-savers. Parenting authors and family therapists have been beating the drum for decades to get parents to spend more one-on-one time with their children. While retreating behind closed doors for private talks can shore up a parent/child relationship, meeting individually doesn't help siblings improve theirs. In fact, excluding brothers and sisters can further fragment the family. Children only need one-on-one time because they don't share much personal information when the family is together. Quieter, less assertive children have a hard time making their way into conversations when boisterous brothers and sisters are around. Some children don't speak up because they are afraid that siblings will tease them. In many households, sibling insults and derogatory comments are standard fare whenever two children are in the same room. If children can trust that their siblings are emotionally safe, they don't need to be alone with a parent to open up.

When a youngster makes poor grades, is being harassed at school, is upset about his weight, or has another personal problem, many parents discuss the matter privately and agree to keep it a secret so his siblings won't humiliate him. If a child doesn't trust his siblings, that is a serious problem that needs to be addressed! Siblings cannot be close if they don't know the important things that are happening in one another's lives. If they must keep their problems a secret, they lose the benefit of having one another's help and support.

When one of your youngsters has a problem, you may be able to set the proper tone and mobilize sibling support by discussing it at a family meeting. Problems become less daunting when children feel that others are rooting for them, so a strong display of family solidarity is often enough to help a troubled child cope. Hearing a sibling say, "Those kids sound like dangerous bullies. You should tell the principal" helped one child immensely. He had thought he was being picked on because something was wrong with him. His parents' advice to avoid them hadn't worked. Because siblings are from the same generation, they often have more information about school and social problems than their parents. They may be more objective about parent/child problems as well and may be able to provide helpful insights and suggestions. When a father solicited suggestions for helping one child bring up his grades, a sibling said, "He needs to study where you can keep an eye on him. When he's in his room, he just plays on the computer." Siblings may be willing to tutor a brother or sister who is having academic problems, include a friendless sibling in their social groups, take on extra chores so an overwhelmed sibling can prepare for exams, or lend an outfit to a sibling who needs something special to wear to a party. The possibilities are endless.

Alert!

When siblings are considerate of one another's feelings, mealtimes, car rides, outings, and time spent relaxing at home can be high-quality family time. If your children can help one another with personal problems, there is less need for private parent/child chats.

Preparing for Family Meetings

Create an agenda by posting a list of topics to be discussed in a central location, such as the refrigerator door. Suggest that family members add items to the agenda as they think of them. Agenda items can include decisions that need to be made, issues to be discussed, and problems that need to be addressed. If a sibling conflict develops during the week, you may need to settle the dispute on the spot. But you might also suggest that one or both children add the problem to the agenda so that the matter can be discussed at the next family meeting, or you can add the issue to the agenda yourself.

Essential

It is best to schedule family meetings on weekends. Choose a time in the morning, afternoon, or early evening when everyone is relaxed and isn't too tired. Sunday evening works well for many families. Follow the meeting with some family fun such as a game of cards, popcorn and a movie, or a bike ride.

For meetings to accomplish the twin goals of solving problems and strengthening sibling relationships, it is important to strive for a balance of fun and serious discussion. If all of the agenda items are about problems, the meetings will be too stressful, and family members will resist attending. How topics for discussion are listed on the agenda can increase everyone's enthusiasm or sour their attitude. For instance, when a child keeps asking you for a special privilege, you might add the problem of whining to the agenda, which sounds very negative. Or you could suggest that your child add his request to the agenda and raise the issue at the family meeting. The latter is likely to heighten his interest in the meeting and give him an alternative to whining.

Structure family meetings in a manner that reflects your values and preferred parenting style and that fits your children's capabilities. To accommodate your children, you may need to provide more or less structure than you would like. As a general rule, the more you can involve your children in running the meetings and making decisions, the better. In some families, parents run the meetings and delegate some of the smaller tasks to the children, such as calling family members together and cleaning up afterward. Children are asked for their opinions, but one or both parents remain in change of the discussions and make all of the decisions. A parent might tell the children what he has in mind for a vacation destination, listen to their opinions and any information they have to contribute, and then announce his decision at the next family meeting. This authoritarian, parent-controlled style may be necessary if the children are very young, unruly, unable to work together, or don't take the meetings seriously. By concentrating on teaching your children to speak in turn, listen without interrupting, and address one another respectfully, they may be able to progress to the point that they can assume more responsibilities. When they do, they may be able to participate in family meetings as decision-makers or problem-solvers and take turns leading the meetings.

At the opposite extreme, parents and children take turns running the meetings and make all of the decisions together. This permissive approach can work well if the children are older or especially mature. It may be necessary if your family includes a defiant teenager who will not adhere to group decisions or even attend family meetings unless he participates as an equal. A permissive parent might ask the children where they would like to go on vacation and then participate as an equal in coming up with a workable, mutually agreeable decision.

Alert!

Children's nervousness may cause them to joke, act out, and not take family meetings seriously at the outset. When they understand what transpires and become accustomed to the format, they settle down. It may be better to keep the first meetings short, keep the decisions simple, and avoid discussing serious problems.

Between these two extremes is the authoritative approach. Parents and children take turns running the meetings, and children are encouraged to participate actively in solving problems. When decisions need to be made, the children may be given a few options and be allowed to settle on a choice. Otherwise, their input is solicited, but the parents make the final decision themselves. An authoritative parent might suggest two or three possibilities for a vacation destination and help the children choose. Alternatively, the parent might ask where the children would like to go, provide information about what is feasible and what is not, supply additional information as they discuss the matter, and retain the right to accept or veto their choice. It can be hard to know in advance whether an authoritarian, permissive, or authoritative approach will work best.

Involving Children

Parents usually need to lead family meetings until the children understand what to do. Then allowing them to take turns being in charge of meetings develops their leadership skills. By pairing a parent or older sibling with a young child, even preschool children can help run the meetings. Even after your approach and set of rules are working well, it is important to remain flexible. Your children's needs and capabilities will change as they mature, and your family meetings need to change accordingly. You can prepare children to run meetings by having them take turns serving as monitor. The monitor helps everyone stay focused by keeping track of the time and letting the leader know when it is time to move on to the next item on the agenda. The monitor also does any other duties the leader assigns. There are many possibilities including:

- Finalizing the agenda by deciding how much time should be devoted to each issue
- Preparing snacks
- Rounding up family members when the leader is ready to call the meeting to order
- Conducting opening and closing rituals
- Pointing out when someone is not following the rules
- Making arrangements and gathering supplies for activities
- Cleaning up afterward

Starting each meeting with a short ritual can help everyone settle down and focus. The ritual might include lighting a candle and saying a special prayer or requesting that everyone direct their thoughts to what is best for the family as a whole during a moment of silent reflection or a brief meditation. A first order of business is to establish the ground rules, such as waiting to speak until called upon, not interrupting, and being respectful. Be clear that condescending and derogatory comments, sounds, and body language are unacceptable. Mumbled comments, hoots, rolling their eyes at one another, and other disrespectful behavior can be as inflammatory as name-calling and obscenities.

 ## *Essential*

The Native American custom of passing a talking stick to the speaker provides a visual reminder of who has the floor. Requiring children to summarize what the last person said before they add comments of their own encourages attentiveness.

Creative Problem-Solving

Family meetings are a good time to solve individual and family problems. There are several steps in the problem-solving process. At first glance, they appear simple enough.

1. Define the problem.
2. Gather information.
3. Brainstorm solutions.
4. Evaluate solutions.
5. Select a solution.
6. Implement the solution.
7. Evaluate the results.

When solving real-life problems, it quickly becomes evident that these seemingly simple steps are hard to follow. Siblings often have a hard time even agreeing on a definition of the problem. When children battle over the condition of their shared bedroom, one may declare the problem to be that his sibling is a neatfreak, while the other child thinks his sibling is too sloppy. Sometimes it helps to proceed to the next step and pay attention to each child's underlying needs and concerns while gathering information. As the siblings describe who made which mess and who cleaned the room last, it usually becomes apparent that their underlying needs are different but aren't incompatible. For instance, one sibling may need a neat room, while the other needs not to be hassled and to put as little time as possible into cleaning and straightening. In that case, the family may be able to proceed to step three and generate some ideas for solutions: The little neatnik might do all of the cleaning in exchange for other favors, the sloppy child might agree to do the minimum needed to satisfy his roommate, they might put up a room divider so that the neatnik doesn't have to see the mess, or the children's bedroom assignments might be changed.

 *Question?*

Can preschool children participate in family meetings?
Many three-year-olds are astute observers of what goes on in their families and have lots to contribute. Be sure to ask for their opinions and ask why they believe as they do. You may be amazed by their thoughtful, sophisticated reasoning.

When brainstorming solutions, it is important to list every idea anyone can come up with, no matter how ridiculous or far-fetched. Sometimes a good deal of silliness emerges as children propose outlandish solutions. Injecting some humor into the problem-solving process helps lighten the tone of the discussion. Don't hesitate to propose an impossible solution and write it down. As siblings laugh together, they forge stronger bonds, soften their hard-line attitudes, and are more willing to work together. Note and record all suggestions. Disallow criticism, which stifles creativity; sometimes suggestions that sound ridiculous lead to excellent solutions. For instance, in the controversy over keeping the bedroom clean, one youngster proposed that his neatfreak brother move his bed into the garage so that he could learn the true meaning of clutter. His suggestion was supposed to be a joke. However, on reviewing their list to look for a workable solution, his parents seized on the idea and decided to convert a section of their oversized garage into a bedroom.

The final step in the problem-solving process, evaluating the solution, is also important. It is easier for children to agree to try a solution when they understand that if it doesn't work the family will resume the search for one that does. Sometimes a solution that sounds great turns out to be a flop, or it works but creates a new set of problems. Flexibility is the name of the game when it comes to problem-solving.

Family Decisions

There are several ways to arrive at decisions: by parental fiat, democratic vote, and consensus. For consensus decisions, everyone comes to an agreement or they find something everyone can support for the time being, even if they don't especially like it. Sometimes that means postponing making a decision. Consensus decisions take a bit longer to arrive at but have some definite advantages over simple votes. Because one person can prevent a consensus from being reached, everyone's needs and wishes are considered, and everyone has an incentive to compromise. For instance, if family members can't reach a consensus about which movie to rent, no movie is rented. Once children experience the consequences of not cooperating, they become very motivated to look for ways to accommodate everyone. They may agree to rent the movie the majority prefers this week and let the child who dislikes their choice decide which movie is rented the next week. Democratic votes, on the other hand, invite coalitions. As soon as two brothers realize they can get their way by teaming up against their sister, they can effectively exclude her from having a say about anything. Furthermore, the losers in democratic votes often refuse to carry out decisions they dislike and undermine family projects by refusing to participate.

Some families limit how long individuals can address a particular issue so they don't dominate the discussion and appoint a timekeeper. If the children grow tired but want to continue a discussion, a short break can give them time to process what has happened thus far and boost their energy level. Breaks are useful for breaking impasses. Unfinished business can be carried over to the following week, or an emergency meeting can be scheduled at another time. What matters most is that children have the experience of working together to make decisions and solve problems. That can be enough for youngsters to begin solving problems on their own outside of the meetings.

Family Fun

To help make family meetings festive, serve a snack. It is important to limit how much time is devoted to discussing problems. Usually, everyone burns out after an hour, and nothing more gets accomplished. To offset the unpleasantness of difficult discussions, make the meetings part of a family night. Play a game of Monopoly or enjoy another fun activity together after the hard work of discussing problems is over. Consider enforcing the same rules as during the formal meetings: no interrupting, derogatory or provocative comments, sounds, or body language. When meting out consequences to rule-breakers, keep them in the same room rather than sending them to time-out. In that way, you can work toward the preliminary goal of helping siblings coexist peaceably even though they are upset with one another. The next step is for them to treat one another with enough respect so that they can work and play together without purposely antagonizing one another. The next challenge is to be able to resolve conflicts that develop when they inadvertently step on one another's toes or disagree. When they can tolerate disagreeing strongly without damaging their relationship, all of their time together can be high-quality time.

CHAPTER 6

Controlling Competition and Rivalry

Parents try to be fair and impartial. Nevertheless, a majority of kids say that their parents have a favorite child and treat him better than the rest. But kids don't always think a sibling is the favorite. Many youngsters claim that honor for themselves. It is important to avoid the obvious pitfalls that cause children to feel that they are losing the battle for parental affection. But simply feeling closer to one child than another can trigger accusations of favoritism. Avoiding charges of "It's not fair!" may prove very challenging.

Young Rivals

Mrs. Dupont loved both of her boys and tried not to show favoritism. Nevertheless, each continually assailed her with accusations of favoring his brother.

> While growing up, Mark and Ron seemed to be on a never ending quest to discover which of them I loved more. If I told Mark to clean his room, he would inevitably ask, "Aren't you going to make Ron clean his room, too?" It wasn't so much a question as an accusation. If I asked Mark to feed the dog, he would usually insist that it was Ron's turn. If I held firm, Mark acted as though I was picking on him. If I bought Ron a new shirt, Mark pouted if I didn't buy him something and complained that his brother got everything. The complaints went both ways. Ron often acted as though I deprived

him and made him do all the work. Both boys made a big issue out of which one I served dessert first and who got the biggest scoop of ice cream. The "winner" gloated, as if he had proof positive that I loved him more. They constantly let me know what the other one was doing wrong to discredit one another in my eyes. In truth, if our ship was going down and I could only save one of my children, I don't know how I could ever bring myself to choose. When I look into my heart, I feel that I love one as much as the other.

One year Mark was very unhappy with his Christmas presents because he only got two and Ron got six. But Mark got a new bicycle, so I actually spent a lot more money on him. The next year Ron wanted some really expensive snow skis for Christmas; so I gave him skis and a couple of other small gifts. Mark had about a dozen presents, but he was still unhappy. He was sure I had spent more on Ron! I realized then I would never win. So every time Mark asked why I was making him do a chore but not his brother or why his brother got a special privilege, I would say, "Because I love your brother more." Whenever Ron wanted to know why I was doing or buying something for Mark, I said, "Because I love Mark more." That actually settled them down for a time. Now that they are grown, the question of which child I love more has become a standing joke. When Mark opens his Christmas present, Ron says, "Aha! Mom must have given you that because you're her favorite." When Ron opens his gift, Mark says, "That's cool! But then, you always were Mom's favorite." They laugh about it now, thank heavens. But when they were growing up, their rivalry was very draining.

Alert!

Some parents feel guilty about being closer to one child than another and are hypersensitive to charges of favoritism. Their children learn that by complaining that they are being treated unfairly, their parent feels guilty and gives in to their demands. Don't let yourself be blackmailed!

Comparing Siblings

It is inevitable that you will compare your children. Because a first-born starts walking at age twelve months, you will undoubtedly expect your next healthy child to do the same. Similarly, if your seven-year-old remembers to brush his teeth and make his bed each day, it is reasonable to assume your next child can handle those chores when he is seven. However, parents tend to assume correctly that a late walker simply needs more time and practice to learn. But they often mistakenly assume that a child who can't remember to brush his teeth or make his bed at the same age as an older sibling is simply unmotivated or irresponsible. Too many parents throw up their hands in frustration and say those damaging words, "Why can't you be more like your brother?" The correct answer is: "Because I am not my brother." If youngsters could give the correct answer, their parents might realize how unfair it is to expect their children to be alike. Some youngsters learn faster than others. Some require more reminders and supervised practice to learn. Some need more discipline to remain motivated to do things they don't enjoy. When youngsters are expected to do things that are overly challenging for them, they end up feeling badly about themselves. If they think they are disappointments to their parents, children may give up trying to please them altogether.

Destructive Comparisons

When parents compare their children, one sibling may rise to the challenge and try to emulate the child who is being held up as a good example in hopes of winning his parents' love. He may even succeed for a time. But changing is no small task. After the surge of determination to tackle a self-improvement project dissipates, it is hard to remain motivated. Moreover, bona fide self-improvement projects may have some definite long-term benefits, but the benefits of changing in order to be less like oneself and more like someone else are highly questionable. If children succeed, they may feel like shams. Sooner or later, most children feel very resentful that their parents tried to pressure them to be more like someone else.

Essential

If you want one of your children to be more conscientious, less emotional, or to change another fundamental aspect of his personality, tackle the issue directly. Bemoaning the fact that he isn't more like his sibling doesn't help him improve.

Comparing your children in your mind is probably unavoidable. But urging them to be more like one another is very hurtful. Asking "Why can't you be more like your brother? He works out regularly and doesn't overeat" engenders the same negative emotions as when a husband says to his wife, "Why can't you be more like your sister? She's such a hard worker and a great mother" or when a wife says to her husband, "Why can't you be more like your brother? He is so much fun to be around!" Spouses commonly divorce when such cruel statements are made. Similarly, many children give up trying to please, rebel, or divorce their parents by becoming so alienated that as adults they stay away for years or even decades.

The Consequences of Comparing Siblings

Children naturally seek acceptance and approval from their parents. Even children who were adopted at birth and grew up in loving families usually struggle with painful feelings of having been rejected by their biological parents. When biological children see the acceptance they crave being lavished on a sibling, they commonly wonder if they were adopted. Many decide their sibling is to blame for setting an impossible standard. They set out to convince their parents that he isn't so wonderful by pointing out all of his small faults and failings. They may try to punish their sibling by repainting his strengths as weaknesses and imperfections, whether real or invented. If the favored child does well in school, his siblings may tease him about being the teacher's pet or undermine him by distracting him when he needs to study. After being teased about the size of their nose, many beautiful children become convinced that they are ugly. Thus, the youngster who is being held up as a good example to the rest usually ends up suffering at the hands of his jealous siblings. When children mature they become aware of how their parents contributed to their suffering. Alienated siblings commonly reconcile. Some close ranks against the parent who engendered the destructive competition that kept them at odds. The parents may end up alienated from all of their children. Comparing your children may be natural, but it is important to keep your conclusions to yourself!

Mom's Favorite, Dad's Darling

In a 1950s study of five- and six-year-olds reported in the book *Separate Lives*, only one-third of the young interviewees felt that they and their siblings received equitable treatment at home. Two-thirds of the children who were interviewed believed that their mother preferred one sibling over another. Not all felt that their sibling got better treatment than they did. Some reported that their sibling received preferential treatment; others considered themselves to be the favorite. When a family therapist notes that siblings are highly competitive, asking which child is the parents' favorite often elicits a very clear answer. Even as the parents are insisting they don't have a favorite, the children are all pointing to the same sibling to indicate that he is the favorite. At the very same moment, the designated child is raising his hand to indicate that he is his parents' favorite. Even if you are quite sure that you treat your children fairly and don't have a favorite, it is wise to ask. If they are uncertain or don't agree which is your favorite, you are probably on a good track.

Since children have different personalities, it is natural for parents to feel closer to one of their children than another. There is only so much that parents can do to hide their preferences because their body language betrays them. The way parents' eyes light up when the child they feel closest to walks into the room, their special tenderness when they hug him, their ability to joke with and accept criticism from him, and their gentle tones as they issue reprimands are often obvious. If you are confronted with the line "You love my brother more than me," it is important to find out what you are doing to convey that impression. Ask your child for feedback. Rather than insisting that you feel the same about all of your children, it may be more helpful to admit that you feel especially close to one child and give your reasons. You might explain that his sibling's personality is more like yours or less like yours. You might say that you find his brother easier to understand and suggest ways that you can get to know one another better. Let your child know what you like and consider special about him, and share your ideas for ways to strengthen your relationship.

Alert!

Many parents get upset because a relative favors one of their children over another. Don't upset your child by pointing out that one child gets worse gifts or less attention. If one of your children complains, suggest that he raise the subject with his relative directly. Otherwise, leave well enough alone.

Setting aside time to talk or engage in a shared activity can help you get to know your child better and strengthen your relationship. Reading *Please Understand Me* by David Keirsey and Marilyn Bates can help you understand why certain personalities click and others clash and learn how to relate to different types of people. The book contains a personality test for adults. A test for children is available from ✍*www.DrSonna.org*. If you dislike certain aspects of your own personality, seeing the same traits in one of your children can be very uncomfortable. The first step to improving your relationship may be accepting or changing yourself. In either instance, a psychologist or counselor should be able to help. In the meantime, supportive counseling may help your child feel better about himself and give him the opportunity to work on his own issues. If you see him headed down a self-destructive path similar to one you took, don't assume you can browbeat him out of it. Get him some real help!

Question?

I feel closest to my middle child. Is that terrible?
All of your children need to feel secure about your love. But since they are likely to have very different personalities, it is to be expected that you will feel closer to one child than another. Being aware of your feelings can help you avoid showing undo favoritism.

Although it may be harder for you to accept and deal with one child's personality quirks than another's, they all need your love and affection. Too many strong-willed, independent children end up feeling their parent prefers a sibling because they are constantly being reprimanded, criticized, and punished. Children who receive more parental kindness and compassion often feel badly that one of their siblings receives a lot less. It hurts them to see their sibling being treated unkindly. They may even feel guilty about the love they do receive if it seems to be coming at someone else's expense. Thus, many favored, good-hearted children would gladly trade their special status for more parental kindness toward their sibling.

Every Parent's Favorite Child

Most parents have a favorite age. Some parents prefer infancy because they find infants so uncomplicated and straightforward to care for. "When a baby cries, he usually just needs food, a diaper change, or some cuddles," one mother said. This particular mother found the whining and endless "why" questions of her preschool children much more taxing. Her husband had a harder time with babies because they can't say what is on their minds. When he couldn't get them to stop crying, he feared they might be ill. He also found the emotional displays of toddlers off-putting. Yet, he loved helping inquisitive preschoolers unravel the mystery of everything from lightning to lightening bugs and helping older children with homework.

While many parents consider teenagers especially difficult, some parents find this age group especially delightful. They transition easily from serving as their tween's protector and teacher to their adolescent's mentor and guide. They accept that a teenager's values are basically formed and don't try to control what their adolescent thinks. They enjoy being able to converse as equals and don't get upset when their child tries out different identities or experiments with ideas and fashions they find strange. Tweens who complain that you favor their siblings may benefit from your honest admission that it's harder for you to set limits or know how to relate to their age group. Teens may benefit from hearing that you find it hard to loosen the reins and accept their emerging independence. Although such admissions may be hard for children to hear, thinking that you dislike them personally will probably be more painful for them.

Research studies suggest that parents tend to treat all of their children pretty much alike at a given age. That is, each parent tends to treat all of their newborns in much the same way and has a particular approach to dealing with each of the other age groups: toddlers, preschoolers, tweens, and teens. Older children don't remember that they were indulged when they were younger. They think that their parents should be stricter with the younger children. "If I behaved that way, I would get in trouble," older children say. Meanwhile, younger children think that their older siblings are favored because they are given more privileges. Setting rules and assigning consequences according to age leads to charges of favoritism because children tend to regard one another as peers. As a consequence, most children feel that they are being short-changed. In fact, they may be, but not in the way they think.

Fair Treatment?

Some younger children fear that their parents favor their older siblings because they have more privileges. Most parents try to solve this problem by reassuring their younger children that they will have the same privileges when they are older. But communicating that privileges come with age rarely satisfies but feeds children's eagerness to add candles to their birthday cake. Many children try to grow up too fast. Children aren't ready for privileges until they can handle the responsibilities that go with them. Telling a child that he can have a later bedtime when he reaches the age of his ten-year-old brother suggests that bedtime privileges come with age. Children look to the calendar and clock to decide when they need to sleep. They need to look inside themselves to see if they are getting enough rest. If a child wants a later bedtime, tell him he can have it when he needs less sleep. Agree to push it up when he can get out of bed in the morning after a single wake-up call, awakens in a good mood, can get ready for school on time, and doesn't become tearful or misbehave late in the evening. Similarly, let a child cross the street unaccompanied when he is conscientious about checking for traffic and uses good judgment. Until then, it doesn't matter if your child is four or fourteen; he shouldn't be allowed to cross alone. Regardless of the number of candles on a child's birthday cake, it is too dangerous to let an eighteen-year-old drive if he is reckless and drinks. Yet, a responsible fourteen-year-old might be ready to drive if the government would license him. Your children may not like you to make decisions based on their capabilities. But they will be more likely to regard your decisions as fair.

Treating Everyone Alike

Some parents try to avoid being charged with favoritism and unfairness by bending over backward to treat all of their offspring alike. They spend the same dollar amount on each child when buying new school wardrobes. They literally count the number of birthday gifts to ensure that if one youngster receives three presents worth $100 that the next child gets three with the same value when his birthday rolls around. If one child needs a new pair of shoes, the parent buys shoes for all the children. All of the children have the same bedtimes, trek to the beauty salon to get their hair cut together, and cannot attend a birthday party unless all of their siblings are invited. If one school-age child has to study an hour each night, so do the others.

Essential

Ironically, making a superhuman effort to treat your children alike may increase their rivalry and competitiveness. Children are individuals. They have different needs and capabilities. By treating them the same, you deny their individuality.

When parents fail to acknowledge and affirm children's differences by treating them as individuals, competitive struggles usually worsen. "If it weren't for you, I could go to the museum with Grandma," children say. "Because she didn't invite you, I don't get to go." "If you hadn't wanted to learn to play the piano, we wouldn't have to take piano lessons." To thwart children's efforts to compare themselves to one another, treat them like individuals. It may be helpful and reassuring to explain: "Your sister needs new shoes; when you need shoes, I will buy them for you." Children need to know that their individual needs are being considered and will be taken care of. Because parents tend to treat twins the same, the children end up fighting in an effort to get their separate needs met. They become more focused on their differences in an effort to carve out separate identities. Being fair while treating your children like individuals is hard. It may prove impossible. But it is definitely a worthy goal to strive for.

CHAPTER 7

Settling Squabbles

Parents say that sibling squabbles make mealtimes unpleasant. Family outings are unpleasant because the children spend so much time arguing. Family vacations are especially stressful because the children won't stop picking at one other. Sibling conflicts tend to become more frequent and intense as the children get older. To teach your children to get along, it may help to abandon your current approach to resolving conflicts and try the technique used in family-centered cultures around the world.

Sibling Strife

Kim and Jennifer's parents tried to be fair and impartial when settling their children's conflicts. But the squabbles intensified at times. The loser often felt misunderstood and sometimes a bit victimized. At age thirty, Kim still remembers an incident that took place when she was ten.

My sister and I didn't get along well as kids. She would start an argument, and then I'd get in trouble if I tried to defend myself. She says the same thing; so who knows? As a kid, it seemed like I usually lost. I still remember the time one of her Barbie dolls got broken. I don't know how it happened, but my sister blamed me and called me a bad name. I called her the same name back just as our dad walked into the room. So I got in trouble for saying a bad word. Then my sister started crying about her broken doll. She was very manipulative and could turn her tears on and off like a faucet. She said that I had taken her doll without permission and broken it. Dad made me give my sister one of my dolls.

One night we were eating dinner when my sister suddenly exclaimed, "Move over! You're hogging all the room." "No, I'm not," I protested. "Yes! You bumped me." "I did not," I countered. But Mom took her side and told me to move over and give her more room. So when dinner was done, I ran to the couch and sat in my sister's favorite spot to get even. She raised a ruckus, and Mom came in. I said I was there first, and Mom sided with me. When she went back into the kitchen, I felt pretty smug. "That'll teach you to tell lies about me!" I said. My sister stuck her tongue out at me. It was always like that. We had this ongoing war. We get along now, though I wouldn't say we're close. She still has a tendency to do little competitive things. When my parents and the family get together at her house, I am always served last. She often interrupts when I am talking to Mom or Dad.

 **Fact**

The squabbles you know about may be only the tip of the iceberg. One study found that parents never hear about most of their children's arguments. They take place behind closed bedroom doors or outside the house.

The Family Court

When siblings can't get along, parents are likely to find themselves devoting a lot of time and energy to settling property disputes. Parents serve as detectives as they gather evidence to try to figure out who took whose toy, who was playing with it first, who had it last, and who should have a turn to play with it next. Parents serve as jurors when they decide which child is the innocent victim and which child is guilty of taking a toy that doesn't belong to him, damaging it, or failing to share. As judges, parents award settlements. They decree which child gets to play with the toy next and for how long. They mete out punishments and levy fines by assigning time-outs and having siblings apologize, make amends, and compensate one another for damaging one another's personal property.

In addition to hearing cases involving property disputes, parents settle numerous land wars when children claim that their personal space has been violated. Toddlers begin filing petitions because the new baby is taking up too much room on mother's lap. Later, toddlers get upset when the baby is riding in "their" stroller or blocking their view of the television. As preschoolers, disputes arise about which child gets to ride the mechanical pony first. During elementary school, battles over space commonly involve accusations that a sibling is taking up too much room at the dinner table, hogging the space in the backseat of the car, getting too many turns to sit in the front seat of the car, or entering someone else's room without permission.

Standard Advice for Parents

Most parenting books and articles assure readers that continuing sibling conflicts are normal and to be expected. Parents are urged to try to reach fair decisions and not side too often with one child. If incessant arguing is overwhelming, authors suggest ignoring the squabbles unless violence threatens to erupt. Many parents resort to minimizing the time their children spend interacting, encouraging them to watch television in their rooms, watch a movie in the car, and stay out of one another's rooms.

 *Alert!*

Holding court may seem like a good way to protect each child, punish bullies, ensure that victims receive justice, and uphold each child's rights. But children don't learn to solve their conflicts. They learn to turn to a parent.

Like any plaintiff who achieves a victory in court, the sibling who is pleased with a parent's verdict is more inclined to turn to the justice system the next time he feels he has been wronged. An occasional victory provides powerful reinforcement. Meanwhile, the loser is inevitably displeased with the outcome. Only rarely does he admit that justice was served. He usually feels that some extenuating circumstances should have changed the verdict or produced a lighter sentence; so he usually appeals. If that fails, he may try to even the score or exact revenge by taking the law into his own hands. When recidivist children pause to ponder why they keep losing sibling squabbles, many youngsters conclude that their parent doesn't like or love them as much, or they conclude that they are bad and embrace the role of a little troublemaker. In either way, they can justify mistreating their sibling. Even the sibling who wins a favorable ruling is often made to suffer.

Producing Fair Verdicts

It is hard if not impossible for parents to produce judgments that both siblings consider fair. Consider the following dialogue:

Sister: Donald took my doll!
Brother: I did not! She said I could borrow it! I needed its battery for my flashlight.
Sister: That was yesterday! Today he took my doll without asking, and he used up the battery!
Brother: Well, yesterday she came into my room without permission and messed up my baseball cards. If she can take my things, I should be able to take hers.
Sister: I didn't touch his baseball cards. Why would I do that? I don't like baseball and could care less about your stupid cards.
Brother: She did so! My cards are all mixed up. The corner of my best one is bent.
Sister: Did not.
Brother: My best card is ruined! You should make her pay me for it.
Sister: You should make him buy me a new battery.
Brother: I only used it for five minutes.

The U.S. Supreme Court itself would probably have difficulty evaluating such conflicting testimony. Overwhelmed parents with too many cases on their dockets might sentence both youngsters to spend some time in their respective rooms until they settle down and can play together nicely. But then both children are apt to feel the verdict was unfair. While a time-out may help them settle down, sitting alone in their rooms doesn't teach them to get along.

Hearing Cases

However long a trial lasts and regardless of the outcome, inviting children to testify against one another is divisive. It encourages their belief that safeguarding their personal possessions and space is the central issue. An older child can usually outtalk a younger one. With a lot of practice, he is likely to become a more artful debater and skilled verbal manipulator. Meanwhile, the ready tears of children who are more emotional serve them well by mobilizing their parents' protective instincts. Over time, they become more adept at crying and appearing helpless. By age three, the baby of the family is likely to be quite masterful at emotional manipulation. His tears are real enough. But so is the effect on their parents. Middle children usually do a poorer job of presenting their cases effectively, which may be why they prefer to negotiate settlements out of court. But many find the best way is to avoid their siblings and parents as much as possible and become alienated from their families.

Accepting a case for trial involving a dispute over a toy confirms that such grievances are important. By ordering that a toy be returned to its rightful owner or shared, you communicate that respecting property rights is more important than respecting a sibling's feelings. This can reinforce children's greed without helping them develop the empathy, courtesy, and compassion needed to get along. It also teaches that it is all right to destroy family peace and harmony if a toy is at stake. Despite the positive values parents want to teach, they legitimize and reinforce their youngsters' materialism.

Making Value Judgments

In most cultures, possessing material objects and protecting personal boundaries are not considered the route to true happiness. "Protecting personal boundaries" includes declaring a bedroom off-limits to siblings, being first, not wanting to share a parent's lap, and maintaining a careful physical distance. In modern industrialized Western countries, arguments commonly revolve around such issues as who gets the first drink from a water fountain and who is taking up too much room on the sofa. In other countries, parents discourage children from competing with siblings by striving to be first. Family members enjoy curling up together on the couch. Parents in most of the world's cultures raise their children to believe that family relationships are the principal source of joy, not possessing objects and safeguarding space. (See Chapter 14 for more discussion of these differing value systems.) This may be because in poorer countries material possessions and space tend to be scarce. But now that families in wealthier countries have become so fragmented, many parents are searching for ways to restore traditional family values.

Parents with family-centered values are unconcerned that toys are in the hands of their proper owners and actively discourage siblings from testifying against one another. When two children fight over a toy, such parents might simply point out to the older child, "Your brother wants that truck." If the older child doesn't automatically hand it over, the parent demonstrates the correct response: find another way to appease the baby. That might involve distracting the baby by offering him another toy or playing with the truck together. If those solutions don't work, the parent takes the truck from the older child, hands it to the younger one, and says, "See? Now the baby is happy. Aren't you glad?" The values being communicated are that older family members must see to the welfare of younger ones, and toys are mere diversions, not routes to happiness—but babies are too young to understand such things.

Of course, a toddler may not understand, either. He may think that he needs the truck to feel happy. So his parent sets out to teach him. "Come with me," the parent says. "I've got something better for you." The parent takes her sobbing toddler to another room to distract him from the disputed toy and gives him something that will make him happier: loving attention. While the baby plays with the truck, mother wipes her toddler's eyes and his nose. She does not berate him for wanting the truck, refusing to share, or being a baby. She doesn't bribe him with another toy, knowing he would only want the truck. She lets him cry and continues wiping tears as she directs him to an activity that is fun and appropriate for someone his age. If she is busy cooking, she may sit him on the kitchen counter (where a baby would never be allowed to sit) so he can help her fix lunch. "I think you're old enough to sit up here," she may say as she invites him to help rip lettuce leaves for a salad or pull pickles out of a jar and set them in a bowl. She may sing or recite nursery rhymes while they work to be sure he has a good time. His relationship with his brother is reinforced at lunch, when his mother proudly informs the baby that his big brother helped prepare the meal. When grandmother telephones, he will be encouraged to share news of his grand accomplishment as a chef.

 **Fact**

In disputes presented to a family-centered parent, the younger child usually gets the toy, and the older child is given positive attention. Alternatively, the disputed toy is put away, and no one gets to play with it. If a toy is divisive and creates conflict, it is considered undesirable.

If mother is washing clothes when a fight over a toy erupts, the toddler may be invited to help her with the laundry. He might get to help measure out the detergent and will surely be allowed to push the buttons on the machines, or his mother might sit down and read him a story. If time is limited, she might take him into the bathroom and fuss over him by combing his hair, perhaps applying a dab of Dad's gel to help cheer up her toddler and reinforce the message:

Babies play with toys; big boys get to do more fun, interesting activities they would find appealing.

When the toddler has settled down, chances are that the baby is already tired of playing with the truck. If not, the toddler may respond like his mother. He may distract the baby with another toy or activity. If the same dispute resurfaces, the mother removes the toy so that no one gets to play with it. But she does not take sides. If another family member learns that a toddler is crying because he wants to play with the same toy as the baby, that family member teaches the same message. He shows the toddler how to try to distract the baby, suggests ways to share it, or says that a ball is nothing to cry about and engages the toddler in another, more interesting activity.

Alert!

Preschoolers who have been raised with the family-centered method rarely cry when a younger sibling takes their toy. They have learned how to handle the situation. If you have been arbitrating disputes and try to switch methods, you will need to help your children adjust.

Sibling Privileges and Responsibilities

Settling disputes by giving the toy to the baby isn't an act of favoritism. Just as parents in Western countries insist that "bottles are for babies" when a weaned toddler wants one, members of family-centered homes teach that toys are for babies. When parents who are accustomed to settling disputes by issuing verdicts on a case-by-case basis first learn about this method, they fear that indulging the younger child will turn him into a tyrant. But family-centered parents don't hold toys in such high esteem; they view comfort and attention from a human as the greater gift. The younger child will be expected to relinquish his toys to the next child in line. Older children and parents take away dangerous objects from the baby; so he doesn't get everything he wants. Older children can't manipulate their parents, but they work hard to master the art of convincing younger ones to share without upsetting them. The youngest child doesn't need to manipulate to win possession of the toys.

 Essential

The family-centered method requires parents to adopt a special mindset. They must believe that family harmony is more important than besting a sibling by being first, older children merit extra responsibilities as well as extra privileges, and it is better to nurture children by giving them positive attention instead of toys.

Older children learn to keep their prize possessions where the baby can't see them so they won't have to relinquish them and risk having them destroyed. Otherwise, all they can do is try to distract the littlest family member with a more fun, interesting activity or try to control the damage as best they can while he plays with their things. If the youngest child persists in taking all the toys, the other children are more likely to feel sorry for him than angry. They have learned from experience that material objects are less satisfying than loving attention. They are secure in their parent's love and don't feel jealous. This method may strike parents in Western nations as bizarre. It requires them to abandon all of their notions about what is fair. Of course, various complications arise when parents apply the family-centered method to daily squabbles. But this method quickly eliminates most sibling disputes. It also teaches children some valuable lessons such as:

- If I fight with a younger sibling over a toy, he will get to play with it by himself, or it will be put away. This deters fighting.
- If I want to play with the same toy as my younger sibling, I have to find a way to keep him from objecting. Older children

are deterred from upsetting the baby, who must be appeased. They work hard to keep him happy.

- If I can distract my sibling with another toy, I can play with the one I want. Children learn to get their own needs met by attending to their sibling's needs.
- If I can talk my sister into sharing the toy, I can play with it, too. Children are motivated to invent cooperative games and compromise.
- If I tell my mother that my sibling won't let me play with the toy, she will comfort me with an activity suitable for an older child. Children learn that people are more satisfying than objects and being older has advantages.

Parents are unifiers, not dividers. Older children learn that they have a responsibility to nurture younger, more vulnerable human beings; younger children learn to mind elder children. No method for managing sibling relationships is perfect, and family-centered parents still serve as detectives, judges, and juries on occasion. Most cases involve charges that an older child failed to care for a younger sibling properly or that a younger child failed to mind an older one. Sibling relationships are hierarchical rather than egalitarian, so older children relate to younger ones more like parents than peers. Children don't squabble as they jockey for position in the pecking order. But there are some disadvantages, too. Even as adults, older children may continue to treat the youngest family member like the baby. Some older children continue to feel overly responsible for their younger siblings decades later. See Chapters 18 and 20 for help overcoming these problems.

Teaching New Values

Changing to the family-centered method midstream can be a challenge. For starters, you might announce that, from here on in, whenever two children argue over a toy, the younger child gets the toy or the toy will be put away. If they argue over what television show to watch or who sits where, the younger one gets to choose. If an older child is playing with his baseball cards and a toddler wants to play, too, the older child will have to try to talk him out of it or supervise very carefully. Otherwise, the cards may be taken away until the older child can care for them without upsetting a younger sibling. He might do that by playing with them in his room and keeping the door closed or waiting to take them out until the younger children are asleep or playing outside.

You might consider taking the extreme step of announcing that all other disputes about which child goes first, gets the first pick, first choice, and first everything will be based on age. From now on, the younger child goes first, and the oldest goes last. Explain that younger children are usually less mature. They have poorer impulse control, have poorer tolerance for frustration, are greedier, and are less able to handle waiting. They don't understand that being served dessert first isn't a big deal—and it won't be if no one can start eating until everyone else is served. Explain that older children have lots of special privileges that younger children don't have, so letting them go first will help compensate them for their many disadvantages, which range from hand-me-down clothes to earlier bedtimes.

Learning to put their wants on hold will prepare older children to be parents and raise children of their own some day. Comfort older children when they are upset and be sure they get lots of extra attention when they are disappointed about having to wait. You will probably find that siblings' determination to be first wasn't because they actually wanted the biggest piece of cake or the first pony ride. Rather, being singled out by you for a special honor made them feel important. The chosen child felt special and reassured of your love. When someone else was chosen, he felt insecure. Once he is expected to wait because he is older, more mature, and more capable, he may not mind going second, third, or last. A family-centered method can be very effective for eliminating squabbles, as well as for helping your children get along, encouraging them to nurture one another, discouraging greed, and encouraging them to share.

CHAPTER 8

Tackling Teasing and Tattling

Siblings may claim they are just kidding when they tell one another, "You're such a klutz" or "You look stupid in those glasses," or roll their eyes at one another condescendingly. But being teased can make children self-conscious about real or imaginary flaws and undermine their self-esteem. Negative comments from a family member are especially hurtful. Children tattle when they believe that family rules are being broken. Rather than simply admonishing tattlers to mind their own business, consider whether they need better instructions about what to do when a sibling misbehaves.

Siblings and Self-Image

Siblings exert a powerful influence on one another's self-image and self-esteem. Eric's story illustrates how children can end up with a distorted view of themselves.

> When we were growing up, my brother and sister and I didn't dare make fun of one another or put each other down in front of our parents. But behind their backs, we were merciless toward one another. My brother Don and I teased our sister about being fat. Even though she was thin, comments about her weight always got a rise out of her. If we saw her eating chips or a candy bar, we would say, "Are you sure your thighs can take it?" If she asked for a second helping at dinner, we

would puff out our cheeks when our parents weren't looking to make our statement. My sister started dieting when she was nine. In high school, she had to get help for anorexia. In a family counseling session, the shrink acted like my parents might be too uptight about her eating or her looks or something. I knew that Don and I were to blame but couldn't bring myself to say anything. I apologized to my sister, but it didn't change anything. She's better now, but I still feel guilty.

Living Their Labels

Being teased about being a poor reader can make it hard for students to concentrate when they are reading; so they make more errors. Being teased about being clumsy makes a child tense and more distracted, so he is more likely to stumble, trip, or miss the baseball that is tossed to him. The predictable result is that children end up confirming for themselves and others that they have certain deficits and deficiencies that didn't even exist initially. Eric's story demonstrates how he and his sister assigned a cruel label to their brother Don and got him to live up to it.

Our brother Don was the studious one. He didn't play a sport and wasn't particularly athletic, and my sister and I teased him about being clumsy. I guess that made Don nervous. After we called him a klutz, he would predictably stumble, or he would spill or drop something. We got a kick out of teasing him, then sitting back and waiting for an accident to happen. Then, of course, we rubbed it in by teasing him some more. One evening Don dropped a plate. I said, "The klutz strikes again." Don looked so mortified that I realized I needed to cut it out, so I stopped. One night when my sister was teasing him, I said, "Hey, why don't you lay off?" That was all it took for Don and I to get to be friends. As an adult, he took up tennis and became a decent player; it's obvious we were wrong about him. He's actually pretty athletic.

Reversing Negative Dynamics

A bit of empathy, some honest self-disclosure, and a simple apology can be amazingly powerful. Eric used these positive methods to reverse negative dynamics and shore up his relationship with one kind comment.

My brother and sister teased me about being a "dumb jock." I was afraid they were right. When I was in high school, I was into sports and was hypersensitive about people thinking I wasn't smart. Ignoring them and telling them to leave me alone never got anywhere. One night when Don and my sister started in on me, I was really exhausted. I said, "Hey, let's not go there, OK?" The next time, I tried humor and said, "Why not pick on somebody your own size?" That got a laugh because I was a full head taller and solid muscle. We actually joked together and had a decent time. One night I was kind of down, and Don started in on me again. I said, "You win; I'm a loser. Are you happy now?" An hour later Don suddenly gave me his favorite CD. "No reason," he said. But I knew he was trying to apologize. I started using the same line on my sister. When I said, "You're right. I'm hopeless," she stopped razzing me. We all got to be friends, but I guess the damage was done. I still worry that people will think I'm all brawn and no brains. My advice to parents is to let your kids know that what they say to each other can stick. Saying "that's not nice" doesn't cut it.

Alert!

If you tease your children about their faults and failings, they are likely to follow your lead and tease one another. Rubbing their noses in their quirks and mistakes will make them feel ashamed without helping them improve.

Joking Versus Teasing

There is a difference between light-hearted joking and teasing. The target of a joke appreciates the humor; the target of teasing feels hurt. Onlookers can easily mistake one for the other; so before staging a rescue, it is important to verify that a sibling feels hurt by what is being said. A comment such as "Now I've got you, you wimpy little squirt" could make a child ashamed of his small stature and disinclination to fight. But these words are probably harmless if uttered during a wrestling match. In fact, they might actually help a sensitive youngster. On the playground, such comments are often part of boys' good-natured banter. Children who overreact alienate others and turn potential friends into enemies by taking offense where none is intended.

 **Alert!**

Some children do not realize that their teasing is harmful. When admonished by a parent to stop, some children feel unjustly accused. Encourage a victimized sibling to say, "That hurts my feelings; please stop." Being directly confronted by a victim is the best way to drive the message home.

The only way to know whether comments that disturb you are negative and destructive on one hand or harmless and benign on the other is to ask the targeted child if he is bothered by what is being said. If he is not upset, there is no reason to intervene. Playful kidding brings siblings closer and brings much joy and laughter to family life. Beware of trying to intervene by saying, "Don't tease your sister about her kinky hair! She can't help having been born that way. You'll give her a complex." In doing so, you paint her hair as a misfortune. It is better to tell her siblings: "A lot of people like curly hair! If you don't, remember the old saying 'If you can't say something nice, it is better to say nothing at all.' Trying to hurt someone who loves you is cruel, and I won't stand for it." If a child who has been teased about her hair has come to dislike it, suggest her siblings take positive action, such as offering to help her comb it or figure out a new hairstyle. But denigrating people for things they cannot change is inherently wrong. Most siblings know one another's "hot buttons"—the special sensitivities and insecurities that elicit a big reaction. Simply saying "four eyes" in the presence of a child who dislikes her glasses can be upsetting. She needs to be helped to understand when she is reacting to innocent comments. She won't understand if children add insult to injury by saying, "I wasn't even talking about your stupid glasses." She needs a proper explanation: "I didn't mean you. I was talking about a boy at school. The issue isn't really his glasses. It's that he's a show-off."

Tackling Teasing

Siblings tease one another for a number of reasons. When a youngster is in a bad mood, he may tease a sibling to discharge tension or to have a temporary distraction from other troubles. If a child is feeling helpless, picking on a sibling can restore a sense of being in control. Some siblings are actually trying to be helpful when they tease, as when older brothers tease younger siblings in an effort to toughen them. This helps some children if they comprehend their siblings' motive. But this tough-love approach can backfire and beat down the child they are trying to help. Some bullies enjoy the feeling of power that comes with being able to upset others. When a child doesn't know how to hold his own against a bigger, stronger sibling, teasing can turn the tables on him. Toddlers often persist in teasing out of curiosity; they are intrigued that scampering off with their brother's ball elicits exciting shouts and a frantic chase.

Time-out

When a preschool child is teasing a sibling, issue a reminder that "that's not nice" and help him develop compassion by pointing out that his sibling is upset. Have him apologize and give his sibling a hug and a promise not to tease him anymore. Compassion is the best antidote for teasing. To stop older children from teasing, you will probably need to put forth some effort to drive home the lesson that teasing is wrong because it is hurtful. When an incident occurs, begin by separating the children and sending them both to time-out. Instruct the child who feels victimized to contemplate his part in the problem; or, if he considers himself innocent, instruct him to consider what he might do or say in the future to get his persecutor to back off. A simple instruction to "think about why your brother teased you" should suffice for younger children. Join the alleged perpetrator for a private chat and ask him if he understands why it is wrong to tease a sibling and is against the family rules. Don't allow yourself to be distracted by the "buts": "But he teased me first," "But all I said was . . .," or "But he took my toy without permission." State that he has been accused of violating the family rule against teasing. Emphasize that you need to be sure he understands why the rule exists: Teasing hurts people's feelings; family members are not to hurt one another; and being teased by a loved one is especially hurtful. Communicate the underlying value: Family members need to feel emotionally safe at home, which they cannot do if they are at risk of being hurt by people who are supposed to love them. Family members must not tear one another down or make them feel badly about themselves. Once the accused can state why teasing is wrong, listen to what transpired and be ready to deliver more lessons.

- **"All I said was . . ."** If the accused thinks that his sibling overreacted, remind him that when he steps on someone else's toes accidentally and doesn't think he did it hard enough to hurt, common courtesy dictates that he apologize. Explain that family members are duty-bound to treat one another with sensitivity and compassion; so when he is being told that he has hurt a sibling's feelings, he needs to apologize. Point out that if someone is especially sensitive about wearing glasses, even a completely innocent comment about shortsightedness can be hurtful. The way to get a sibling to stop overreacting to innocent comments about his poor vision is to explain: "I didn't suggest you put on your glasses to make fun of you. I just think you could read the sign yourself if you would wear them."

- **"But he was bugging me." "But he started it."** Listen as the accused describes what provoked him. Respond empathically with a simple statement, perhaps by saying "I can understand how you felt." But stick to the issue at hand by pointing out that teasing doesn't solve anything; it makes a conflict worse. Point out that starting conflict is easy but that resolving it is more challenging. Once he learns, he'll have some great skills for getting along with other people he finds difficult. Tell him to call you the next time he doesn't know how to handle a problem and feels tempted to tease.

- **"You always take his side."** Many parents become distracted from the issue at hand and begin defending themselves when they are accused of hurting their child. Demonstrate the proper way to respond. Apologize and explain your intentions, just as you want your child to do when he is told that he inadvertently hurt his sibling's feelings. For instance, you might say, "I'm sorry if I hurt you. I love you and do not mean to side with your sibling against you."

Reassure your child that if he is teased and needs help, you will be glad to assist him, but he needs to let you know. Then return to the subject at hand. To help your child develop empathy and compassion, instruct him to think of a time when someone outside the family teased him and hurt his feelings. If he is impervious to teasing, ask him to think of ways to help his sibling become similarly immune to it.

Alert!

When parents take a strong stand against teasing, many children appear to comply but continue to tease one another in private. Be sure that all of them understand you are willing to help them if they are teased.

Pausing to Ponder

Meet privately with the child who claims to have been teased. Help him consider his part in the problem. Discuss how his sibling might make amends and how to respond if his sibling teases him in the future. If the victim is very sensitive about a particular issue, he may have over-reacted to a benign comment. He needs to let his sibling know to avoid that subject. To that end, he might explain: "I hate having to wear glasses. Please don't bring them up." Role-play some possibilities. Then, if his sibling continues teasing him, at least the matter will be clarified: The issue isn't being nearsighted or needing glasses; his sibling purposely tries to make him feel badly about himself. Although that would be a hard lesson, it is probably healthier to conclude "My brother is teasing me again because he is mean and likes to upset me" than "My brother loves me and keeps mentioning my glasses because they are ugly."

Conflict Resolution

After you have talked to each child individually, sit down together with them to discuss the matter. Restrict the conversation to the current incident. Otherwise, an endless list of complaints is likely to emerge, with the accused child claiming he teased his sibling because he cheated at cards, the victim saying he cheated at cards because his sibling entered his room without permission, and so forth. Charges and countercharges escalate tensions and make it impossible to resolve anything. Instead, empathize with the fact that both children have been getting their feelings hurt a lot. Stress the importance of dealing with issues as they arise rather than letting them fester.

Usually, an apology and a handshake is enough for a sibling to forgive and move on. If the child who has been accused refuses to apologize, he may be innocent. Or he may be guilty but unwilling to accept responsibility for his cruelty, intentional or not. Short of administering a lie detector test, there is no way to know for sure. Moreover, knowing the truth doesn't serve a useful purpose. Your jobs are to teach that teasing is against the rules, help your youngsters develop empathy for one another, encourage them to accept responsibility for their part in disputes, and help them find enduring solutions to their conflicts.

 **Fact**

Punishing children can curtail problem behavior such as teasing in the short run. In the long run, punishments increase aggressiveness; so teasing is likely to worsen. Efforts to teach good values, especially empathy, compassion, and respect, are usually more effective.

If the accused child refuses to apologize, ask him to demonstrate his understanding that teasing is hurtful by recounting an incident in which being teased hurt his feelings. If being teased doesn't bother him, encourage him to share how he manages to shrug it off. He may have some valuable advice that could be of benefit to a more sensitive sibling. Ask him to commit to not tease his brother in the future. In the event that hard feelings persist and the boys remain stalemated, set up a time to continue the discussion the next day. After having had time to think about the incident, they may have a different perspective. Often they would rather drop the matter rather than endure another intense discussion. It is important to ask them how they got over being mad. If they shrug and say, "We just started playing a video game, and we forgot all about it," suggest that when someone starts teasing in the future, they may need to switch to a different activity. If a sibling says, "I went in my room to listen to music, and when I came out, he left me alone," support their wise decision to separate for a cooling-off period. If the victim says, "He just started being nice to me," it may be that even though the accused never admitted any guilt, the message that teasing hurt the victim was successfully conveyed and the youngster repented. Let him know that you are glad he is getting along with his brother.

Tackling Tattling

It can be irritating to have a child continually seek you out to report that a sibling left the bathroom without hanging up his towel, is eating a cookie without permission, or is jumping on the bed again. Don't assume that a little informant merely enjoys getting his siblings into trouble. Most elementary school children are genuinely concerned about rules. Children may have trouble following rules themselves but nevertheless believe that rules are important and need to be observed. Children under age twelve also tend to be very literal. If you say that no one is to have anything else to eat or drink until dinner, they may think their sibling is committing a high crime by drinking a glass of water. Accusing an informant of tattling sends a confusing message. Youngsters wonder why parents set a rule if they don't care that it is being broken. It is more helpful to clarify the rule (e.g., beverages such as soda and milk are to be avoided so as not to ruin their appetite; it is always OK to drink water). Otherwise, explain why this particular transgression doesn't need your attention (e.g., "I told your sister she could have a cookie since she didn't eat lunch"). If a rule is being broken but you don't wish to tackle the problem, you can simply state, "Your brother shouldn't be doing that, but I'm too tired to deal with this problem right now." That frees your child to decide whether to relay the message "Mom says you shouldn't do that" or follow your lead and ignore the problem. Discouraging your children from letting you know what their siblings are up to is a definite mistake. During adolescence, you may want to be informed that a sibling is using drugs, sneaking out at night, shoplifting, or breaking other important rules. By then, most have learned that to inform a parent is tattling, and they expect to be regarded as snitches and "narks." They try to help troubled siblings on their own rather than finding an appropriate resource.

Another type of tattling involves accusations of having been mistreated by a sibling. Complaints of "Larry took my hula hoop and won't give it back" or "Susana won't give me a turn to play with her new toy" sometimes arise when children are in a bad mood. They find one another's behavior to be irritating because they are irritable. Suggesting they separate for a time may help. But often, children really don't know how to solve everyday problems on their own. After being given lots of simple solutions such as "Tell Larry to give you back your hula hoop" or "Tell Ana she either needs to get the stain out of your blouse or give you one of her blouses," children should learn to solve small, everyday problems themselves. To speed up the process, encourage your youngsters to say what they think should be done to fix a problem rather than handing them readymade solutions. If they have good ones of their own, help them develop confidence in their ability to settle disputes by pointing out that they seem to know how to handle this type of situation themselves. If they are at a loss as to what to do or their ideas don't sound reasonable, suggest some alternatives or recommend that they bring up the matter at a family meeting. The point is to guard against accusing your children of tattling when you lack the time, energy, or motivation to provide the help they are requesting.

CHAPTER 9

Uniting Siblings

Even warring siblings tend to come to each other's defense if one is being threatened by an outsider. It is common for siblings to unite when a major illness, divorce, or a death threatens a family's well-being. But you don't need to wait for a crisis to help your children discover that they care about one another. Help your children bond, de-emphasize competitive activities, and do team-building exercises so they can learn to cooperate. Your dream of having your children relate like friends may be easier to fulfill than you think.

Forging a Bond

Like many U.S. children, Haley and her sister didn't get along very well. In fact, they didn't even seem to like one another. But Haley stepped forward to help her sister when she was injured. When tragedy struck, they turned to one another for support, became close, and struck up an enduring relationship.

> *When I was young, I used to wish I was an only child. I didn't like my little sister coming into my room and bothering me and my friends. I thought my parents spoiled her. She was three years younger than me, and whenever we argued, they always took her side. I called her "Do-do bird" just to upset her. But I was also protective of her. If other kids bothered her and I found out about it, I stepped in and made sure they left her alone. When she was seven, she fell off a swing and broke*

her arm. I couldn't stand that she was in pain. I let her hang out in my room and was nice to her until it healed. Then I told her to stay out of my room, and we were back to squabbling about everything under the sun like before.

Mom and Dad began having problems when I was in sixth grade. The living room was near my sister's bedroom, and I started hanging out there to hear what they were arguing about. I was afraid they might get divorced, and I wanted to know what was going on. My sister was afraid, too, but hearing them argue made her nervous and kept her up at night. One night she came into my room and asked to sleep with me. I let her, and I read her a book to help her fall asleep. She started sleeping in my room every night, and we got close. Maybe having our parents act like kids helped us shape up.

Teaming up gave us lots of power. Our parents were at the point where if Mom said "white" Dad would say "black" and vice versa. So if my sister and I sided with my Mom about something, we outvoted Dad three to one. He couldn't take the pressure and would give in. If we sided with Dad, Mom couldn't take the pressure and would give in. Once they were arguing because Mom said my sister could go roller-skating after Dad had grounded her. My sister really wanted to go. I said, "Let her go," and that ended the argument. My sister got to go. Sometimes my sister and I felt kind of nervous about having so much power. All we really wanted was for them to get along. But it was great getting our way.

Alert!

Instead of the usual board games and decks of cards that end up with one winner and one sobbing child, see the selection of cooperative board games by Family Pastimes at *www.life.ca* or call (800) 215-9574 for a catalog.

United They Stand

Crises have been called opportunities in disguise, and this is often the case for siblings. When confronting a family crisis, children are often able to set aside their petty differences and put even serious, long-standing disagreements on hold. Tweens and teens that couldn't be in the same room without arguing suddenly become allies when a family member is seriously injured or gravely ill or when a family move, divorce, or death threatens to disrupt their way of life. Adult siblings manage to mend fences that have been broken for decades when one of them or a parent has a personal crisis. This is not true across the board, of course. Children who are too young to understand what is happening typically respond to increased family stress by becoming crankier, which worsens their relationships with one another. Some children side with different parents during a divorce and end up at odds. When some adult siblings try to make joint decisions for an ailing parent's care, they end up arguing over every detail. But in general, even children who never were close show an amazing ability to work together when serious family troubles develop. The big question for many families is how to get their offspring to show similar concern for one another on a daily basis.

Competition Versus Cooperation

Many siblings don't get along because they are constantly competing with one another. They spend their days trying to outdo one another and relate like bitter rivals. Some parents believe that sibling competition is healthy and beneficial, so they encourage it. Competition can in fact motivate children to do their best. But there is a difference between trying to live up to a successful sibling's example and trying to compete with him. Human beings have won the age-old battle for survival of the fittest by cooperating with members of their own family, clan, or tribe and competing with outsiders, not with members of their own group. Throughout human history, working as a team increased a family's ability to hunt down dinner; defend its food supply, water, and women from outsiders; and care for members who couldn't care for themselves. Competitions within a family group were ritualized events rather than no-holds-barred attempts to best one another. Rules kept competitions from degenerating into destructive free-for-alls.

Times have changed, but cooperation within family groups still helps individual members. A child is more likely to be able to compete successfully in the outside world if he has a supportive group of family members working on his behalf. To cite one simple example, a student will have a better chance of rising to the top of the academic heap at school if his siblings advise him about how to get along with teachers and peers, provide study tips, and help him with homework. Simply being quiet so a sibling can study and get some sleep the night before a test can make a critical difference. If siblings regard one another as rivals, they have a vested interest in having one another fail. Instead of helping, they may try to undermine each other.

Competition Run Amok

Competitive games and activities can be sources of great fun and excitement for children of all ages. If siblings can observe rules of good sportsmanship, playing competitive games can bring them closer while encouraging them to stretch and grow. However, some children are too insecure to enjoy competitive pastimes. They look to victories for confirmation of their personal value, investing their egos in each throw of the dice or race toward a finish line. They can only feel good about themselves as long as they are winning, and competitive games produce a lot of tension and anxiety but little joy. When insecure children lose, they see themselves as losers or believe they are losing at the game of life itself. Beating or one-upping a sibling provides a temporary emotional boost, but it doesn't last. They may turn every situation into a competition in an effort to garner the continuing affirmations they need to feel good about themselves. A child is likely to receive more affirmations of his personal self-worth and value if he is friends with his siblings rather than if he competes with them. Encourage your children to work together. When they are racing to bed, discourage them from playing "last one in bed is a rotten egg." Instead, have them play "beat the clock" so that they are both trying to get there before a timer goes off. In this way, they have an incentive to work together.

 *Question?*

Do some children enjoy arguing?
Some children, especially boys, enjoy a sort of verbal roughhousing that can sound to adults like arguing. But the children don't feel threatened or intimidated and don't get their feelings hurt. When asked about their "argument" later, they say they were having fun.

Overly competitive children alienate their siblings by casting them in the role of opponents, treating them like adversaries, and constantly trying to show them up. When two children are instructed to set the table, one child may put more energy into pointing out everything his sibling is doing wrong than into the chore. Some children continue this pattern of faultfinding into adulthood. When they gather at holidays, they take exception to or find flaws in almost everything their sibling says or does. In so doing, they engender ill will by turning conversations into win/lose debates. When confronted about their nit-picking and negativity, some insist that they are simply correcting their sibling's mistaken notions. But if each time a child says "white" a sibling feels compelled to say "black" or "gray," he is clearly more interested in scoring points during a conversation than in having one.

It can be tempting to try to put "know-it-alls" in their place, but attempts to show up your children merely reinforce the same competitive pattern. When dealing with minor children, take a strong stand against criticism. Affirm each youngster's right to have and express his own views. Require chronic debaters to summarize what their sibling said before stating their own position. This encourages them to listen when their sibling speaks instead of spending the time compiling lists of items with which they disagree. Ask adult children not to interrupt one another, and studiously ignore those who do. Ignore competitive comments, too. When a sibling makes a positive contribution to a conversation, provide reinforcement with an approving smile, nod, and verbal acknowledgment.

Alert!

When children turn everyday events into competitions and argue over who gets the biggest piece of cake, look for ways to turn them into cooperative activities. For instance, if you have two children, let the older one cut the cake and the younger one choose his slice.

Some firmness may be required to prevent arguing in the car. To solve problems with arguments about who sits where or which radio station to listen to on the way to school in the morning, put the children to bed fifteen minutes early so they can get up earlier. Let them spend the extra time working out a mutually acceptable plan. The obvious solution is simply to take turns, but it is important that the children learn to resolve their differences and enforce whatever rules they come up with themselves.

Team-building for Siblings

Encouraging your children to compete is like pitting members of a football or basketball team against one another. Infighting and attempts to undermine one another undermine the team as a whole. For a winning season, team members need to work together and help everyone do their best. In the 1960s, managers of *Fortune* 500 companies began recognizing that competition in the workplace has the same negative effects on a firm's success that competition among team members has on a team's success. Having employees cooperate with one another enhances a company's ability to compete with other firms. Sports and organizational psychologists have determined the characteristics of productive groups and have developed methods for helping individuals function as good members. You can use the same strategies at home to help your children work together.

Symbols that create a shared identity such as uniforms, logos, and large portraits of important founding fathers and distinguished members help build a sense of shared identity for sports teams and company employees. Similar strategies for families such as dressing alike for outings, painting a family crest on a wall, and hanging up imposing portraits of ancestors are no longer in fashion. But there are other things you can do to give your family a special identity. You might put a sign on your house with your family's name. Create some in-jokes. Provide lots of contact with relatives. Go through the family photo album from time to time to acquaint your children with their ancestors. Describe members of previous generations to help your children take pride in their shared heritage. Tell stories about your own growing up years. Preface discussions of values with "our family believes" and "our family likes to do it this way."

Rituals also help children see their family as special while helping to unify them. This can be anything from smoking a turkey for Thanksgiving to visiting an amusement park on the first day of summer vacation each year. Consider adding a Siblings Day celebration to your list of yearly holidays. The governors of twenty-six states have designated a special day to honor siblings. The Siblings Day Foundation Web site states: "The purpose of Siblings Day, April 10th, is to set aside a day to pay special tribute to honor our brothers and sisters who are living and memorialize those who have died. This day is set aside to remember the utmost importance of this relationship and to cherish, love and respect our brothers and sisters. Siblings share our earliest experiences in life with a bonding that grows stronger into adulthood and throughout our golden years."

Building Trust

A basic requirement for a successful group is for the members to trust one another. According to the Euroregional Center for Democracy, they are less defensive when trust is high, as well as more productive, creative, spontaneous, and willing to assume responsibility and express ideas. A lack of trust impairs efficiency and productivity, and members feel alienated. The best way to build trust is by making your home emotionally safe. To do that, you need to disallow critical comments. Instead of yelling, "Mom, he's doing it wrong," children need to learn to remain focused on their duty to help one another learn and grow. Instruct them to give respectful, noncritical feedback by saying something like "It might work better if you did it this way."

One mother was very weary of her two boys' incessant fighting. They were close in age and highly competitive with one another, and they took every opportunity to try to show one another up. Instead of doing their homework and chores, they spent their time complaining that their sibling wasn't doing his. Instead of enjoying a snack, they spent the whole time complaining that their sibling had received a bigger piece of cake. One day their mother announced that they were to spend their evenings with their hands tied together with a scarf for one week. She hoped that spending several hours at one another's side, having to do everything together, and having only two free hands between them would force them to work together. After spending some time stalemated at the bathroom door arguing over who would enter first, they realized it was better to let their brother go first than to waste time arguing about it. Instead of fighting, they started working out compromises. They had to agree which television program to watch. Flipping coins solved many but not all of their problems. Because they only had one free hand, they had to work together help one another cut their meat at dinner, put on their pajamas, and unscrew the cap on the toothpaste. They became so adept at coordinating their movements that they managed to play some video games together. As they grew more trusting of each other, their mood lightened. There was plenty of clowning and joking along the way, and their mother reported that they went from being archenemies to friends by the end of the week.

Essential

To help solidify your family's identity, create a brief family mission statement. Read it at the start of family meetings or incorporate it into bedtime prayers, such as "Help our family fulfill its mission to ..."

Many parents end bickering in the car by putting on videos so the children don't have to interact. But most youngsters spend too much time passively staring at television and movies as it is, and isolating children doesn't teach them to get along. Many disputes that arise in the car stem from crankiness and irritability, but children need to learn to handle their emotions without upsetting others. A simple solution is simply to pull off the road and wait until the children figure out how to solve whatever they are arguing about at the moment. Many parents are amazed how easily children forge treaties and call a truce when properly motivated. After listening to her children's nerve-racking arguments and bickering for two solid days on a cross-country trip, a single mother declared that she would not drive as long as an argument was in progress. Every time the children began picking at each other, she pulled off to the side of the road and simply refused to budge. The first time she stopped the car, the youngsters spent ten minutes arguing before they became impatient and said they would settle down so she would drive on. Five minutes later they were bickering again, and she again stopped. They complained that they might never make it to California. She was concerned they might be right but said that was up to them. They bickered for a few more minutes before they reassured her that their latest problem was settled and then managed to get along until it was time to decide where to have dinner. She again pulled off the road and refused to budge until everyone could agree. From then on, the children took charge and managed to nip arguments in the bud. At home, she began calling time-outs when the bickering began. If they argued about what to watch on television, she turned it off until they decided. If they argued about which video game to play or who got to play next, no one played until they could agree.

Cooperative Games

Cooperative activities give siblings a chance to have fun and learn that working together is often the best way to get things done. With a little creativity, almost any endeavor can be turned into an opportunity for shared fun. Here is a small sampling:

- Put your children in charge of making dinner once per week. Let them come up with a menu, figure out the list of ingredients, and do the actual food preparation. If one child tends to dominate the rest, have them take turns serving as head chef.
- Have your children work together to bake the cake or make the cookies for special celebrations.
- Washing the family car gives kids a chance to play in the water and perhaps even get the car clean.
- Make holiday greeting cards a shared endeavor by having the children collect the addresses, address envelops, affix stamps, sign their names, dictate portions of the family letter, or write notes on the cards. Relatives are sure to find cards that the children made themselves far more appealing than the store-bought variety.
- On picnics, try activities like flying kites and throwing Frisbees.
- Instead of keep-away and dodge ball, try balloon toss. Blow up several balloons and see how long family members can keep them all in the air. To increase the challenge, make a rule that older children cannot use their hands.
- Keep joke books in the car for the children to read to one another when they are bored.

For a bit of family fun, have everyone lie down with their head on someone else's abdomen. The first person says "ha," the next person says "ha-ha," and the third person says "ha-ha-ha." When the last person finishes, start over. See how many rounds you can go without anyone laughing—a virtual impossibility.

When your children laugh uproariously over a shared joke and engage in a bit of silliness, avoid admonishing them to settle down. Don't put a damper on your children's moments of shared joy! Having fun together creates strong, long-lasting glue. It brings them together, and the pleasant memories create a bond that can last a lifetime.

CHAPTER 10

Raising Super Siblings

S hould you allow two of your children to try out for the same part in a play, given that at least one is bound to be disappointed? Does it help or hurt siblings to compete for the same honors and awards or strive for fame in the same field or career? Should you try to wrest one child from the shadows of a successful sibling? The stories of superstar athletes, artists, writers, scientists, and politicians highlight the issues that arise when siblings reach for the sky.

Finding a Niche

Carrie's story highlights problems that arise when a child grows up in the shadow of a highly successful sibling.

> *My mother played the piano and taught me to play a little. She wanted me to get serious and take lessons from a regular piano teacher, but I wasn't interested. I was busy with dancing, drama, singing lessons, Girl Scouts, and homework. I thought that having to practice everyday would be boring. Mom convinced my younger brother to take piano lessons. He hated practicing, but nevertheless progressed rapidly and won some major competitions. He achieved so much success so fast that some experts hailed him as the next Van Cliburn.*
> *The piano was a regular topic of conversation at home, and I started to really appreciate piano music. So I decided I wanted to take piano lessons after all. But Mom said, "You are older, make better grades, and seem to outshine*

your brother in everything. He finally has something of his own, and I don't want you honing in on his territory or worse—outdoing him."
I had never stopped to think that my successes might be hard on my brother. I tried to be more sensitive to his feelings. But I still had a burning desire to learn the piano. Mom held firm, so I decided to teach myself. I used my brother's beginning music books and practiced an hour every night. About a year later, I reached Book 4 and got stuck. I couldn't go further without lessons. I went back to the first book and started over again, but couldn't get past the first song in Book 4 again. My brother quit the piano at age twelve and never touched it again, but at that point, I assumed I was too old to start learning. Most concert pianists start taking lessons by age seven.

Two decades later, my best friend bought a piano. "I didn't know you played," I said. She said she didn't, but even old dogs could learn new tricks. I was thrilled! I bought a piano and found a teacher that very week. I studied for four years, practicing several hours each day. Finally, I accepted that I had started too late to make a career of the piano. Since then, I have just played for fun. I've often wondered if I missed my true calling, but I can't say Mom made the wrong decision. If I had taken lessons as a child, it might have been a problem for my brother, and I might have lost interest or turned out not to have any talent.

 **Question?**

Will being in the same activities encourage sibling rivalry?
If your children are overly competitive, they may do better with separate activities. Otherwise, having a shared activity can bring siblings closer. Encourage the loser to take pride in the winner's victory, and help the victor to be sensitive toward the loser's feelings.

The Parent Factor

Many siblings end up with similar activities and hobbies, working in the same field, or even pursuing the very same career they were exposed to while growing up. If a husband and wife have a special interest, their youngsters see related magazines and newsletters on the coffee table, overhear telephone conversations, and hear the subject discussed at dinner. Some children gain a lot of hands-on experience as well. For example, kennel owners commonly enlist their children's help grooming and feeding show dogs. The children go with them to the vet and accompany them to dog shows. The youngsters end up learning the finer points of canine diets, obedience training, health issues, conformation, and showing. Soon they are longing for a champion of their own. If they continue in the field as adults, their background and experience give them an edge, making it more likely that they will distinguish themselves. Some parents make a concerted effort to groom their children to continue their life's work. Joe Kennedy had long been active in politics. He served up family discussions on the subject with most meals. He succeeded at molding his boys into political leaders, with son John serving as a U.S. president, Edward as senator from Massachusetts, and Robert as U.S. attorney general.

Alert!

Shared family activities bring siblings closer. A little mathematician may not want to join in when family members jog. But he might enjoy holding the stopwatch and recording their times as they prepare for a marathon. With some creativity, you may be able to find ways for all of your children to participate.

Because children share their parent's genes, they commonly inherit some of their special abilities and talents. One modern example is the Jacksons. Joe Jackson worked in a steel mill by day and played in an R & B band at night with his brother Luther. Joe's older children took their father's guitar without permission when he was at work and taught themselves to play by accompanying the radio, while the younger siblings sang and danced. Their father eventually found out, recognized their talent, and began working them. The Jackson Five took the world of rock by storm. The youngest sibling, Michael Jackson, went on to win eighteen Grammy awards and achieved worldwide fame as the undisputed king of pop. Each of his siblings produced solo albums of their own.

On the Same Path

Some superstar siblings gravitate toward the same activities on their own. The Brontë sisters, Charlotte, Emily, and Anne, jump-started their distinguished literary careers by visiting libraries together and devoting untold hours to writing stories for their little newspapers, magazines, and chronicles. They had few outside friendships, and their lives centered on one another and their shared passion. As adults, they pooled their poems to publish a poetry book and produced enough individual books to fill a library shelf. The youngest daughter, Anne, enjoyed the most success during their lifetime, but several of her older sisters' books, including *Wuthering Heights* and *Jane Eyre*, became enduring classics.

 **Essential**

> If your children cannot pursue their individual interests due to time and money constraints, try to find an extracurricular activity they all enjoy or look for a way to compromise. Some children prefer to support a talented sibling's passionate interest than pursue an activity.

Even if your children have very different interests, they may have to be in the same activities due to scheduling, transportation, and money problems. You may need for your children to play the same sports, attend the same karate class, go to the same summer camp, or join the same scouting troop. Having to attend disliked activities because of a sibling can engender resentment and exacerbate problems with competition, rivalry, and self-esteem. Many siblings rise to the occasion when they are asked to make a sacrifice on behalf of a brother or sister. One family of very modest means poured all of their extra cash into skating lessons so that one of their daughters could pursue her dream of an Olympic gold medal. The family even uprooted their household and moved across the country so that she could study with the best possible coach. There was no money or time to indulge her younger sister's interests, but she wholeheartedly agreed with the family goal, happily supported her sibling, and could not have been more proud of her sister's victories. Not all siblings would be so gracious, but many gladly rally to the their sibling's cause. Not every child aspires to superstardom.

It is probably a mistake to try to manipulate one child into participating in activities that have actually been chosen to benefit a sibling. One parent tried to convince both of her children to play soccer. She claimed that both children loved the practices and games. But one child was a budding athlete, and the other was a budding artist with no interest in the game. He kept losing his equipment, forgot to inform his parent about his matches, and dragged his heels when it was time to head out the door. If you lack the resources to help each child develop his talents, there are merits to discussing the matter truthfully. You might explain that although the artistic child would undoubtedly prefer a painting class, you only have time and money for one activity and want his sibling to play soccer. Describe the possible benefits and drawbacks for your child. You might tell your little artist that "the exercise would do you good, you might enjoy being on a team, and if you worked very hard, you might discover that you also have the makings of an athlete." Help your little athlete appreciate that because she cannot be in separate activities, that playing soccer will entail a sacrifice on his sibling's part. Discuss both children's preferences and needs and have them suggest solutions. Success really is only 10 percent inspiration; 90 percent is grit and determination. You may discover that a talented athlete isn't all that motivated. If he is, perhaps a young artist would be content with a how-to art book and a new set of paints. If he is passionate about learning, he might join a local group of adult artists and paint with them once per month for free. If you have more money than time, he might benefit from an online cartooning course.

Alert!

The adults-only movie, *Hilary and Jackie,* explores a range of issues faced by superstar siblings. It demonstrates the disasters that ensue when childhood rivals enter the same field and envy one another. The movie is based on Hilary's memoir of her world-famous sister, cellist Jacqueline du Pré.

Superstar Sibling Rivalry

There are many headlines about superstar siblings becoming embroiled in vicious battles. Brothers Orville and Wilbur Wright made aviation history by working together to build and fly the first motorized airplane. Orville served as the pilot at Kitty Hawk, managing to remain in the air for twelve seconds and traveling 120 feet. Orville has been memorialized in North Carolina's license plate slogan "First in Flight." However, because of their intense rivalry, a more fitting slogan might have been "First in Fight." After Wilbur died in 1912, Orville set out to claim all of the credit. When a scandal developed because pilots were crashing and dying in planes built by their company, Wright Aviation, Orville tried to blame the problems on his older, taller, and brighter brother. Orville went so far as to burn letters attesting to his brother's positive contributions. The truth was eventually revealed when a sister refused to destroy letters the boys had written to their father. After their father's death, she helped to set the record straight by donating them to the Library of Congress for the world to see.

Serious squabbles among superstar siblings abound. According to a 2004 article by Corrine Sweet in *The Independent,* actress Julia Roberts and her brother Eric have been estranged for years. Eric believed he was on the path to stardom until his sister "stole his lime-light." He continues to work at less glamorous Hollywood studios. Such headlines create the perception that intense competition and destructive rivalry are inevitable when superstar children pursue careers in the same field. However, it is hard to know whether their small differences of opinion are being blown out of proportion by reporters who dredge up such stories. Some superstar siblings are content to remain in the shadows, and some actually prefer to be there. Paul McCartney's brother changed his last name because the worldwide obsession with the Beatles prevented him from living his own life. Although Paul's brother was also a musician, he denies ever having felt overshadowed by his superstar sibling.

Alert!

The press commonly exaggerates minor squabbles among superstar siblings. Some siblings do well sharing a spotlight, some become alienated on the way up or down from the top, and others begin and end their careers as bitter rivals. Whether being constantly compared undermines their relationship undoubtedly depends on their personalities.

Some superstar siblings are fierce competitors yet manage to remain dear friends. One of the most stunning examples in recent times is the dynamic duo, tennis athletes Serena and Venus Williams. Each of their matches produces one winner and one loser. Many people have a hard time accepting that they have dedicated their lives to trying to beat one another on the courts but manage to remain very close. Ex-tennis star John McEnroe commented, "This is unheard of. It's never happened in tennis, and I don't think it's happened in sports, when the number one and two [contenders for a world title] have to face off against each other, and are so close, and who apparently still love each other so much." The idea that the sisters are such intense rivals and good friends seems to strain people's credibility. McEnroe has not been the only one to intimate that because the sisters sometimes seem to lack the desire to kill each other on the court they might be colluding. One headline proclaimed, "Lackluster Final Missing Sibling Rivalry."

Yet, it is quite possible that these sisters are in fact able to remain close while being fierce competitors. The girls' father took pains to nurture their relationship as well as their game. When his daughters were growing up, he did not allow them to play against each other in order to reduce some the competitive pressures. When Serena left the court in tears after losing to Venus in the 2000 Wimbledon semifinals, it seems safe to assume that she was deeply disappointed about losing. Perhaps she was disappointed in her own performance as well. But whether she also felt envious and resented her more successful sister as some observers suggested is an open question. In commenting on the pair, former U.S. Open champion Tracy Austin, who won the Wimbledon Mixed Doubles with her brother John, said, "I don't think we can ever hope to understand the emotions that they go through when they play each other."

Of course, superstar siblings may perceive one another as rivals even though they are in completely different fields. A medical researcher with a long, distinguished career at an Ivy League university confessed to his siblings that, compared to them, he felt like a complete failure. His astounded brother and sister asked how he could possibly feel that way. They only had bachelor's degrees and worked in low-paying professional jobs, while he jetted around the world to deliver papers to scientific gatherings. Their brother replied, "I'm the only one of us kids to blow my marriage and end up divorced."

If siblings with high aspirations cooperate, they benefit from being in the same field or pursuing similar goals. They are in a unique position to help one another.

- Sibling athletes receive a motivational boost by working out together and coaching one another.
- Sibling authors read and critique one another's work, and they introduce one another's manuscripts to their agents and editors.

- Sibling actors share tips on technique, alert one another to auditions, and provide important contacts and introductions to each other's agents, directors, and producers.
- Sibling academics tutor one another and discuss each other's ideas and research.

In the Shadow of a Supersibling

It is generally assumed that an ongoing competition with a more talented sibling delivers too many crushing blows to the self-esteem of the less talented child. Accordingly, many parents nudge their children into different activities to try to protect them and to remove obstacles to their relationship. Although every child is different, many siblings are not harmed by being lost in the shadow of an exceptionally talented sibling. Antonia Kidman followed her older sister Nicole into drama school, but instead of becoming an international star, she does small programs in Sydney, Australia. Nevertheless, she says, "It's what you want for yourself and what makes you happy."

Alert!

For better or for worse, many siblings capitalize on the fame of their superstar siblings. Sean Connery's brother turned his home into a museum to honor his famous sibling and starred in a spoof on James Bond called *Operation Kid Brother*. President Carter's alcoholic brother Billy used his reflected fame to promote Billy Beer.

It seems easier for younger children to cope with coming in second to an older sibling than for older children to cope with losing out to a younger brother or sister. Perhaps this is because older children are accustomed to being more competent and capable; as long as they continue to outshine younger siblings, the relationship remains unchanged. When a younger child overtakes an older sibling, the older child's concept of himself as being the more capable of the two must change. Sometimes the younger sibling proceeds to try to help the older brother or sister by giving advice and suggestions or offering to provide important contacts. Such a role reversal may insult an older child, who is accustomed to being the teacher and mentor. But again, these trends do not apply to every set of siblings.

Alert!

Although older children tend to have more difficulties adjusting to the success of a younger brother or sister, this is not true for everyone. Some older children applaud the successes of their younger, more successful siblings as enthusiastically as parents.

There are some things you can do to nurture the relationship between siblings who are trying to make names for themselves in the same field. First, encourage them to be clear about their goals. It is fine for each child to strive to be successful, but if the goal is simply to outshine one another, they stand to lose their relationship. Encourage them to use their own progress and achievements as benchmarks for evaluating their success. Comparing themselves to one another is likely to result in hard feelings. Encourage them to take responsibility for their own losses and failures rather than blaming the winner. Thinking "It is his fault that I didn't win" leads to hard feelings, smoldering resentments, and vindictiveness. Accepting that "It is my fault that I didn't win" can spur children to work harder or lead them to decide to put their energies into another, more rewarding activity. Point out that some winners owe their success to chance and circumstance, but most succeed by doing their best despite daunting odds and heady competition. Envious people sometimes win by using underhanded tactics to undo their rivals, but their victories are often short-lived and hollow. They usually lose at the larger game of life.

 **Fact**

> Envious siblings seek to undermine one another. Envy is not a given among siblings. A child can admire his more attractive, talented, or capable siblings and appreciate their gifts. By trying to learn from them, he is more likely to rise to their level.

In general, research has found brothers to be more competitive than sisters. Eric Douglas, the drug-addicted, alcoholic half brother of actor Michael Douglas and son of Kirk Douglas, was never able to get an acting career off the ground despite his fabulous contacts. In an interview, Eric once said that his family contained two Oscar winners and one "social embarrassment." Although sisters tend to be more cooperative than competitive, plenty of girls continue their childhood rivalry into adult life. In the biography, *America's Queen: The Life of Jacqueline Kennedy Onassis,* author Sarah Bradford noted that Lee could not hold her own against her sister Jackie, who went on to become the first lady and wife of a billionaire business tycoon. Their relationship during childhood was contentious. At one point Jackie knocked Lee unconscious for two days by hitting her with a croquet mallet. Jackie was four years older, stunningly beautiful, and accomplished in an area of great importance to their father: equestrianism. Lee's father required her to jump fences repeatedly, even though the horse kept stalling and she was repeatedly thrown. Although Lee recalls sharing some special moments with her father, she was hurt by his expectation that she match her older sister. Lee said, "I revered him and just longed for his love and affection."

The best way to wrest your other children from the shadow of a supersibling is to help them find their own niches. This may simply entail helping them appreciate their personal talents. It may mean helping them pursue special activities so they can develop in areas that interest them. You may need to begin by rethinking your values and expanding your notion of what constitutes success. If you value academic achievement above all else and have one child who is an academic superstar, you may inadvertently consign the rest to the shadows because they lack similar abilities or interests. It can be especially hard to accept that some of your children have great talent but lack interest in an area that you personally cherish. For instance, if you hold athletic or academic talent in high regard and have several children with outstanding physical or intellectual abilities, you may heap praise on the sibling who goes out for sports or makes good grades and deride the others for being lazy because they are not similarly motivated. Many adults rise to the top of their fields but cannot appreciate their accomplishment because their families will not acknowledge their success in an area they did not choose. Encourage each child to follow his own dream, and all of them will know you regard them as superstars. For many children, that is enough.

Alert!

Some children want to succeed in the same area as a supersibling, although they lack his talent. If they are willing to pay the price by dedicating themselves to their goal with the kind of single-minded commitment superstardom entails, they may succeed. Encourage them to be realistic about the amount of work involved.

Superstar Siblings

Siblings are in a position to help one another with their careers. Many brothers and sisters have been instrumental in helping one another achieve superstardom as entertainers, businesspeople, scientists, athletes, politicians, and writers. Here are some famous siblings.

- Gregg and Duane Allman
- Sandy and Alberto Alomar (baseball)
- Maxene, Patty, and LeVerne Andrews (The Andrews Sisters)

- James Arness and Peter Graves
- Kevin and Michael Bacon (The Bacon Brothers)
- Alec, William, Stephen, and Daniel Baldwin
- Lionel, John, and Ethel Barrymore
- Sid, Edward, Robert, and Lee Bass (The Bass Brothers)
- Jeff and Beau Bridges
- Emily, Charlotte, and Anne Brontë
- George W. Bush and Jeb Bush
- Karen and Richard Carpenter (The Carpenters)
- Keith, David, and Robert Carradine
- Patrick, Ryan, Shaun, and David Cassidy
- Hillary Rodham Clinton and Hugh Rodham
- Joan and Jackie Collins (actress, writer)
- Jim, Sharon, Caroline, and Andrea Corr (The Corrs)
- Kieran and Macaulay Culkin
- John and Joan Cusack
- Dizzy and Daffy Dean (baseball)
- Phil and Tony Esposito (hockey)
- Don and Phil Everly (The Everly Brothers)
- Ralph and Joseph Fiennes
- Jane and Peter Fonda
- Joan Fontaine and Olivia de Havilland
- Esther Pauline and Pauline Esther Friedman (Ann Landers and Dear Abby)
- Crystal Gail and Loretta Lynn
- George and Ira Gershwin
- Andy, Maurice, Barry, and Robin Gibb (The Bee Gees)
- Jacob and Wilhelm Grimm (The Brothers Grimm)
- Paul and Morgan Hamm (gymnasts)
- Robbie, Kenny, Johnny, and Tom Hanson (The Hansons)
- Mark and Christine Harmon
- June Haver and Gypsy Rose Lee
- Eric and Beth Heiden (skaters)
- Rudolph, O'Kelley, Ronald, and Vernon Isley (The Isley Brothers)

- Jackie, Tito, Jermaine, Marlon, and Michael Jackson (The Jackson 5) and Janet Jackson
- Ashley and Wynnona Judd (actress, singer)
- Stacey and James Keach
- John F., Robert F., and Edward M. Kennedy
- John F. Kennedy, Jr. and Caroline Kennedy Schlossberg
- Ronnie and Reggie Kray (gangsters)
- Betty and Linda Lovelace
- Mike and Marilyn Madsen
- Tom and Ray Magliozzi
- Barbara, Louise, and Irlene Mandrell (The Mandrell Sisters)
- Wynton and Branford Marsalis
- Groucho, Harpo, Chico, Gummo, and Zeppo Marx
- Shirley MacLaine and Warren Beatty
- Frank, Malachy, and Alphie McCourt
- John and Patrick McEnroe (tennis)
- Hayley and Juliet Mills
- Ricky and David Nelson
- Aaron, Arthur, Charles, and Cyril Neville (The Neville Brothers)
- Mary Kate and Ashley Olsen
- Donny and Marie Osmond (The Osmonds)
- Michelle and Dee Dee Pfeiffer
- Mackenzie and Chynna Phillips
- River Phoenix and Joaquin Phoenix
- Anita, Ruth, June, and Bonnie Pointer (The Pointer Sisters)
- Dennis and Randy Quaid
- Vanessa, Lynn, and Corin Redgrave
- Julia and Eric Roberts
- John D., David, and Nelson D. Rockefeller
- Emilio and Javier Sanchez (tennis)
- Charlie Sheen and Emilo, Ramon, and Renée Estevez
- Dick and Tom Smothers
- Sly and Frank Stallone
- John and Ellen Travolta

- Vincent and Theo van Gogh (artist, art dealer)
- Kevin, David, Kerry, Mike, and Chris von Erich (wrestlers)
- Rusty, Mike, and Kenny Wallace (race car drivers)
- Alec and Evelyn Waugh
- Venus and Serena Williams (tennis pros)
- Brian, Carl, and Dennis Wilson (The Beach Boys)
- Edgar and Johnny Winters
- Wilbur and Orville Wright (aviation pioneers/inventors)
- Harry Moses, Samuel, and Jerome Howard (The Three Stooges)

CHAPTER 11

Birth Order Blues

W hen siblings are close in age, their birth order is likely to affect their personalities. The firstborn child tends to be more responsible because he is frequently called upon to help with chores and younger siblings. Because middle children tend to get substantially less attention than the eldest and the baby, many are more free-spirited and independent. The lastborn typically gets a lot of attention at home for being so very cute and darling. The baby is likely to proceed to charm outsiders as well—or to bully them with tantrums.

Perfectionists, Peacemakers, and Clowns

Some researchers say that birth order isn't as big a factor in molding personality as popular books on the subject suggest. Nevertheless, when parents describe the personalities of siblings who are close together in age, it is often clear that their children fit the stereotypes. This was the case for the Gonzales children.

Ruben and Patricia Gonzales believe that they raised their three boys alike. But the children's personalities are so different that it is hard to believe they grew up in the same home. Even as a toddler, Gabe was anxious to please. He remained conscientious about doing things correctly and continues to be a perfectionist now that he is in high school. Whenever he misbehaves, a little discipline goes a long way. His parents are proud of his good grades and pleased with his determination to get into a good college and have a professional career. However, his parents wish he would take things easier and not be such a worrywart.

Relaxing is a definite talent for the Gonzales' second son, Miguel. At age fourteen, he is a sweet-natured, easygoing child. Actually, his parents and teachers consider him a bit too laid back and wish he would apply himself more in school. When it comes to his studies and chores, he seems to do the minimum required to slide by. When his parents confront him about a poor grade or an unfinished chore, he seems properly contrite. But that doesn't mean his behavior improves. His parents complain that he only shapes up when he is grounded or has a privilege revoked. As soon as his punishment ends, he is back to his old self. His parents worry about his lack of goals and ambition. His main interest is hanging out with his friends. He has been warned that if he doesn't buckle down he won't get into college, but Miguel doesn't seem concerned.

Angel, the Gonzales' youngest son, has never known a stranger. Even as a toddler, he turned everyone he met into a friend with a flash of his winning smile. His delightful sense of humor earned him the title of class clown in elementary school. He kept his classmates entertained with his antics. Even Angel's teachers have a hard time staying angry with him when he disrupts the class because he is so charming. He loves being the center of attention, and his parents think he would do well as an entertainer. But Angel is also moody and has quite a temper. His brothers complain that at age twelve he shouldn't act so spoiled. But when his parents ground him or revoke his television and video game privileges, they have a hard time following through. Nobody can stay mad at Angel for long.

 **Fact**

Siblings who are close in age spend more time together. This increases the potential for positive intimacy on one hand and for tension and conflict on the other, according to research reported in the *Journal of Counseling and Development* in 2004.

Personality, Birth Order, and Spacing

Research on how birth order affects personality remains in its infancy. Studies of oldest children, middle children, and youngest children suggest that birth order alone isn't as important as some psychologists originally thought. The spacing between the children is also important. When both birth order and age differences between the youngsters are jointly considered, some fairly consistent personality differences emerge. These differences undoubtedly reflect how parents in Western industrialized nations typically interact with their children when they are close together in age. When the age difference between two siblings is more than six years, the usual birth order affects do not apply. The family dynamics differ in other cultures. For instance, in most white U.S. families, the oldest child is given a lot of responsibilities for helping around the house and caring for siblings, while the baby of the family gets a lot of reinforcement for simply being cute. In some Hispanic cultures, the oldest boy gets a lot of doting attention and isn't expected to do many chores.

Alert!

Personality characteristics relating to birth order only apply when the age differences between the siblings are less than six years. If you have a seven-year-old and an infant, each will probably develop more like an only child. See Chapter 12 to learn about the personalities of only children.

When siblings are spaced six or more years apart, a firstborn doesn't have to share his parents' time and attention during his most formative years. He lacks a live-in peer to serve as his rival and playmate. With a six-year gap, an older child will probably relate to his infant sibling more like a parent. Because the firstborn is in school all day, the younger child gets a lot of undivided parental time and attention. Thus, if a family has a twenty-five-year-old, fifteen-year-old, twelve-year-old, five-year-old, and three-year-old, the twenty-five-year-old is likely to have the personality of an only child. Both the fifteen-year-old and the five-year-old will probably both develop personalities like firstborns. The twelve-year-old and the three-year-old will both develop like lastborns. No one will act like a typical middle child.

Parenting the Firstborn

An old joke has it that parents greet their firstborn with a camera in one hand and a video recorder in the other. They take pictures of their first little miracle morning, noon, and night to capture him in the act of performing all sorts of feats they find tremendously impressive, such as eating and sleeping. Enough photos quickly pile up to fill several file cabinets and enough home movies to stock a video store. Parents carefully label and file every photographic treasure. They are equally fastidious about every aspect of their firstborn's health and welfare. First-time parents are prone to devour child-rearing articles and avidly compare notes with other parents. They try to do everything correctly, wanting to be the best parents possible and fearing that a small error might have disastrous consequences. If the child development books say that babies benefit from playing with blocks and puzzles and eating peas, parents spend hours helping their firstborn stack blocks and put puzzles together. They will work hard to find a way to get lots of peas into their baby's diet.

A few small burps can alarm first-time parents, and they have been known to rush a hiccupping baby to the doctor. First-time parents may walk a crying baby for hours to try to get him to sleep, fearing that too much upset might harm him. If they use a pacifier at all, they are careful to sterilize it before putting it in their baby's mouth. First-time parents worry about whether he is developing normally. Their outpouring of delight when their youngster says his first word and takes his first step is genuine. It is very important to them that their baby does everything on schedule or early.

The Firstborn Personality

By the time a second child arrives, a firstborn is able to understand a lot of what is said to him and may even be able to carry on short conversations. Parents tend to continue to chat with their firstborn even after a sibling is born. They go from telling their firstborn "You need a diaper change" to telling their firstborn "Your baby brother needs a diaper change." So much conversational practice boosts firstborns' verbal skills, which gives them an advantage in school. Moreover, as the family grows, a firstborn's ability to converse keeps him in close contact with his parents. Parents often confide in their firstborn as well, which strengthens his verbal skills and their relationship. The fact that parents tend to be so close to a firstborn may help explain why firstborns tend to embrace their parents' values. Even if parents and firstborns have many conflicts, they are likely to share an especially deep understanding.

Question?

How can parents help firstborns develop more relaxed personalities?
Try to relax and enjoy your child. Avoid turning every activity into an educational experience. When you go outside, let him explore the flowers and bugs without lecturing him about botany and zoology. When he runs, don't keep reminding him to be careful so that he doesn't fall.

Parents are apt to call upon a firstborn when they need someone to keep an eye on a younger sibling. They put firstborns in charge of protecting and disciplining younger siblings during their absence and hold firstborns accountable when something goes wrong. "You shouldn't have let your little brother play with that!" they exclaim. "I told you to watch him!" As a result, firstborns get a lot of experience giving orders, making decisions, enforcing rules, and leading. They end up being more responsible, industrious, and controlling than their siblings and are likely to have good leadership skills. Those traits, combined with their desire to follow the rules, their ambition, and good verbal skills make them good students and hard workers. The firstborn is likely to do better in school and be more successful occupationally than middle children and lastborns.

Common behavior patterns of first-time parents correlate well with the typical personality characteristics of firstborn children. First-time parents tend to be nervous; firstborns tend to be tense. First-time parents tend to take child-rearing very seriously and attend to all the details; firstborns tend to be very responsible and conscientious. First-time parents try to be perfect; firstborns tend to be perfectionistic. Parents tend to hover and scrutinize their baby; firstborns tend to be self-conscious. Parents try to raise their first-born by the book; firstborns tend to be conservative. First-time parents are intent on having their baby do everything on or ahead of schedule; firstborns are ambitious.

Parenting Middle Children

When a second child arrives within six years of a firstborn child, parents have their cameras ready just as they did for child number one. But with two young children at home, parents don't have time to take many pictures. Because they aren't amazed when a middle child rolls over, sits up, crawls, or walks, they don't feel moved to capture such mundane accomplishments on film. Parents are too busy to organize their few pictures, which are heaped in a box to be sorted sometime in the next four decades. A common characteristic of middle children, according Kevin Leman, author of *The Birth Order Book*, is that they have the fewest pictures in the family photo album.

Parents are much more relaxed with their second child. Instead of working night and day to teach him to walk and put on his socks, they trust that he will figure everything out sooner or later. They also know that little humans aren't nearly as fragile as they thought when they were dealing with their first bundle of joy. They don't check their middle child every few minutes to be sure he is still breathing or pick him up every time he looks like he might cry. In fact, when a middle child howls at 2:00 A.M., his parents may decide that letting him cry himself to sleep has some merit. It's not surprising that middle children tend to be more self-sufficient and independent. They have difficulty asking for and accepting help.

Busy parents take shortcuts with middle children that they wouldn't have dreamed of trying with their firstborn. The firstborn probably had carefully coordinated outfits, was kept immaculately clean, and was nursed for as long as possible. But parents dress their middle child in whatever hand-me-down clothes are within reach at the moment and wait to remove all of the dribbles on his chin until bath time. They may prop the baby's bottle to feed him, hand off the chore to a sibling, or rinse a pacifier before plopping it into his mouth. Since he chews on the dog's toys every time their backs are turned, parents figure a few more germs won't hurt him.

The Dilemma for Middle Children

Unlike firstborns and lastborns, middle children never have their parents' exclusive attention. The firstborn gets to be in the limelight until a sibling is born. The youngest child gets to be in the limelight after the older siblings leave home. Research suggests that this has drawbacks as well as benefits. Parents don't spend as much time talking to and reading books to middle children; so they receive less language stimulation. This puts them at an academic disadvantage and may partially explain why they are more likely to fail a year in school, complete fewer years of education, and achieve less occupational success than first and lastborns. Also, more relaxed child-rearing tends to produce more relaxed, easygoing children. Relaxing and taking life easy tend to be special talents for middle children. They are generally less driven, perfectionistic, and ambitious than firstborns, less motivated academically, and less intent on pleasing others than eldest children and lastborns.

Middle children do want to please their parents and teachers, but they are also more concerned with pleasing themselves than the eldest and youngest. When they are given chores, middle children tend to do exactly what their parents have been doing while raising them: they take shortcuts. Middle children can be quite artful about figuring out ways to do the minimum amount of work needed. Another fact of life for most middle children is that they are not as big and strong as the eldest; so they usually lose sibling fights. They aren't as verbal; so they lose arguments. In *The Birth Order Book*, Kevin Leman notes that middle children often become artful mediators and negotiators in an effort to hold their own against their older sibling. Holding their own in the struggle for their parents' time and attention is harder. Middle children don't have much time alone with their parents; so it is hard for them to form the kind of very close relationship that the firstborn enjoys. Middle children have trouble making their way into family conversations by describing all of the exciting things they are doing. Family members are enthralled when a firstborn talks about his first day at school, first class picture, first field trip, first soccer practice, first Little League tournament, and first driver's education class—the list goes on and on. But they yawn when a middle child tells the same stories. Middle children are constantly told that they are too young for the many privileges a firstborn enjoys. When they try to get attention like the lastborn, their parents don't laugh and clap. Instead, middle children are admonished to act their age. Many turn to peers for friendship and support.

 **Fact**

To determine a child's birth order personality, consider whether other children were present during early childhood. A lastborn may develop the personality of a middle child if he lived with an older sibling and a younger foster sibling or cousin during his most formative years.

The most reliable way for middle children to get attention is to do something wrong. That does not mean they misbehave on purpose as many parents and therapists suppose. Firstborn and lastborn children might prefer to be yelled at than to be ignored. But middle children can't usually hold their own in arguments and fights with the firstborn, and their parents step in when middle children take on the baby. They learn to solve disputes by negotiating. When negotiations break down with a parent who is upset about poor grades or unfinished chores, middle children may respond by handing him a verbal pacifier—some soothing words that provide comfort. "I'll start bringing my books home and studying," they say. Parents feel better but feel betrayed when nothing changes. But just as parents don't try to trick middle children into thinking that a pacifier contains milk, middle children are trying to pacify their parents, not trick them. Middle children are often wrongly accused of being oppositional and rebellious. But many eventually live up to their labels.

 *Essential*

Firstborns commonly engage their parents through talking, while last-borns get attention by being cute. Middle children can easily get lost in the shuffle. They commonly complain that they are only noticed when they do something wrong. They need lots of positive attention!

Middle children tend to be wonderful friends. They may not be great conversationalists, but they have lots of practice listening while others talk. They probably gave up trying to be the center of attention long ago and are happy to remain on the sidelines as enthusiastic supporters and cheerleaders. Peers appreciate middle children's easygoing, independent personalities and indifference to rules. Many middle children create surrogate families from their peers and are very loyal friends.

Helping Middle Children

Criticism is not likely to alter their basic personalities but may well alienate them. Don't assume that their different values and lack of motivation are signs of rebellion. The secret to engaging middle children is to talk less and listen more. Remember that experiences that seem old hat to you are new to them. They have lots to say but take longer than a firstborn to express themselves. If you were somewhat haphazard about your middle children's care early on, they will probably be haphazard when they do things. If you were rather disorganized, often let things slide, and cut lots of corners, they are probably more easygoing than conscientious. If you were somewhat indifferent to their accomplishments, they may not be very ambitious. If you gave them a lot less attention than your oldest and youngest, they may not be as bonded to you or share your values. If you gave them a lot of space to develop in their own way, they are probably more free-spirited, self-sufficient, and independent. If you didn't make educational activities priorities, they may not enjoy them or consider them especially important.

Trying to separate your middle child from a surrogate family of friends may lead to open rebellion. An older child will probably resent having you suddenly take charge. It is wiser to lure him back into the fold by accepting and supporting him. Try relating to him like a friend.

Keep your fears for a middle child's future to yourself. Telling him that his lack of ambition and irresponsible behavior will make him a failure may cause him to live up to your negative expectations. In fact, because of their easygoing personalities, they may be better positioned for happy marriages and good friendships. Who knows? They may get a college degree around the time you finally get their few fuzzy baby pictures organized.

Parenting the Lastborn

When the last child arrives, the camera is likely to be dusted off. Parents now realize that the baby years end in a flash. They are a bit hazy on what transpired with their middle children, and capturing their last child's important moments on film becomes a priority. A baby's "firsts" now hold little interest. Many parents focus on the golden moments that make having children such a joy. Parents may have been horrified when their first child climbed onto the counter and licked raw cake batter straight from the bowl. He could have fallen! Eating raw batter is dangerous! It took an hour to bathe and change him! Parents may have looked the other way when their middle child did the same. He was already a mess, their last child didn't get sick, and the parents needed a break. They took one while their middle child entertained himself.

 **Fact**

> Seeing a big kid about to attack a little one triggers parents' protective instincts. They understandably take his side. By elementary school, a lastborn may only need to threaten to tell his parents to get his way. The lastborn may be the smallest, but he is likely to be a tough competitor.

Other family members may be too busy even to notice what the lastborn is up to until the damage has been done. When they discover him up to his elbows and ears in cake batter, they see a great photo opportunity. As parents clap and clown to get their lastborn to smile and say cheese, the older children are appalled that he isn't being punished. But they understand that the baby is special, and the usual rules don't apply. Soon the lastborn understands this, too, and babies learn that being charming and even outrageous are guaranteed ways to get positive attention, not only from parents but also from everyone else. Soon he is delighting everyone with his antics. He can't hold his own against older siblings with fists or words. If he can't charm them into getting what he wants, he may grab it and howl for a parent before he is pummeled to a pulp.

Exhausted parents tend to do what they can to avoid scenes. If the baby wants something, his parents may prefer to give in than to struggle. If he is five and still wants his pacifier, they may quickly hand it over without even insisting that he first rinse it off. An upset child is stressed and stressful. Most people know that stress is bad. Ergo, if both crying and a dirty pacifier are unhealthy, why not take the easy route and risk the germs? Parents have lots of excuses for indulging their lastborn, and most boil down to exhaustion. They may regret not setting limits if they end up with a little tyrant who rules the family with his temper fits. Once that happens, the project of reining him in can be daunting. When crossed, lastborns may hold their breath until their faces turn blue, become so enraged they strike out at a parent ten times their size, or engage in some other intimidating manipulation. It can be hard to remember that they do benefit from discipline in the long run.

Alert!

Lastborn children's affectionate, charming personalities and enjoyment of being in the spotlight can serve them well in their careers. They often make outstanding salespeople, as well as actors, comedians, and entertainers. In fact, lastborns tend to do well in almost any occupation requiring people skills.

Parents are often very tired of nursery rhymes and children's stories by the time a lastborn is ready for Mother Goose. Lessons on how to put on socks, use the potty, put puzzles together, and count to ten may be neglected. Like middle children, lastborns commonly enter school with some serious educational gaps. But lastborns are accustomed to having everyone think they are wonderful, and failing to impress the teacher can be a big blow. Many children become very insecure and frustrated. They want to be constantly admired but lack the background or self-discipline required to make an academic splash. Many get positive attention by charming their peers by being the class clown.

Helping Lastborns

If you can't motivate yourself to spend hours every day working with your lastborn as you did with your firstborn, an academically oriented nursery school can help fill in his educational gaps. If your child has academic problems in school, sign him up for tutoring sooner rather than later. It is important to hold firm with limits and to avoid giving into temper fits. Plenty of lastborn adults have full-blown tantrums when challenged. Lastborns are usually very open to asking for help since they are accustomed to being mothered by their parents and older siblings. If your youngster collapses into tears because he doesn't want to button his coat or do other simple tasks himself, provide instruction, emotional support, and some help. But avoid doing everything for him.

Don't assume that a lastborn's behavior problems at school stem from being high-spirited and underappreciated by his teachers. He may in fact be a bit spoiled. To help a lastborn develop self-discipline, provide some small daily chores and insist they be done regularly. Set up a quiet time each evening for studying and doing homework until he can manage his school responsibilities. Teach your child to control his temper with simple anger management strategies: taking a deep breath, counting to ten, and accepting that the world won't end if he doesn't get his way. Sooner or later, lastborns learn that charming the pants off everyone is wonderful, but it is not enough. You do your child a great favor by ensuring that he develops other talents.

CHAPTER 12

Surrogate Siblings

Y oungsters without a brother or sister close to their age and those who have no siblings miss one major benefit of growing up with a peer: the boost to their social development. But children raised as "onlies" get more verbal stimulation and tend to be closer to their parents. You can help your youngster learn to initiate and maintain friendships by providing extra opportunities to interact with other children. Start organizing those playdates! If this isn't enough, see if you can round up a surrogate sibling.

Lonely Onlies?

John describes what growing up without siblings was like for him.

> *These days, there is a lot of talk about the loneliness and isolation of being an only child. I think this stereotype is wrong. I didn't feel lonely or isolated when I was young. I've known plenty of other only children, and they didn't feel that they suffered from not having a brother or sister. In my case, my parents made sure I had plenty of social outlets. They encouraged me to invite kids over to play. I had a lot of sleepovers, and got to bring a friend along when we went to the zoo or museum and even on our family vacations. My parents and I were much closer to one another than most of my friends with siblings were to their parents. I not only had lots of friends my own age, but I also had the blessing of an especially warm relationship with my parents. From*

hearing my friends complain about their brothers and sisters, I don't think I was missing much.

Living in a college dorm was a big adjustment. I was accustomed to quiet and keeping my room clean and tidy. Having a messy roommate who blasted his stereo and took my things without permission drove me crazy. But lots of other students had the same problems with their roommates; so it's hard to know whether having grown up with other kids would have made me more tolerant. Getting married was also a big adjustment. I value my privacy and really need to have some space to call my own. Even when my wife and I lived in a one-bedroom apartment, I created a private retreat by putting my stereo and a comfy chair in an oversized closet. There again, it's hard to know if that's because I never had to share or whether I would feel the same way even if my circumstances had been different during childhood.

Now that my parents are getting up in years, I worry about having to take care of them all by myself and making all the hard decisions about things such as nursing homes. But there again, when I hear how siblings fight tooth and nail over such heavy-duty issues, I think maybe I'll be better off. Because I'm so close to my parents, I know what they would want. Anyway, if not having any brothers or sisters deprived me, I didn't know it. It's hard to miss what you never had. I've got a loving wife, a good job, lots of friends, and am pretty happy. So I think I turned out OK.

 **Fact**

When there is a difference of six years or more between children, they commonly relate to one another more like little parents and children than like peers. Each is likely to develop like an only child despite having siblings.

Onlies on the Rise

According to Carolyn White, editor of *Only Child Magazine* and author of *The Seven Common Sins of Parenting an Only Child*, single-child families are the fastest growing type in the United States. *Time* magazine predicts that one-third of new U.S. families will opt to have just one child. The trend toward having fewer children is taking place in other countries as well, according to research reported by the U.S. Statistics Division. Japan now averages just 1.33 children per household. The birthrate has even fallen in some countries where families have historically been large because of the Catholic Church's stance against using reliable methods of birth control. Spain has an average of just 1.13 children per woman, and Italy has 1.2.

Fact

The *Washington Post* recently reported that the number of families with an only child has nearly doubled in the last twenty years. There are an estimated 20 million single-child households in the United States alone. Large age differences between siblings can create an only-child mentality.

The most dramatic increase in single-child families has been in China. There, the government attempted to quell the country's burgeoning population growth by limiting city dwellers to one child per couple beginning in 1979. Less than one decade later, an estimated 30 million of the 337 million Chinese children under age fourteen were without siblings, according to a December 1987 article in *Time*. The children from this giant generation of onlies were dubbed "'little emperors" because so many of them ruled their families with their terrible temper tantrums. Chinese teachers began confronting U.S.-style classroom behavior problems—a new phenomenon in a country known for its highly respectful, dutiful, conscientious children. On Chinese buses, children outfitted like princes and princesses clutch expensive toys and take up two seats while their aging grandparents dressed in rags stand, tending them like servants. The Chinese experience is not necessarily applicable to other countries, however. In China, large families have been the norm. The sudden reduction in family size meant that a single cherished child was doted on by two parents, four grandparents, and literally dozens of uncles and aunts. The Chinese experience exemplifies the tendency to pamper only children.

Social factors account for the increase in only children in the United States and other industrialized countries. One factor is the trend among women to pursue careers during their twenties and early thirties and postpone starting a family. Older females have a harder time conceiving and are more likely to have complications during pregnancy. If they do have a child, the tremendous energy required to care for a little one often deters them from having a second. For other couples, the high cost of raising and educating youngsters drives their decision to limit themselves to one child. The same goes for adoptive couples, who often find the financial as well as the emotional cost of adoption overly taxing.

Many children have siblings but grow up as onlies because of the large differences in their ages. These "onlies with siblings" may have become more common in recent years. Besides the straggler children born to older couples, many couples with children from a previous marriage decide to have a child together.

Despite the presence of half-siblings in the home full-time, the new baby doesn't have to share so much parental attention if the siblings are quite a bit older. They are not competing for toys and privileges like peers.

Myths and Misconceptions

Myths about only children abound. They have been stereotyped as selfish, spoiled, egotistical, lonely, and socially inept, according to Darrell Sifford, an only child and author of *The Only Child*. Sifford points out that some therapists in recent decades have gone so far as to liken being an only child to a disease. The "symptoms" supposedly include low self-esteem, depression, egotism, and an insatiable need to be the center of attention. The research has not demonstrated that only children are actually more prone to these problems, and some noteworthy individuals demonstrate how completely without merit these stereotypes can be. Far from being selfish or socially inept, onlies such as Indira Gandhi and Franklin Roosevelt devoted their lives to social change, to cite just two examples. Many only children are high achievers. They set and pursue high goals. The single-minded drive and determination of only child athletes such as Lance Armstrong, Kareem Abdul-Jabbar, and Maria Sharapova are often mistaken for egotism. Onlies such as Albert Einstein, Charles Lindbergh, and Lillian Hellman have been labeled as loners, when the real issue may be their dedication to solitary work. Would such individuals have turned out differently if they had grown up with siblings? There is no way to tell. However, plenty of children with siblings are selfish, spoiled, socially inept loners, have poor self-esteem, and suffer from depression. Falbo and Polit examined numerous older studies on only children and reported their findings in the *Psychological Bulletin* in 1986. They concluded that only children actually had an edge on youngsters with siblings in the areas of achievement, intelligence, and character.

Author Carolyn White, an only child who raised an only child, publishes *Only Child Magazine* (available from onlychild.com). White believes that her loving relationship with her parents increased her capacity for sharing and her sense of loyalty to others. Screenwriter Kirsten Smith agrees. Smith noted that as only an only child her parents instilled her with the belief that she could accomplish anything she wanted to in life. It is not unusual for only children to have especially close relationships with their parents and to set high goals for themselves. Children who enjoy warm relationships with their parents tend to get along better with other authority figures, including teachers, and are more conscientious about complying with their rules and fulfilling their expectations. Not having to share parent's attention with siblings means that only children are talked to and worked with more at home. As a group, they arrive at school with an intellectual and verbal edge on their classmates. Since academic success lays the foundation for occupational success, it is not surprising that lots of onlies go on to high-level careers. Like lastborns in larger families, the extra doses of parental attention make them comfortable being the center of attention.

Alert!

Only children tend to be well-adjusted when raised by parents who wanted just one child. However, the situation seems to be less rosy when couples try but fail to have additional children. Many look to their only child to fulfill all of their hopes and dreams.

Too much pressure to fulfill all their parents' expectations can leave a child feeling like a failure. For instance, common parental goals are to have a child attend a good college, take over the family business, and provide them with grandchildren. An only child may feel pressured to meet all these expectations whether or not he is college material, suited to carrying on the business, or interested in having children.

Overindulgence

Parents have a natural tendency to lavish their firstborn child with as much attention and as many material goods they can afford. When another sibling arrives, the firstborn must share the limelight. He loses a lot of the undivided attention to which he was accustomed, and money becomes tighter. Firstborns who were accustomed to getting most everything their little hearts desired begin to hear "no" when they request toys, money for a gumball machine, and rides on mechanical cars and horses. Once a sibling arrives, there are a host of new rules and demands that teach firstborns to be considerate of others. Firstborns are admonished to hurry because mother needs to attend to the baby, wait because mother is busy with the baby, be quiet so as not to awaken the baby, and be careful not to bump the baby. As the new sibling matures, firstborns lose control over their toys. They walk into the living room to find the baby playing with them, and they may be required to share. You may need to make a conscious effort to set limits and avoid catering to your only child's every whim in order to avoid the overindulgence that leads to spoiling. Having young visitors come to their house to play ensures onlies share parental time and attention and their toys.

Question?

Does giving children too many things spoil them?
Children growing up in luxury aren't necessarily spoiled. The secret is not to give in instantly to your youngster's every whim. Teach him to wait, work for some items, take care of his things, and share.

Setting Limits

Psychologists point out that having parents remain in charge is important for children because it helps them feel safe and secure. Little tyrants who rule their families with their pouts and tantrums may seem to enjoy being in control. But inside, they may feel afraid of having so much power over the adults in their lives. Parents do their children an important service by teaching them to cope with limits. Instead of giving in to all of your child's demands, consider having him earn special toys by doing chores and saving his money so he can buy them himself. Otherwise, he may expect everything to be given to him. He won't understand the need to take care of his belongings either, if a replacement appears every time he loses or breaks something. When parents refuse to buy their child a toy they could easily afford or withhold a privilege they could easily grant, some parents feel guilty. But children must learn to delay gratification, tolerate frustration, and cope with everyone's least favorite word: "no."

Picking up after one child and doing all of the housework yourself isn't so challenging when you aren't simultaneously caring for a baby. It may actually be easier to take care of your only child's toys, straighten his room, and do his chores for him. Teaching these skills and struggling to get your child to handle these responsibilities can be much more time-consuming. But youngsters need to be taught to care for their possessions and organize their space, and some children need to have some regular responsibilities to develop self-discipline. Teaching your child to adhere to schedules is important, too. While it might be tempting to indulge your youngster's preference to skip a nap, stay up past his bedtime, watch an extra television show, or have dinner early, learning to follow routines is important. He will need to move in sync with his classmates at school and with other children in extracurricular activities.

Alert!

For answers to questions, to get advice, and to chat with other parents of onlies, go to ✐*www.essentialbaby.com.au*. To chat with parents who are giving up the dream of having a second child, see ✐*www.raisingkids.co.uk*.

Even if your child grumbles and resists having to do chores, doing them is important. Contributing to the household helps your child master basic self-care skills, experience the pride of accomplishment, and teaches him to be responsible. Many parents are afraid to set limits for fear of damaging their child's self-esteem. If so, they are misunderstanding what healthy self-esteem involves. Egotists, narcissists, and sociopaths have excellent self-esteem and tremendous self-confidence. They believe everything they do is wonderful and consider themselves deserving of praise and admiration, even if they haven't put forth much effort and haven't accomplished anything. Such children preserve their overblown, grandiose self-images by blaming their setbacks and failures on other people or events. Children with healthy self-esteem take pride in their accomplishments and appreciate when they have made a genuine effort.

The Burden for Onlies

Parents have a tendency to want their only offspring to be good at everything they consider important. They want him share the interests they feel passionate about and embrace the values, attitudes, and opinions they hold dear. Parents with more than one child are better positioned to accept the best qualities in each child instead of expecting them to excel in everything and live out their dreams. If a firstborn child likes reading and quiet indoor activities but the second child loves sports, the pressure on the first child to meet his father's desire for a playmate to toss balls to or a budding athlete to coach will probably ease. Inappropriate expectations can create an enduring sense of not being good enough or of being a disappointment to beloved parents. Some children defend against such painful emotions by rebelling. "I have to go to college; it's not my choice," one only child said angrily. "Mom went to Smith; Dad is a Penn State alum. My grades are okay because of all the tutors and summer school and books they've made me read, but I want to be a welder. Welders make lots of money, but they don't care. It's my parents' way or the highway. Hitchhiking to make it on my own would be better than years of misery to get where I don't want to go. I've considered just taking off."

In some cultures, children expect to have to follow their parent's choices for their education, careers, hobbies, and even spouses. But mainstream U.S. values hold that each person has the right to pursue happiness in his own way. Ignoring your child's individual traits and rejecting his personal goals is a common cause of alienation and family rifts. The divided attention that comes from having more than one child makes it easier for parents to let each youngster develop in his own way and establish his own goals. Resist the temptation to hold your youngster under a microscope and micromanage the details of his life. This is especially important during adolescence, when children are trying to define their own values and plan their futures. Maintain other involvements so your child doesn't feel responsible for providing you with a reason for being. Knowing that you have sources of meaning will make it easier for him to continue along his path toward independence unencumbered by guilt for having left. The best way to avoid living vicariously through your child is to find additional sources of fulfillment.

Alert!

Because only children tend to be so close to their parents, they are especially concerned with pleasing them. Because there isn't a sibling to fulfill some of their parents' dreams, an only child may feel obligated to fulfill all of them. When they can't, they may feel like failures. Beware of overburdening your youngster.

Strengthening Social Skills

Do only children have more difficulties getting along with peers? Most studies have found no differences. However, when Ohio State University sociologist Douglas Downey had teachers rate 20,000 kindergarteners, the teachers observed what the general public has long suspected. In an interview which appeared in a 2004 United Press International article, Downey said, "Children without siblings were consistently rated as having poorer social skills." Downey pointed out that although siblings have lots of conflicts, they also figure out how to resolve them. It makes sense that relating to a sibling just a few years younger or older helps prepare children to get along with their peers in school and in the neighborhood. Siblings have daily opportunities to practice important interpersonal skills that onlies also need to master such as:

- Approaching other children and asking them to play
- Taking turns
- Sharing

- Empathizing
- Respecting others' personal space and possessions
- Asserting themselves to protect their personal space and possessions
- Accepting differences of opinion
- Making joint decisions
- Compromising
- Resolving conflicts
- Continuing to work together despite being angry

Onlies have opportunities to relate to peers at school during recess and lunch, during extracurricular activities, when playing in the neighborhood, and on playdates with classmates, friends, and cousins. Unfortunately, when conflicts develop, other children may simply pick up their marbles and head for home. If there is too much unpleasantness, they may cut off contact altogether. Sibling relationships force children to continue to relate to one another, even though they are put out with one another or are embroiled in a serious conflict. They may have been fighting tooth and nail, but when they sit down to dinner, they are expected to remain civil. An only child isn't likely to have this type of experience very often. Onlies need to learn to resolve disputes so they can maintain intimate relationships through thick and through thin. Roommates and married couples must continue to rub elbows and work together, even if they are very upset with one another. Only children need longer, more intense involvements than the usual friends and neighbors to develop the interpersonal skills needed for intimate, long-term relationships.

Surrogate siblings can benefit onlies. Cousins who live nearby or visit for extended periods during the summer commonly fulfill this role. A young friend who stays at your home for a week or accompanies your family on a vacation can do the same.

Alert!

Not all youngsters growing up as only children are lonely. Many have more than enough peer interaction in day care centers, nurseries, school, after-school programs, extracurricular activities, and from playing in the neighborhood. Only children tend to enjoy especially warm relationships with their parents as well.

Foreign exchange student programs can provide only teenagers with a surrogate sibling for a semester or an entire school year. Your family can serve as a host for a foreign student, or your child can live abroad with a foreign family. Reputable nonprofit agencies such as Peoplelink (*www.peoplelink.org*) will help to match students who share similar interests. If your child plays in the band at school or is on the basketball team, chances are that an agency can find an exchange student with similar interests. Such relationships often endure. Many children continue to communicate and visit one another long after the school year has ended. As a bonus, your entire family will learn about a different culture.

Volunteer mentors can also provide sibling experiences for onlies. Teen mentors can be of special benefit to onlies born to older parents who lack the energy for youthful activities and have difficulties relating because of the extreme generation gap. Big Brothers/ Big Sisters of America was once regarded as being a program for disadvantaged youth, but its vision is to "provide a mentor for every child who needs or wants one," according to the organization's Web site. Children gain companionship, support, and positive role models while learning to appreciate volunteerism. See *www.bbbsa.org* for help locating a mentor in your community. Contact your child's school counselor to learn about other ways to locate a mentor. Many school districts have mentoring programs.

Foster Siblings

Families take in foster children for many reasons. Often, parents hope to help a youngster in need of a home while providing their only child with a surrogate sibling. In 2001, 542,000 children spent time in foster care, according to a 2003 U.S. Department of Health and Human Services AFCARS Report. Taking in a foster child has special challenges and rewards. In some cases, the stay is short—the child may be back at home in a matter of a few days, weeks, or months; others remain with their foster families for years. Most foster children have been removed from their birth parents due to abuse and neglect. They are not allowed to return home until a judge is convinced it is safe for them. If the home situation does not improve, legal guardianship may be turned over to other relatives, or a young-ster may be freed for adoption. In that case, some state policies make it easy for the current foster parents to adopt. However long a foster child is in your home, your family must provide the love and care a troubled child needs to grow and develop. Besides having a sur-rogate sibling, your natural child can benefit from learning to empa-thize with someone less fortunate.

 Essential

Help your youngster understand that his foster sibling's parents could not care for her properly. When they can, the court may decide that she can go back home to live. Explain that until then it is your family's job to provide her with a safe and loving home.

Settling In

When a new foster child first arrives, he will likely be reeling from the shock of all he has been through. The sudden loss of home and family, worries about other family members, the trauma of past abuse and neglect, and nervousness about the future are likely to sap most of his energy. If your natural child is eagerly anticipating the arrival of a great new playmate, he may be disappointed to find that his new brother is too preoccupied, angry, or despondent to be a good companion. Help your child understand that his foster brother has a lot on his mind. Help your child understand, too, that it will take his foster brother awhile to learn all the new household routines and rules. Explain the importance of making some allowances for his behavior and being especially kind and gentle. His foster brother is probably scared about living with strangers. Worse, if he has been abused, he may expect to be treated badly. He may be especially meek and compliant until he feels safe, or like an animal that has been mistreated, he may act tough to try to ward off the attacks he anticipates.

The typical pattern of adjustment for foster children is the same as for new adoptive children. At first, there is a honeymoon period, during which a foster child's good behavior reflects his uncertainty about how to handle himself in an unfamiliar environment. Next, there is likely to be a period of escalating tensions as homesickness deepens and the stress of so much change piles up. Then you can look for a gradual improvement as your family adjusts to the newcomer and the foster child settles in. In recent years, social workers and mental health professionals have urged foster parents to spell out their rules clearly and impose swift, consistent consequences. The point is to combat behavior problems that foster parents find overwhelming. However, children raised in chaotic environments may have marked difficulties following rules, adhering to routines, and accepting limits. Expecting a foster child to follow the same rules as your natural child may not be realistic. A better approach is to select one or two problems to work on and put the others on hold for a time. Sometimes scaling back expectations and working to gain a child's trust and cooperation is a more effective way to motivate her to behave as you would like. After spending some time in a stable, loving home, many traumatized children begin to act out their problems, and their behavior worsens. Meanwhile, many children who appeared extremely troubled on arrival show few or no signs of emotional disturbance. Many go on to lead full, productive lives, and some gain celebrity status. See the list of famous people who were adopted or spent time in foster care in Chapter 16. Beware of first impressions, which can be markedly deceptive.

Alert!

Children who have been abused may be more at ease with their new foster siblings than their new foster parents. Suggest that your natural children help a foster child feel welcome by showing him to his room and providing a tour of the house.

Foster Sibling Issues

A foster child may display some behaviors, attitudes, or problems your natural child has never encountered. He may wonder why his new sister sings herself to sleep, has nightmares, or wets the bed. Focus on teaching your child respect, empathy, and compassion—the key ingredients of positive sibling relationships described in Chapter 2. Explain that her birth parents weren't able to care for her properly, and she became fearful and unhappy as a result. Encourage your youngster to include a foster sibling in her activities, and make it clear she is not to be teased about any unusual behaviors. If a foster child exhibits more serious problems, she may need counseling. If your child feels left out or misplaced because a lot of attention is being focused on his foster sibling, spend some special time with him doing something he enjoys. Let him pick out the movie or game for the whole family. Compliment him on something he has done well.

Saying goodbye to a child who has come to feel like a member of the family can be hard, but there is value in learning to love and let go. Your child is likely to feel sad even if he had difficulties getting along with his foster sibling and is anxious for her stay to end. If the time was brief or the relationship was contentious, it is still very important to set aside time for proper goodbyes. Doing so can help to dispel any lingering guilt or hard feelings so that both children can move on. Encourage them to describe a happy memory or something they wish had been different, and have them say something they liked or appreciated about one another. If necessary, this can be handled in a telephone call. You can share that you, too, will miss your foster child, but that you are happy she will be with her own family or might have prospects for a happier experience in a different foster home. After the foster child has left, compliment your child on the positive things he did for his foster sibling, and encourage your child to talk about his feelings about the departure. Even if the children didn't get along, they typically experience some grief when they part. That doesn't negate the benefits of having had a foster sibling. Part of the usual sibling experience entails saying goodbye to beloved older brothers and sisters as they depart for college and move away from home to begin lives of their own. Many of the life lessons siblings and surrogate siblings teach one another are in fact very painful. But that doesn't make them any less valuable or important.

Famous Only Children

The fact that so many only children have achieved fame and fortune dispels the myth that growing up without a sibling is a terrible handicap. Here is a small sampling of only children who have become superstars.

- Kareem Abdul-Jabbar
- Lance Armstrong
- Lauren Bacall
- Burt Bacharach
- Elizabeth Bishop
- Adrien Brody
- Dick Cavett
- Van Cliburn
- Robert De Niro
- Laura Dern
- Marlene Dietrich
- Albert Einstein
- Myrlie Evers-Williams
- Lillian Hellman
- Elton John
- Shirley Jones
- Vivien Leigh
- Charles Lindbergh
- James Michener
- Cole Porter
- Natalie Portman
- Rex Reed
- Franklin Roosevelt
- Jean Paul Sartre
- Maria Sharapova
- Frank Sinatra

- Clark Gable
- John Kenneth Galbraith
- Indira Gandhi
- Rudolph Giuliani
- Tipper Gore
- Cary Grant
- Alan Greenspan
- William Randolph Hearst
- Emile Zola

- Alexander Solzhenitsyn
- Roger Staubach
- Robert Louis Stevenson
- Jacqueline Susann
- Charlize Theron
- Paul Verlaine
- Malcolm-Jamal Warner
- Robin Williams

CHAPTER 13

Stepsiblings

Expect some rocky times when you tie a new marital knot and the children officially become stepsiblings. Issues relating to the loss of their first family and ambivalence about having a stepparent often color children's attitudes toward one another. Counseling can help them resolve emotional conflicts so they can embrace their new family. They will need time and help to adjust to all the changes. Spend time alone with your youngsters to keep your relationship strong, and spend time alone with your stepchildren to bond with them.

Identifying Issues

Some children readily embrace their new stepparent and stepsiblings and happily settle into their new life. But for many youngsters, a new family presents a number of trying emotional issues. This was the case for Haley.

> *My parents divorced when I was seven and my brother was five. My Dad remarried soon after. We saw him regularly for awhile, then he and his wife had a baby, and he sort of faded away. It was just my mom, my brother, and me for a couple of years. Everything was fine until Mom started dating Chuck. He and my brother did a lot of guy things together and got along okay, but I didn't like Chuck hanging around all the time. Sometimes he had his two kids on the weekends. Dana was two years older than me, and I thought she was really cool.*

We got to be friends, and my brother hit it off with Ricky. When Dad found out that Mom and Chuck were getting married, he threatened to get custody of us. I had complained to him about Chuck, but I didn't want to live with Dad. I could tell his wife didn't like me. I was really scared. When Mom didn't call off the wedding, I knew all she cared about was Chuck and his kids, and she wanted me and my brother out of the way. I can't tell you how that hurt.

Dad didn't get custody, but my brother and I had to start visiting him again on weekends. After being basically gone for years, Dad thought he could just start acting like my father and telling me what to do. My stepmom was mean to me, but their son could do no wrong. They always took his side. Mom and Chuck needed a bigger place. We moved, and I lost my friends, my school—everything. But Dana and I still had to share a room. Even though Dana only came on weekends, she acted like she owned the place. One day Chuck told me to clear out a drawer so she would have a place for her stuff. I told him he wasn't my father and couldn't tell me what to do. Mom said I needed to show Chuck some respect and be considerate of my stepsister. We had a huge blowup. I said I would live go live with Dad, but they talked me out of it.

Things started to settle down a bit, and then Dana came to live with us full-time. Chuck let her do whatever she wanted so that she would stay and not go back to her mom's. I hated having to share my room with her. Then Mom got pregnant. That was the worst. I figured she wouldn't want the rest of us kids once the baby arrived. The school counselor got me into a group for divorced kids. It helped a lot. I opened up to Dana and found out she was worried about how things would be after the baby, too. We talked to my mom and Chuck, and finally we started working things out. Now we all get along. I'm glad I have a stepsister and brother, and Chuck and I got to be close. But it was hard, hard, hard for a long, long time.

Finishing Old Business

It is not unusual for children to cling to the hope that their parents will reconcile long after a divorce, and a remarriage can come as a serious blow. Some teenagers impulsively respond to their mother's wedding announcement by exclaiming, "But what about Dad?" even though he remarried and hasn't been involved with them for a decade. Their question isn't as strange as it might seem. Just as many people comfort themselves over the death of a loved one with thoughts about being reunited in the afterlife, some children reeling from the blow of a family breakup comfort themselves by imagining a reunification at some unspecified time in the future. When the custodial parent announces wedding plans, youngsters begin to face the fact that their original family will never be restored. Until they come to terms with the loss of their old family, they are likely to resist a new stepparent and stepsiblings.

Even though your children know your fiancé well and like him a lot, they may still balk at having him enter the role of stepparent. It can be hard for children to trust that your new love story will prove more enduring than the last one. After having been through one family breakup, children tend to be more cynical about committed relationships. Many children avoid getting too close to new family members for fear of being hurt again by another major loss. In fact, youngsters have reason to be skeptical. At a time when about 50 percent of first marriages fail, about 80 percent of second marriages end in divorce. Yet often, children's fears that the new marriage will fail turn out to be self-fulfilling prophecies. By rejecting their stepparent and stepsiblings, youngsters cause much of the marital stress that leads to divorce.

Other issues can also lead children to reject their stepsiblings. Single parents and their children tend to be very close, and they resent having a new spouse usurp their parent's time and attention. Supervision is often lax in single-parent homes, and youngsters tend to feel uncomfortable having another adult act as an authority figure. They commonly resent attempts to shore up discipline. After serving as their parent's confidants, friends, and helpmates, they resent having someone else take over their role and treat them like children. A stepparent can also threaten the natural parent of the same sex, who may fear being replaced or losing his children's affection. Ex-spouses may undermine the new marriage by being overly sympathetic to their children's complaints about new family members. Even if your ex is not in the picture, your children may feel that loving their stepparent is an act of disloyalty to their biological parent. Many youngsters save a special place in their heart for their absent parent, continuing to hope that he will some day appear and finish raising them. They reject anyone who tries to step into that role. To further complicate matters, the good feelings that come from being nurtured by a loving "stranger" can intensify children's sense of having been deprived due to their natural parent's absence. Feelings of anger over having been abandoned conflict with the idealized image of the parent that commonly develops when there is little or no contact. Your children may need a therapist to help them untangle and resolve their many complex emotions. Until then, they may be unwilling to accept being part of a blended family.

Question?

Shouldn't kids call their stepparent "mother" or "father"?
Many children feel that these words are sacred. Using them for a stepparent feels disloyal. Most children prefer to use their stepparent's first name, or they settle on a nickname, such as "Mama Sue" or "Papa Joe."

Advice and Consent?

Given that so many children are so successful at undermining a new marriage by driving a wedge between their parent and stepparent and by alienating their stepsiblings, some parents seek their youngsters' consent before marrying. Most parenting authors think this is a mistake. They believe that adults should be the ones in charge of making such an important life decision, not children. Because youngsters lack the maturity and wisdom to know what is best, it doesn't make sense to let them dictate to their parents regarding such a major issue. If children nix the marriage, knowing that they deprived their parent of a life partner can produce too much guilt, which can be psychologically harmful. If they give their consent, they may feel they have the right to withdraw it and expect their parent to comply by getting a divorce. Nevertheless, it is important for your minor children to get along with the future members of their stepfamily before you say "I do." If they are seriously opposed to your marriage, ask them to commit to making their new family work. If they refuse to cooperate and are intent on driving off their new stepparent and stepsiblings, it will be that much harder to get your new marriage off the ground.

Engaging Minor Children

To increase the children's commitment to their new family, involve them in the wedding. Have them serve as ring bearers, flower girls, ushers, or bridesmaids or be in charge of the guest book. Some companies now make special jewelry to help solidify the stepsibling bond. Medallions and rings with the unity sign are especially popular, and they make meaningful wedding gifts for the children. Consider holding a ceremony to validate their new relationship, perhaps having the children pledge to accept their stepsiblings as family members. Suggest they refer to one another as "my brother" or "my sister."

 **Essential**

Because you are happy about your new family and anxious for your children to share your views, it can be tempting to try to deny difficulties. But it is better to respond to complaints by acknowledging the truth: Many of the changes will take some getting used to.

After the wedding, create some new rituals to begin establishing your new family's identity. This could be a special daily prayer when saying grace at meals, a weekly walk around the block, a monthly trip out for donuts, or a yearly anniversary celebration. Spend one-on-one time with your new stepchildren to begin bonding with them. Hold family meetings regularly to resolve conflicts. Use mediation to settle disputes. Avoid taking sides during arguments when at all possible. This may calm the children down in the short run but will escalate ill will and competition in the long run. Instead, try calling a time-out, separating the children, and having them try to think of a solution.

Engaging Adult Children

Even if your adult children don't live with you, they can be significant sources of stress if they are unhappy about being a part of a blended family. Even if you only see them occasionally, your new marriage will affect them. During holiday visits, some of your family's special traditions will need to change to accommodate your stepchildren. Installing a new spouse in a home or apartment that your children are attached to may make them feel like guests instead of like returning family members. Even if they never actually lived in your previous home, they may still have come to feel connected to it and in some sense consider it theirs. If you and your spouse move into a new home, your children lose their connection to a place that may have been important to them. Being in an alien environment can contribute to their feeling of being alienated.

 *Alert!*

Children never outgrow their need for parents and a sense of family. Chances are that you won't outgrow your desire to have your children in your life either. Introduce your fiancé and stepchildren to your children and give them opportunities to get to know one another.

Some adult children are as conflicted about the breakup of their family due to divorce as minor children who are still living at home. They may view a new marriage as a betrayal of their other parent or fear that the inheritance they expected will go to your new spouse and stepchildren. If you want your children to participate in holiday celebrations and family reunions and be a part of your lives, introduce them to your fiancé and stepchildren. They won't feel close to you if they don't know the new people who figure so prominently in your life and won't feel comfortable visiting you and a group of strangers.

A New Family Identity

A sense of stability and security is a basic need for children, as is a sense of belonging. With all of the divorces and remarriages, it can be hard even for adults to make sense of the complex web of family relationships. It's no wonder that when middle school children are asked to say the names of their parents and siblings, some have difficulty recalling them all. When elementary school children are asked to draw a picture of their family, many are at a loss as to who to include. When told to include everyone, some children draw themselves far off to the side of the paper, while three or four family constellations dominate the center. Such youngsters may feel that they really don't belong anywhere. When ten-year-old Ed described his family, his confusion was readily apparent. He explained, "That's my dad and stepmom and my new sister Jessica. She's two. That's a girl who sometimes comes to visit, mostly on weekends. That's another boy who lived with us last year. I'm not sure if he's my brother or just a friend." In actuality, the girl was his stepsister, who lived with her father full-time. The boy was his stepbrother, who lived with his stepmother's second husband and occasionally appeared for visits. It goes without saying that the children need to be properly introduced and to have the relationships clearly defined. Children can easily become confused when they meet many people in a short period of time. You may need to explain who is related to whom with several repetitions for them to grasp where they fit in.

Stepparenting Challenges

Keep your relationship with your own children strong by spending time alone with them so they can have you all to themselves for at least a few minutes every day until they adjust. Continue to follow some of the rituals that have been important to them. For instance, if your children are accustomed to piling into a bed with you for a bedtime story, try to continue this custom. Your children will probably dislike having to share your time and attention with their stepsiblings. But rather than directing their anger toward you, they may direct it toward your stepchildren. There are some other steps you can take to ease their adjustment. If you are talking to a stepchild and one of your children bursts in the room and starts talking, avoid admonishing him for being impolite. Probably he is doing what he has always done. Learning to wait while you attend to someone else will take time. Consider kindly saying "just a minute," while giving him an inviting smile or special wink, tousling his hair, or putting a friendly arm on his shoulder to let him know you are glad to see him. Or treat him as you would an adult. When two adults are talking and a third joins them, the etiquette is to acknowledge the newcomer, summarize the conversation for her benefit (e.g., "Hi. We were just talking about how cold it has been lately."), and find a way to include the newcomer in the conversation. Alternatively, the newcomer is briefly acknowledged, the first conversation is quickly concluded, and the newcomer is invited to chat via a welcoming comment and perhaps a question on another subject likely to interest her, such as "So, how are you? I heard that the Dallas Cowboys are having a good season."

Children's attitudes toward having a stepparent are often influenced by stories. In fairy tales and cartoons, stepparents are commonly portrayed as showing gross favoritism toward their own terrible children and being cruel toward the hapless stepchildren who fall into their evil clutches. Joseph Campbell, the distinguished professor who investigated comparative mythology, has suggested that the widespread appeal of such stories around the world may be because they reflect children's innate fears of being cared for by an adult who is not a blood relation. Their fear may stem from the fact that the strong bond between biological children and parents mobilizes parents' protective instincts. Biological parents are inclined to make great sacrifices to nurture and protect their young. Without a strong, loving attachment, an unrelated adult may be indifferent to a youngster's welfare or even respond cruelly when stressed by the many demands of child-rearing. Although the stepparent/stepchild bond can be as intense and loving as any parent/child bond (and can actually be much stronger and healthier), stepparents are statistically more likely to be abusive than natural parents.

Alert!

Stepparent/teenager relationships tend to be stormy, but that doesn't mean a boy is better off without one. The presence of a stepfather is a protective factor for adolescent boys, who are less likely to get involved in delinquent activities or drop out of school than those without any sort of father.

Solidifying Blended Family Relationships

Your first order of business as a stepparent is to try to bond with your stepchildren. Biological parents spend the first year developing a warm, trusting relationship with their infant. You may need to do the same before attempting to discipline your stepchildren. For discipline to be useful, children must believe that it is meant to help them. Until your stepchildren are bonded to you, they are likely to have difficulty trusting your good intentions and think you are merely trying to hurt them. You are likely to be more effective serving as a mentor, guide, kindly friend of the family, or beloved uncle. Once a strong, positive attachment is formed, your stepchildren will be probably more willing to accept you as an authority figure, especially if they understand that you are not trying to replace their natural parent. In the meantime, communicate with your spouse about disciplinary needs, make joint decisions, but avoid delivering the reprimands, giving the lectures, and imposing the consequences and punishments yourself. Be careful, too, about pressuring your spouse to take a firmer hand with your stepchildren. They are likely to blame you for turning him against them if you induce him to be stricter. At a time when so much is changing in your children's lives, it is better for parents not to alter their customary methods of disciplining.

Alert!

Natural parents can usually tolerate more difficult behavior from their children because of their strong bond. Avoid asking your new spouse to discipline your children until they are bonded. Until then, attempts to discipline them are apt to cause more problems than they cure.

Even if you have the exact same sets of rules for your children and stepchildren, you can expect to be accused of favoritism. This is not surprising since children commonly also accuse their natural parents of playing favorites. Stepparents who are working overtime to be fair and are intent on treating all of the children the same are likely to find such accusations upsetting. However, if you are honest with yourself, you probably feel closer to your own children. This is to be expected. You and your children share a past and probably enjoy the kind of heartfelt, wordless understanding that comes with having lived together for many years. Your special bond will undoubtedly be readily apparent to your stepchildren. They way your eyes sparkle when one of your own children walks into the room, your ready smile when you greet them, the effortlessness with which you run a hand through their hair, and your spontaneous hugs undoubtedly speak volumes. Insisting that you treat all of the children alike is one thing. Denying that you feel closer to your children is likely to undermine your credibility with your stepchildren. If you are confronted by a stepchild, it is probably better to admit you are closer to your children because you have known them longer, while expressing the hope that the two of you can develop a similarly close relationship.

Essential

Children's temperaments undoubtedly have a lot to do with how quickly they adjust to stepsiblings. Some children are highly adaptable, while some find change very stressful. Some of the specific issues children face when they acquire stepsiblings relate to their birth order.

The New Baby

Spouses in a second marriage often hope that having a baby together will cement their new relationship. In fact, having a baby is a protective factor for second marriages, at least during the first few years. However, a new baby creates another challenge for the children who live with you full-time. A new baby can be especially threatening to children who don't live with you full-time. They commonly fear that they are being replaced. Sensing that a new arrival may upset their children, many parents hold off telling them about a pregnancy for as long as possible. This is risky because if your children discover that you are sharing such important news with others and not bothering to tell them, they are likely to conclude that you no longer consider them as part of your family. Let them be the first to know. Involve them in the preparations since this can reassure them that they are part of the family while helping them bond with the baby. Refer to "your baby sister" to help them understand that even if they don't live with you full-time, the relationship is very real. Consider soliciting their advice about what to name the baby. Accepting their suggestion will affirm their relationship with the new baby. Being able to nix some of your suggestions can also have a positive impact on the children's relationship. They can spend the next twenty years feeling proud that they spared their new sibling from being named Rover or Chiquita Banana, and the sibling will spend the next twenty years feeling ever-so-grateful.

CHAPTER 14

Large Families

Unless you are well-off financially and can afford housekeepers and maids, you will need to embrace a different set of values and raise your child differently from people with just one or two children. Don't let other people's doubts about your family cause you to doubt your decision to have a large brood. A large group of loving siblings is more valuable than closets stuffed with pricey toys. Organization is the key to holding the chaos in check, but avoid the regimentation that saps the joy from family life.

Supersizing Benefits

Like many children with a passel of siblings, Wanda feels a bit sorry for youngsters with just one. Because she has a good job and aspirations for a demanding career, she isn't sure she will follow in her mother's footsteps and have eight children. Nevertheless, she wouldn't have traded her childhood for the world.

> As a child, I was closest to the two sisters nearest my age, and I am still closer to them than to my other sister and brothers. But I love each of them. We remain close even though our family is scattered now. Our "hub" switched from the hometown where I grew up to another city when my parents moved several years ago. One sister and brother live near them, so that is where we go for most major holidays and hold family reunions. Sometimes my husband, children, and I visit my

*other siblings during summer vacations. Between visits, my broth-
ers and sisters and I let our fingers do the walking, staying in touch
by phone.*

*Having friends wasn't as important to us as it seems to be to
kids who only have one or two siblings. Mama encouraged us to
play with other children outside, but they weren't allowed to spend
the night. I don't think any of us minded. Given the size of our family, there was never a shortage of kids to play with, and every night
was sort of like a sleepover anyway. I knew that money was tight,
but it wasn't that much of an issue for me. Actually, we were poor,
but I didn't realize it until after I was grown. We shared clothes and
toys, and Mom shopped at thrift shops. If you get nothing else out
of growing up in a big family, you learn to make do with used toys
and appreciate hand-me-downs! When we asked for things our
parents couldn't afford, they suggested ways we could earn money.
We babysat, had paper routes, mowed lawns, and washed cars.
My two sisters and I made a ton of money one summer with a pet-
sitting service. I didn't feel deprived, maybe because I assumed I
could work if I wanted something my parents couldn't afford.*

*The lack of privacy was a problem. We had a girl's bedroom,
boy's bedroom, and nursery. There wasn't any way to be alone until
I dreamed up this idea of tacking curtains to the ceiling above my
bed and closing them when I wanted privacy, Otherwise, I tied them
back, and it looked like a canopy bed. My sisters copied me, and
my brothers enclosed their bunk beds. Mom even ended up hanging
curtains around the crib so she could use the nursery as a sewing
room without disturbing a sleeping baby. Intruders paid big time
for violating our "cocoons," as we called them! We each stored our
personal treasures under our beds. But of course, the boys knew
exactly where we girls hid our diaries. Privacy is impossible with
that many kids around.*

Alert!

To place calls to any telephone number in the world for a very low charge, plug a microphone into your computer and install the free, easy-as-pie software from skype.com. You can talk online to people who have the program installed on their computer for no charge. The sound quality is perfect!

Better by the Dozen

Most research and popular wisdom is negative about large families, but it seems clear that children benefit from having lots of siblings. Whenever a youngster needs hugs for a hurt, help with homework, a bandage for a boo-boo, a marathon game of Monopoly, or a quick game of catch, he rarely needs to look farther than his own backyard. Humans are social animals, and too many youngsters from small families spend too much time alone. Modern lifestyles leave latchkey kids with working parents isolated for many hours each day. Their contact with other children is highly structured in day care centers, nurseries, classrooms, after-school programs, and extracurricular activities, allowing them little time for free play.

Interacting with older and younger brothers and sisters at home provides some of the benefits that were lost when large families and the one-room schoolhouse fell out of fashion. Then, older children nurtured younger ones, whereas modern children have few opportunities to interact with children in different age groups. Age-segregated environments are more limiting and stressful. In the absence of more mature children to serve as role models and assistants, a lone adult usually has to do everything. Quiet, well-behaved children get lost in the shuffle, while those who act out and misbehave usurp the lion's share of everyone's time and attention. Instead of emulating older children, toddlers, tweens, and teens turn to one another as role models and pick up a lot of very negative behavior. In age-segregated settings, more mature, intelligent children are often bored. They could benefit from playing with their intellectual and emotional peers. Meanwhile, less mature, less intelligent children tend to get trapped at the bottom of the social heap. If given opportunities to play with younger children, they could practice their social skills and have turns serving as the leader. They would receive the emotional boost that comes from being looked up to by younger children.

Alert!

With many children to care for, you won't have time to wait on each one hand and foot or pause to debate every rule. This helps youngsters learn self-reliance and to cope with limits. Too much mothering can result in smothering.

Few parents of large families are willing or even able to drop what they are doing at a moment's notice to run to the store so they can satisfy one child's desire for a new pack of baseball cards. Nor can they cook six different meals to satisfy picky eaters who don't like what is being served. Because they can't cater to their children's every whim or spend time debating every rule, they practice delaying gratification, adhering to routines, and coping with structure. In the process, they learn another important interpersonal skill: to accept "no" for an answer.

Having your children do chores and care for their younger brothers and sisters will probably be a necessity. Doing essential jobs and making real contributions to the household helps children appreciate their personal worth, thereby boosting their healthy (as opposed to self-centered, narcissistic) self-esteem. Through helping to take care of younger children and one another, siblings become more firmly bonded. They learn the skills needed to run a household and nurture babies, which will serve them well when they have homes and families of their own.

Rethinking Family Values

A variety of social changes has contributed to the popularity of small families in the United States and other industrialized nations. The ready availability of birth control, the mass entry of women into the workforce, an economy that necessitates two incomes, and the trend to delaying childbearing until later in life have all contributed to a lower birthrate. People used to feel sorry for children who only had one or two siblings. Now that large families are in the minority, opinions about their acceptability have changed, according to Katherine Schlaerth, author of *Raising a Large Family*. Many people look askance at parents with more than two children, as if they are violating some sort of social taboo. This may be because most U.S. parents have what cross-cultural psychologists refer to as an individualistic worldview. If you have chosen to have many children and make your family your number one priority, you probably have a collectivist worldview or will move in that direction as your family grows. Because collectivists are in the minority, they may feel they are letting their children down by not fulfilling the parenting goals of the individualistic majority. But different does not mean worse, and collectivist families have much to recommend them.

 **Fact**

At the end of the 1700s, the average U.S. mother had seven children. Today, just three children are enough for a family to be considered large.

Individualistic Worldview

Most U.S. parents subscribe to the belief that children need to be able to fulfill themselves as individuals. Most people think it is sad for a child to have to sacrifice his personal wishes, desires, and ambitions for the sake of his family. Having serious responsibilities for household chores and child care is viewed as a misfortune since it interferes with children's ability to devote themselves to more personally gratifying pursuits. Individualistic parents may assign a small regular chore since this is considered important for a child. Otherwise, they solicit help as a favor and acknowledge their youngster's gift by saying "thank-you," sometimes even paying their children to motivate them. One-on-one time is considered imperative to ensure children are treated as individuals and are freed from having to function as a member of the family for at least a few minutes each day. Parents dislike having their children sacrifice their personal goals for the family. Having their teenager forego an extracurricular activity to care for younger siblings or help around the house after school would seem cruel. A teen with individualistic values would probably feel resentful about being asked to make such a sacrifice. If family obligations cause a student to miss so much school that his grades suffer, his parents can be prosecuted for neglect.

Because of the emphasis on individual fulfillment, people with an individualistic worldview consider teenagers deprived if they contribute a portion of their paychecks to the household. Children are expected to move out soon after turning eighteen, and failing to do so is viewed as a misfortune for parents who must cope with the burden of a child who has failed to become properly independent. Similarly, for adult children to devote a lot of energy or income to helping aging parents and needy siblings is considered a trying if noble sacrifice. But if their spouses and children are affected, the sacrifice is apt to be regarded as foolish, if not pathological.

People who subscribe to this worldview tend to be oriented toward the future rather than the present or past. Many parents dream of what their children might become even before they are born. They open college savings accounts for their newborns, put their one-year-olds on waiting lists for private preschools, and try to jump-start their toddlers' education with alphabet blocks. Since parents regard childhood as a time to prepare for adulthood, they consider it important to do what they can to help them become successful adults.

It's not surprising that people with this worldview tend to plan their families around their pocketbooks. Children are considered underprivileged if they must make do with hand-me-down clothes and used toys since this prevents them from dressing according to their individual tastes and pursuing their preferred leisure time activities. Parents with an individualistic worldview uphold their individual children's property rights, keeping siblings out of one another's rooms and from touching one another's toys and clothes. Disputes over a shared toy are settled by determining who had it first, who had it last, who deserves a turn, and so forth.

 ***Fact***

Parents with an individualistic worldview define success in economic terms and have a future orientation. They prize children with special abilities that might lead to future financial success. Collectivist parents define success as having a strong family; they are oriented toward the present. They prize loving, well-behaved, loyal children.

Collectivist Orientation

In most cultures of the world, people subscribe to a collectivist worldview. This is the case for most inhabitants of Asian, Spanish-speaking, and indigenous cultures, as well as for some minority groups in the United States. Collectivist parents regard the welfare of the family as a whole as more important than that of any individual member. When there is a conflict between a child's personal needs and the needs of the family, the family's needs are expected to take precedence. It is considered proper for a child to put his desires and wishes on hold for the sake of the greater family good. To do so is a sign that the child is loving and loyal—two traits that are highly prized as signifying good character. Parents do not request favors for themselves and their other children by saying "please" and asking for "help." To do so would suggest that it is up to the parent to do all of the household chores so the children can pursue their own interests and prepare for their futures as independent people. Instead, children are expected to contribute to the family according to their capabilities throughout their lives. This is not regarded as a sacrifice, but as a duty.

In the collectivist worldview, the present matters more than the future. Collectivist parents are more likely to believe that if the present is properly attended to the future will take care of itself. The family's well-being is primary, and even family obligations that interfere with a child's academic progress are not viewed as problems, since children can simply make up the work or repeat the year in school. In cultures where collectivists are in the majority, children are expected to remain at home to help until they are ready to start families of their own, instead of becoming independent at age eighteen or shortly thereafter. In fact, a child who never moves out is considered loving and loyal, and neighbors consider his parents fortunate. Even married children are expected to care for their parents and siblings when needed. Adult children are pleased to be able to share their money with extended family members, and contributing is considered a necessary expense, not a sacrifice. It is understood that siblings and parents would help them if they were in need. Perhaps because children are expected to contribute to the family throughout their lives, they are considered blessings to be enjoyed, not expensive luxuries to be tended until they can take care of themselves. Children are raised to be interdependent rather than independent.

Parenting Large Families

If you have many offspring, you are likely to feel that you are failing your children if you have an individualistic worldview. If you have a collectivist orientation, you will realize that you are not depriving your children because you lack the time and money to indulge everyone's desires and fulfill all of their individual goals and ambitions. Unless you have a hefty income, your youngsters will probably have to share toys and clothes. Little materialists may be very unhappy about having recycled toys and clothes from neighbors, yard sales, and thrift shops, but having few flashy new toys can also build character. Having less can help children appreciate what they do have, motivate them to take better care of their things, find creative ways to satisfy their wants, and be more discerning about which material goods they set their hearts on. Suggesting that they work at small neighborhood jobs to earn extra spending money can help them feel more in control and nurture self-reliance and an entrepreneurial spirit. Not having all of their materialistic desires fulfilled on demand teaches children to tolerate frustration and delay gratification—two essential aspects of emotional intelligence. With less money to go around, there is less parental overindulgence that causes children to be spoiled and the earth to be despoiled.

Big Family Blues

Children in large families are frequently called upon to help with household chores. Larger families tend to be poorer, and some children are very resentful about the cramped living quarters, lack of privacy, hand-me-down clothes, used toys, and lack of funds for specialized lessons and activities. But social scientists are concerned by the parents' inability to afford the items that give students an educational edge, such as books, tutors, private schools, special learning aids, and good colleges. Nor can the average family with many offspring foot the bills for the cars and apartments that speed children down the road to financial independence and toward the upper tax brackets. Having the family's financial pie cut into so many pieces means each youngster gets a smaller slice. "Researchers have found a very strong tendency for those from a large family to do worse in school (and in life) than those from smaller families," according to Dalton Conley, author of *The Pecking Order: Which Siblings Succeed and Why*. Conley also states: "For almost as long as sociologists have been studying who gets ahead, they have found that kids from large families do more poorly than those from small ones."

Alert!

Most studies of large families define "success" as years of education completed and salary. By those criteria, children are better off with one sibling or none at all. No studies seem to assess health, marital satisfaction, volunteerism, or sense of personal well-being, which collectivist parents consider especially important.

When success is measured in terms of education and income, a youngest child in a large family does as well as children from a small one. Perhaps the lastborn reaps the benefit of having so many older siblings serve as quasi-parents. The reason is unclear, but it seems likely that the older siblings give the baby of the family a lot of special attention. By talking to him, reading to him, helping him with homework, and chipping in to send him to college, they boost his occupational prospects. The children born in the middle get a lot less individual attention and must cope with a noisy environment. Young children need lots of conversations to master language skills. They need to be read to and helped to learn nursery rhymes. They also need a quiet environment so they can separate what is being said from the background noise. If your time is limited, have older children take turns reading and teaching nursery rhymes. Confine televisions, radios, and stereos to children's bedrooms, insist children turn off the sound on video games and computers, and forbid children to conduct telephone conversations in common areas. Keep the radio off in the car so the children can talk, and control the hubbub during meals. Youngsters cannot make sense of what is being said when everyone is talking at once. Don't let older children talk for or interrupt younger ones. Insist that they be given the time they need to collect their thoughts, formulate their ideas, and speak. Emphasize the importance of doing well in school so that your children can qualify for college scholarships. Inform them of low-cost options for higher education, such as community colleges.

Chaos Control

The portrayal of a happy, giant-sized family delighted audiences in the original version of the movie *Cheaper by the Dozen*. But there is another, darker side to the story of growing up with so many siblings. The recent remake of the old classic film is short on realism but nevertheless shows how chaotic life can be when parents don't remain organized and in charge. At the same time, the movies *The Sound of Music* and *The Great Santini* suggest what happens when parents go overboard in the other direction and regiment their youngsters. Running a household like a boot camp makes life easier for those in charge. But being marched through their days in lockstep formation kills the spontaneity which can be the source of so much joy and laughter. Life itself is messy, and trying to contain it with too many ironclad regulations leads to a very dour environment. Nevertheless, some sanity-saving rules designed to maintain order will be needed.

Preventing Mealtime Madness

If a child has special nutritional needs, they must be met. Otherwise, trying to create menus to suit individual tastes is unrealistic. If your children are very hungry, they will eat what you serve; so, disallow snacking for children over four. Choosing not to eat won't cause children to starve or even make them slightly malnourished. To accommodate individual tastes, pair older children with younger ones and rotate the task of planning menus and cooking.

Quiet Time, Quiet Zones

Mark Twain astutely observed that nothing is worse than someone else's music. The same might be said for someone else's television show and radio station. A lot of noise is overly stimulating and makes for a very stressful environment. Headphones are likely to be essential sanity-savers. Send noisy children outside to play so they can whoop and holler to their hearts' content. You need to ensure that younger children who are light sleepers are not disturbed by the older ones with later bedtimes. You need to ensure that the house is quiet enough so that school-age children can study and do their homework. One way to accommodate everyone is to declare a quiet time after the younger children are in bed. On school nights, the older ones can use the time to read or study or pursue another quiet activity until lights-out.

Keeping the Peace

To avoid destructive free-for-alls that can become very dangerous as children get older, strictly forbid physical violence. Violence includes pinching, pushing, shoving, and tickling (after a child says "stop"). To make the rule stick, you must also disallow the words and deeds that children use to incite one another to violence: sarcasm, name-calling, harassment, and destruction of one another's property. To make that rule stick, you must impose consequences each and every time there is a violation. Require the rule-breakers to replay their conflicts using noninflammatory words. They need to be taught how to communicate appropriately when they are angry, which is to say assertively rather than aggressively. Children who share bedrooms may have trouble coexisting. As long as you try to address their litany of complaints, as is the custom for typical problem-solving methods, you will have to put out one fire after another. Instead, work toward enduring solutions by serving as a mediator, or hold family meetings so everyone can help them figure out how to divvy up their space!

 Essential

Whenever a hot-tempered child handles a small disagreement without lashing out, point it out. This will help him develop confidence in his ability to control his temper. Help him figure out how to use his strategy in more contentious situations.

Cramped Quarters

Unless you live in a very large house, you will probably find space a problem. The bathroom tends to be an issue, especially in households with teenagers. You can make a huge dent in the time each child spends in the bathroom by putting mirrors in their bedrooms and storing their combs and brushes there. Supply teens with small dressing tables so they can comb their hair and apply makeup in their bedrooms. Post a bathroom schedule for baths and showers. Teach children to close the shower curtain when they are taking a bath so that the toilet can be used while they are bathing.

You will need to mobilize all of your creativity and organizational skills to make room for everyone's everything. A good first step is to visit The Container Store. Even if you can't afford their expensive wares, seeing what is available can still give you some great ideas for organizing clothes, toys, and household miscellanea into small spaces. In addition, organizational experts work with families to help them figure out how to manage their homes. The consulting fees will save a fortune if the advice saves you from building an addition to your home or moving. Little pack rats may have to face the hard choice of containing their clutter or waiting until they have a home of their own before fulfilling their wish to hoard and save. Yelling at children to clean up their rooms is of little use if they don't know how to straighten and organize. *The Everything® Tween Book* provides a detailed explanation of how to help them master the skills they need.

Taking Care of You

Research studies suggest that how well children get along in large families is strongly related to their parents' mental health. The problems of overwhelmed parents ripple through a sibling group, and events that disrupt children's lives, such as alcoholism, domestic violence, and mental illness, apparently take a special toll on children in large families. This may be because children emulate their parents; so a youngster with a violent parent is likely to have some violent older siblings to contend with as well. If you must decide between spending money on some much-needed clothes for the children or a babysitter so that you can take a break, they might benefit more from having you attend a yoga class or simply sit in the library to peruse a magazine and soak up the sounds of silence. Join a parent support group—the chance to commiserate with other moms and dads while your children play can be invaluable. If you're trapped at home, check out the online resources for large families by searching for the phrase words "large families" or see:

- **Love at Home** (*www.loveathome.com*)—advice about parenting large broods.
- **4 or More** (*www.4ormore.co.uk*)—suggestions and support.
- **Large Families** (*www.essentialbaby.com.au*)—discussion forums for moms.

CHAPTER 15

Twins and More

Misconceptions about twins and other multiples abound. Even children who have identical genes and grow up together don't end up with identical personalities. Whether the youngsters turn out to be best friends or sworn enemies depends on whether they learn to tolerate and appreciate their differences. Multiples are less likely to end up as bitter rivals when given space to develop in their own way instead of being pressured to be just alike. Every child needs to be treated like an individual!

Separate but Equal

When twins and other multiples are dressed alike, they draw lots of attention from admiring passersby. Some youngsters thrive on inspiring so much delight and awe in other people. But when children look alike, people treat them alike, and that can cause a lot of problems, as it did for Laura and her identical twin, Lisa.

From the time we were infants, our mother cut and combed our hair exactly alike and dressed us in the very same outfits, from barrettes to dresses to shoes and socks. We both got our ears pierced when we were six years old, and Mom even chose duplicate pairs of tiny gold earrings for us. No wonder everyone but my parents and our babysitter had trouble telling us apart! When we started school, our teacher asked Mom not to dress us alike so people could tell us apart. Mom refused. She said that once everyone got to know us they would be able to tell who was who. As it turned out, Mom was right.

Fact

Three children born at the same time are called triplets, four are quadruplets, five are quintuplets, and six are sextuplets. The risk of premature birth goes up with the number of infants being carried. In the entire world, there are only two sets of septuplets in which all seven children survived.

In our childhood photos, my sister always looks fresh and presentable in her little ruffled dresses and lacy tights. She was always very "girly" in her interests and continues to choose very feminine clothes and pastimes. I preferred sports to dolls. I spent a lot of time playing outside with my older brother and his friends. My dresses were wrinkled, my ruffles were rumpled, my shoes were scuffed, and my tights had runs and bagged at the knees from getting stretched out when I yanked them on. I can easily spot myself in our early photos by the scraped knees, messy hair, and grass stains. Because Mom insisted that my twin and I dress alike, we argued over what clothes to buy, and we argued every day over what to wear.

My mother couldn't stand that I looked so untidy. "Why can't you take care of your things like your sister does?" she would ask. I didn't know what to say at the time, but the answer was simple enough: Most of our clothes were no good for bike riding or playing ball. I felt that Mom liked Lisa more than me. I criticized Lisa mercilessly about being clumsy so she wouldn't want to take ballet lessons so that we could quit. We fought because I was trying to get her to be more like me, and she was trying to get me to be more like her. We would have gotten along better if we had been allowed to be individuals instead of feeling that we had to be identical. When I see school-age twins dressed alike, I want to take their mothers aside and tell them that they should let twins be themselves!

Multiples on the Rise

Multiple births have become much more common in the last few decades. The number of twin births increased more than 50 percent between 1980 and 2000. Now, one baby out of fifty is born with a twin. During those same two decades, the number of triplet births more than quadrupled. According to the National Vital Statistics Reports and The Centers for Disease Control and Prevention, in the United States alone there are more than one-half million multiples under the age of five. The rise in multiple births is due to two major factors: infertility treatments and the trend toward delayed childbearing. Fertility-enhancing drugs produce follicle-stimulated hormones which trigger ovulation. The drugs increase the number of eggs a woman produces each month. Ten to 40 percent of twin pregnancies are caused by fertility-enhancing drugs, depending on which prescription is taken. In vitro fertilization, which involves placing multiple fertilized eggs into the womb to increase the chance of pregnancy, also results in more multiple births.

The trend among women to delay having children until they are in their thirties and forties has also contributed to the increase in multiple births. Even without the use of fertility drugs, later-in-life pregnancies are more likely to result in multiple births. Other factors such as race determine the likelihood of having a multiple birth. For instance, African-American women are more likely to give birth to twins. Having a history of fraternal twins on the maternal side, regardless of race, increases the chances of having twins in later generations. Identical twins are believed to happen at random rather than being hereditary. Since the likelihood of a multiple birth increases with each subsequent pregnancy, the more children you have, the greater the odds of having twins. Six percent of babies born in the United States are twins, according to a 2005 article in the *Journal of Counseling Development.* There were 6,742 triplet births, 506 quadruplet births, and 77 quintuplets and other higher order births in the United States in 2000, according to pediatrician Vincent Iannelli.

The Biology of Multiples

Fraternal twins result when two different eggs are fertilized by two different sperm. These babies can be conceived at different times and can even have different fathers. Fraternal twins can be of the same sex or of opposite sexes. They are no more alike than any regular pair of brothers, sisters, or sisters and brothers. While they often resemble one another, they can also have very distinct appearances, abilities, and personalities. Fraternal twins are the most common type of multiple births, occurring in approximately two-thirds of the twin population. Triplets and other higher-order multiples can be fraternal, identical or a combination of the two. Triplets, who are sometimes referred to as "super twins," are the most rapidly increasing type of multiple, occurring about once in every 7,000 deliveries.

Alert!

Because they look so much alike, people outside the family may not be able to tell identical twins apart, which encourages people to react to them like a unit instead of treating them as individuals. That can thwart the children's ability to gain a sense of themselves as individuals and form one-on-one relationships with others.

Identical twins occur when a single fertilized egg splits in half within the first two weeks after conception. Identical twins are always the same sex and share the same genetic makeup. Nearly 25 percent of all identical twins are "mirror twins." Because of the way the egg splits, the children are exact reflections of each other. They still have the same genetic makeup, but one twin is left-handed, and the other is right-handed. Their internal organs and skeletal features are on opposite sides, and even their hair curls in opposite directions. They have highly similar IQs, but because life experiences are so formative, their personalities and interests can be very different.

Occasional press reports about identical twins living parallel lives at a distance are fascinating. Some stories describe twins separated at birth who share uncanny similarities, even though they were adopted into different households. For instance, British twins Barbara Herbert and Daphne Goodship, who have been extensively studied by the University of Minnesota's Center for Twin and Adoption Research, were separated at birth and didn't meet again until age forty. It turned out that both sisters had left school at age fourteen, injured their ankles when falling down a flight of stairs at age fifteen, were sixteen when they met their future husbands at a town hall dance, worked at local government jobs, had miscarriages in the same month, and ended up with three children—two boys and a girl. When they met, both were wearing cream-colored dresses and brown velvet jackets. Besides their shared inclination to drink coffee cold and being uncomfortable with blood and heights, they both a habit of pushing up their nose with the palm of their hand. They both referred to this gesture as "squidging."

Nevertheless, genes turn on and off in response to the environment; so there are small differences among identical multiples even at birth. Those differences can set a chain of different life experiences into motion, causing them to become even more different as time passes. For instance, parents may be more protective of the child that is smaller or less healthy at birth. Other differences in life experiences can also give rise to large differences. If one twin is in a highly stressful classroom, he might develop a dislike of school, develop learning problems, and drop out at age sixteen. Meanwhile, the other twin's positive school experiences might lead to a love of learning, good grades, a college diploma, and a professional career.

Preparing for Multiples

The more children a pregnant woman carries at a time, the greater the risk of complications. Carrying multiples to term is more difficult than carrying a singleton. There are more premature births, low birth weights, and subsequent health problems among multiples. Thanks to advancements in medical technology, the survival rate for premature triplets has improved considerably. Quadruplets and quintuplets continue to be rare, but doctors are more successful than in the past at saving more of them. Nevertheless, respiratory ailments, serious infections, anemia, jaundice, cerebral palsy, neurological complications, and other health issues with long-term consequences for health, behavior, and learning are common. It is important to obtain good medical treatment throughout your pregnancy and follow your doctor's advice carefully.

You can prepare your toddler by reading him storybooks about twins. Explain that Mommy and Daddy will be tired when the babies first come home, and talk about how helpful he will be as a big brother. Perhaps he can help choose colors and playthings for the babies' room and assist with organizing diapers and baby clothes. After the babies arrive, he will be able to lend a hand by fetching items for you. If he understands that his role will be important, chances are he will be more excited about embarking on his new adventure as the oldest of three siblings.

Alert!

Keeping up with one infant challenges most families; keeping up with two or more is exhausting. Before your babies arrive, line up as much help as you can from friends and extended family members. You will need it!

Before the babies are born, schedule shifts for people who volunteer to assist you. This will be of immense help during those first few weeks and months, which can be extremely hectic. Create a daily schedule of anticipated feedings, naps, diaper changes, laundry, and other household chores. Consider which tasks you can delegate and assign them to friends and relatives who offer to help. Also, try to schedule some time away from the babies so you can reconnect with yourself as a person and safeguard your physical and emotional well-being. Although finding enough babysitting help can be challenging, it is equally important for you and your spouse to have some time away from the children, whether to take a walk, visit with friends, go to the gym, or just to sit quietly. Afterward, you will have more energy for the babies. Marital satisfaction tends to decline after children are born and doesn't improve until they are in high school. Having twins or triplets is decidedly more stressful through the toddler years when the children's need for physical and emotional care is continuous. It is important that you and your spouse stay connected.

Welcome Home!

Your family will change dramatically with a multiple birth. Given the demands of caring for more than one infant, chances are that you will rely heavily on your other children. Help them build relationships with the babies immediately by encouraging them to hold them. Let the older siblings know that the babies need and appreciate their assistance. You might be pleasantly surprised at how eagerly older children, including toddlers, rise to the cause of nurturing their new siblings. However, don't be discouraged if your other children need time to adjust. It is easy for them to feel neglected due to the loss of attention. When visitors come calling, make sure that your other children aren't pushed aside and forgotten. Let them show off the babies. Draw the other children into conversations by encouraging them to answer questions about the babies instead of answering yourself. Point out to the visitors how lucky the little ones are to have such special big brothers and sisters and how lucky you are to have their help.

Even small amounts of help from grandparents, uncles and aunts, and friends of the family can be of tremendous assistance, so accept all reasonable offers. Perhaps a neighbor can come over for half an hour at about the same time a few mornings each week while you shower. In that way, you can take care of yourself without having to worry about the babies and your other children. If a neighborhood teen shows a lot of interest in your adorable newborns, invite her to visit after school. While she watches the babies, you can prepare dinner, have some uninterrupted time with your other children, or simply sit quietly in another room to gather your thoughts. Encourage your older children to accept invitations to go on outings with other adults. This will temporarily ease your load while ensuring that the big brothers and sisters get extra attention at a time when you are too exhausted to give them much.

Essential

Life can become very hectic and chaotic when you are caring for two or three newborns. A routine will provide a sense of order for your older children. Try to get the babies to eat and sleep on a schedule as soon as possible.

Parents understandably worry how the baby of the family will adjust to the arrival of two or more new younger siblings at once. The good news, according to research reported by Judy Dunn in her book *From One Child to Two*, is that firstborn children usually adjust much more easily to twins and display less envy and hostility than to a single new baby brother or sister. It may be that because they are more involved in caring for them they become more attached and have a new role to replace the one they have lost. Self-esteem comes from real accomplishments, and doing important work helps promotes children's feelings of being capable and needed.

When you are struggling with the demands of multiples, it can be hard to find other parents who can relate to what you are going through. Many parents struggle in isolation at a time when they need a lot of guidance and support. Because they are so busy at home, attending meetings seems like a luxury. But the child-rearing tips and camaraderie can make a world of difference. Visit the National Organization of Mothers of Twins Web site at *www.nomtc.org* and use the directory to locate a support group in your community for parents of multiples. Find out if there is a local chapter of the Mothers of Multiples Society (MOMS, which is also for dads) by typing the name of that organization and your town into an Internet search engine. Be sure to subscribe to *Twins Magazine.*

Competition

It is important not to compare multiples, since doing so encourages the children to compete. Unfortunately, one of the most common questions people ask is which twin was born first. Since being "first" is so important to children, even this innocent question immediately sets up an implied comparison. Consider each child's achievements in relation to his peers, not his twin, and encourage outsiders to do the same. Try to balance special acknowledgments by pointing out an area in which the other child has excelled. Spend time alone with each child so you can relate to them individually. Scheduling special Mommy and Daddy time also gives you a break since it is less stressful to take care of one child than two. The one-on-one time can be spent on routine activities, such as going grocery shopping, running errands, doing laundry, preparing meals, or doing yard work. Toddlers can participate in household chores by separating clean socks, tearing lettuce leaves for a salad, and picking up trash from the lawn. If your children play well together and share the same interests, there is no reason why they can't share the same toys, friends, and activities. If their interests take them in separate directions toward different activities and friends, don't discourage them from leading their own lives. Just as all siblings are different, so, too, are all twins.

Issues in Psychological Development

Most infants arrive in the world by themselves and must learn to develop intimate relationships with other human beings. In fact, psychologists consider bonding with other family members to be a critical emotional task for the first year of life. Multiples have the opposite challenge. They arrive in the world together. They are bonded to one another, and their intimacy is a given. The childhood challenge for twins and other multiples is to develop a clear concept of themselves as separate individuals and to expand their network of attachments to include others. In fact, the article "Twin Loss: Implications for Counselors Working with Surviving Twins" in the Winter 2005 issue of the *Journal of Counseling and Development* reported that twins tend to be more closely bonded to one another than to their parents. Most twins enjoy an extremely warm, close relationship throughout their lives. But their closeness can have some drawbacks. Because twins do such a good job of entertaining one another, their parents and older siblings tend to interact with them less than singletons, which can cause language delays.

Autonomy and Independence

Because twins spend so much of their time together as infants, babies, and toddlers, they naturally serve as one another's security blankets. Learning to rely on themselves can be a problem. They need to spend time apart, practice tackling situations on their own, and gain experience reaching out to others. Otherwise, their extreme dependency on one another continues. Some adult twins say that they are only at ease when they are together. When they are apart, they feel as though they are missing an arm or a leg. They feel lost and overwhelmed without their "other half" close at hand, especially in unfamiliar environments. "My identical twin was the assertive one," one woman explained. "I never had to stick up for myself. Looking back, I can see that even at home she fought my battles for me. But I didn't have a sense of her fighting for me at the time because I didn't have a sense of myself, only of us. She did the anger for both of us, and I cried the tears. To this day, she cannot cry, and I can't assert myself."

At some point, multiples must be able to function independently. If the children have different interests, they will need to be able to attend activities without their sibling at their side. They will need to be in different classrooms if they have different learning needs, which is not uncommon even for identical twins and triplets. As adults, their opportunities and options will be severely limited if they cannot hold separate jobs, marry, and raise families of their own. Multiples may always be closer to one another than to anyone else. But they need to spend enough time apart so they can learn to handle a variety of situations and people without depending on one another.

Alert!

Multiples need to practice building and maintaining one-on-one relationships with other children and adults in order to develop the social skills they need to relate to outsiders. For multiples to gain a clear sense of themselves as individuals and to practice functioning on their own, they need to have a variety of solo experiences.

Identity Formation

Ideally, multiples will have what researchers Schave and Ciriello called an "interdependent identity." Such children are best friends and depend on each other. They can handle being apart but are happiest when together. Twins with a "competitive identity" retain their strong bonds but appreciate their differences and encourage one another to excel as individuals. Twins with a "sibling attachment identity" relate like very close siblings. Their primary identity is of being an individual, not a twin. Twins with a "unit identity" think of themselves as halves of a whole and experience separations as so painful that they may return to living together after brief marriages. The notion of the "evil twin" hails from twins with a "split identity," wherein one twin sees himself as good and the other sees himself as bad. They often have a deep-seated distrust of one another but are locked into their unhappy relationship. Twins with an "idealized identity" believe they are special because they are twins. They may be more attached to the idea of being a twin than to one another and suffer a loss of identity when they embark upon separate lives.

There are differing schools of thought on how to help twins and other multiples establish healthy identities. Many experts advise against referring to multiples as "the twins" or "the triplets." Some psychologists believe that lumping them into a group encourages their tendency to view themselves as a single unit. Lynn Lorenz, author of *The Multiples Manual,* is an identical twin and the mother of triplets. She enjoyed the notoriety of being referred to as "a twin" while growing up. She points out that most families refer to their singletons as "the kids" or "the children" without causing them to develop identity problems. Nevertheless, some twins and multiples do find the label inhibiting. No two sets of twins or multiples are alike, so it is important to determine whether your youngsters are doing a good job of developing as individuals. Here are some signs that may suggest they are having problems.

- They complain about being treated alike.
- They wish they did not have a twin.
- They quarrel frequently.
- They have no separate activities or friends despite being very different.
- They compete by trying to undermine one another.
- One child feels like a winner; the other feels like a loser.
- They resist being separated for any reason.

You may think that your twins have firm, separate identities because they often argue. But people argue when they are intent on trying to convince someone else to think, feel, or act like they do. If twins are constantly battling with one another, it probably means that they are not comfortable with their differences. They are pressuring one another to be "just like me" because there isn't room for two in their relationship. The question is which personality will prevail.

There are some simple steps you can take to ensure that each child develops a comfortable separate identify. Allow the children to pursue their own interests. Buy them separate toys and encourage them to make separate friends. Call the children by their names, make individual eye contact when speaking, and avoid the shorthand reference "the twins" or "the triplets" that lumps them together. Doing so may help you and other family members remember that they are individuals and need to be treated accordingly. This can also reassure the youngsters that they are viewed as being unique. As your youngsters mature, let them participate in picking out their clothes so they can develop their own tastes if they are so inclined. Some preschools and primary schools recommend placing twins in different classrooms, while others have no policies concerning this decision. If the children need help to develop separate identities and friends, it is best to separate them. There is nothing wrong with multiples feeling closer to one another than to anyone else and preferring one another's company. But if their tendency to stick together prevents them from forming other meaningful relationships and pursuing their individual interests, more separation is in order.

Notable Multiples

The reality of being a twin has advantages and disadvantages, and raising twins is no small challenge. Nevertheless, most little girls long for a twin and dream of having twins when they grow up. Twins have a definite mystique.

Celebrity Twins

A number of famous people have a twin. In some cases, both twins are famous. Here is a small sampling.

- Mario and Aldo Andretti
- Karen Black
- Jenna and Barbara Bush
- Montgomery Clift
- Maurice and Robin Gibb
- Jerry Hall
- Paul and Morgan Hamm
- Ann Landers
  and Abigail Van Buren
- Ashley and Mary-Kate Olsen
- Elvis Presley
- Ed Sullivan

- Tiki and Ronde Barber
- Heloise Bowles
- Jose and Ozzie Canseco
- Brittany and Cynthia Daniel
- Deidre Hall
- Linda Hamilton
- Scarlett Johansson
- Liberace
- Alanis Morissette
- Parker Posey
- Isabella Rossellini
- Keifer Sutherland

- Jim Thorpe
- Billy Dee Williams
- Thorton Wilder

Celebrities Who Have Children Who Are Twins

Many notable people have raised twins.

- Madeleine Albright
- Lance Armstrong
- Adrian Barneau
- Corbin Bernsen/ Amanda Pays
- George W. and Laura Bush
- Kerry Kennedy Cuomo
- Geena Davis
- Donald Faison
- Michael J. Fox and Tracy Pollan
- Marcia Gay Harden
- Bruce Hornsby
- King Hussein
- Christine Lahti
- Loretta Lynn
- Dave Matthews
- Julia Roberts
- Jane Seymour
- Cybill Shepherd
- Tilda Swinton
- Margaret Thatcher
- Denzel Washington
- Muhammad Ali
- Ed Asner
- Ingrid Bergman
- David Birney/ Meredith Baxter
- Bing Crosby
- Beverly D'Angelo and Al Pacino
- Robert De Niro
- Mia Farrow and André Previn
- Andy Garcia
- Mel Gibson
- Patricia Heaton
- Ron Howard
- Julio Iglesias
- Ivan Lendl
- Henry Mancini
- Jane Pauley and Garry Trudeau
- Ray Romano
- William Shakespeare
- Donald Sutherland
- James Taylor
- Stanley Tucci

CHAPTER 16

Adopted Siblings

Opening your home to an adopted child adds richness and complexity to family life. When a youngster joins your family, there is likely to be a difficult period of adjustment. It is important not to overreact to sibling conflict. Like biological siblings, the youngsters will undoubtedly get along well on some days and be very unhappy with one another at times. The attachments are likely to be as intense as among biological siblings. Everyone benefits from the expanded circle of love.

Preparing for a New Sibling

Being told that a new child will be joining the family without taking the time to discuss how your natural children will be affected is likely to be very upsetting. Nicole's story emphasizes the importance of preparing your youngsters for such a momentous event.

> *I was nine years old when Mom told my brother and me that six-year-old Susie was coming to live with us. Mom was at the stove at the time, cooking dinner, and I was setting the table. My brother, who was then seven, was playing on the floor with our half-grown Labrador retriever. Mom's tone was serious as she explained that Susie's parents weren't able to take care of her; so she needed a new home and a family to call her own. I felt scared but tried not to show it. Nothing further was said until we all sat down to dinner. As my brother*

munched a piece of fried chicken, he suddenly announced, "Susie can't stay here. There aren't enough bedrooms!"

When my brother brought up the bedroom problem, my mind raced. I realized that since Susie was a girl and I was a girl my parents would have to put her in my room. That meant she would need a bed and space for her toys. Having Susie in my room would be too crowded. I thought about my stuffed animals lined up on my bed. My special rock collection was arranged on my dresser top exactly the way I wanted. A little kid would mess with my things. I wanted to yell, "Susie can't stay in my room! She'll wreck my stuff!" Instead, I timidly asked my parents, "Where will Susie sleep?" Dad answered calmly, "We'll work it out." Mom quickly diverted the conversation by saying, "Let's eat some of this yummy apple pie." I did, but it didn't stop me from worrying. After Susie moved in, I was pretty resentful. It took a long time to accept her being there. It did work out in the end. I came to love Susie. She is as much a part of the family as my brother. But those first months were miserable.

 **Fact**

127,000 children were adopted into U.S. families in 2001 (according to the U.S. Department of Health and Human Services, National Adoption Information Clearinghouse, 2004). Hundreds of thousands of children are waiting for families to call their own. State subsidies may help with medical expenses for children with special needs. For information, contact your local Department of Health and Human Services.

Discussing Adoption

You may decide to adopt a child for a variety of reasons. Perhaps you have a niece, nephew, or grandchild who needs a home. You may be unable to have more children of your own and want your youngster to have a sibling. You may be attached to a foster child or have a special relationship with a youngster who has been released for adoption. If you are a stepparent, you may decide to adopt your stepchild. Many families simply decide that sharing their home with a child in need is the right thing to do. Whatever your reasons, it is important to discuss them with your natural children. Otherwise, they may fear that you decided to take in another youngster because they weren't enough. They may take your decision to adopt as a personal rejection and think they are being replaced.

Older children may have some mistaken notions about how life with a new sibling will be. Some imagine it will be like having a friend come for a party that lasts forever. If so, they may be disillusioned when reality sets in. Others fear that the newcomer will bring unwanted changes that lessen the quality of their lives. Honesty is probably the best policy. Discuss the benefits while admitting that having to share toys and space may at times be hard. Encourage your children to ask questions and express their concerns about having a new sibling without becoming defensive.

 *Essential*

If you paint an overly rosy picture of how life will be with a new sibling, your natural children may end up feeling betrayed. It is usually better to admit that there will be some drawbacks: less money to go around, needing to share their space, and your time and attention will be divided.

Don't be surprised if your natural children say little when you first share your plans to adopt. They may need to ponder the matter before they can formulate questions and verbalize their feelings about such a major change. Stay open to questions, and remain alert to signs that they are ready to discuss the matter. Later, while they are getting ready for bed or involved in another activity, you are likely to hear a comment. Even if they are very enthusiastic on one hand or negative on the other, their feelings may change once they have had time to think about what it might mean to have a new sibling. Be honest when addressing their fears about the household changes and describing the personal sacrifices a new sibling may entail. Let them know how you expect them to benefit, and describe the rewards you anticipate for the adopted child and for the family as a whole. Reassure your children that you are not trying to replace them.

Readying the Household

Some basic decisions need to be made before an adoptive child arrives. By discussing some of the specific arrangements with your natural children, you can help them begin to prepare for the changes while readying the household. Details that seem minor to parents are often major issues for children such as:

- Where the new sibling will sleep
- Where the new sibling will store her clothes
- Where the new sibling will keep her toys
- Where the new sibling will sit at the dinner table
- What can each family member do to help the new sibling feel welcome

Like adults, children are more cooperative with decisions when they are involved in making them. Even if your youngsters are less than enthusiastic about an adoption, you can involve them in the planning. Implementing some of their suggestions will give them a stake in a successful outcome. They may not be able to participate in the big decisions, but solicit their opinions about where their new sibling's toothbrush should go, where to hang her towel, and what to serve for dinner when she arrives. See if your natural children will take on the responsibility of making a welcome sign or baking a cake.

Settling In

Even if you have tried to prepare your children in advance, having a new child move in will be a source of confusion for toddlers and preschool youngsters. Despite your explanations, they may be unable to grasp what is happening. "Who is this stranger at the dinner table?" they may wonder. "Why does she play with my toys?" "Why doesn't she go home to her own house?" Young children may also wonder whether the next guest who arrives for dinner will end up moving in. You can help speed comprehension that this newcomer is now a member of the family by repeatedly referring to the adopted child as "your sister" or "your brother."

Grandparents, aunts, uncles and other extended family members are likely to be curious and a bit nervous about the new arrival. They will undoubtedly have some concerns about how the youngster will fit into the family. They may worry about current or future physical or mental problems. The implication that the adopted child might be damaged can be upsetting. Your close friends will undoubtedly be affected by the fact that you are busier and have a new favorite topic of conversation. You have had lots of time to prepare. Give others time to adjust.

Alert!

The possibility that a youngster you have already embraced as your own might not be accepted as a member of the family can be disturbing. Patience and understanding are required. Their concern is likely to include worries that you will be burdened by a child with physical or psychological problems.

On the home front, you can expect a new sibling's arrival to usher in a honeymoon period. It is common for the other children to be on their best behavior for the first few days or weeks as they strive to make the newcomer feel welcome. They may enjoy showing the newcomer around the house and introducing him to neighborhood friends. Your adopted child is likely to feel like a guest and enact the part by doing his best to follow the rules and get along. Once the newness wears off and the children are comfortable enough to be themselves, the hard work of adjusting to the many changes begins in earnest. Everyone's behavior typically worsens for a time.

For the adopted sibling to adjust to a new environment, he must learn to cope with a whole new set of rules and routines at a time when he is mourning the loss of his old life. That doesn't mean he should be cut off from the people who were important to him. Honor and support relationships with your adopted child's biological siblings by helping the children visit regularly or at least remain in contact. If you are reluctant about allowing your adopted child to visit his natural parents, watch the movie *My Flesh and Blood*. This documentary about a woman who adopted a dozen handicapped children does a good job of presenting the pros and cons of this thorny issue.

During the first few months, all of the children are likely to show stress reactions. The may feel more irritable and sensitive, which can lead them to overreact to small frustrations. Some youngsters act out by becoming angry and defiant. Your natural children may tease and harass their new sibling, even going so far as to suggest she be returned to wherever she came from. The adopted sibling may tease and harass your natural children, threaten to run away, or demand a different adoptive family. Other youngsters internalize their negative feelings, becoming quieter, more anxious, more fearful, or more tearful. Try to ensure that everyone gets plenty of sleep, eats well, and gets lots of exercise. Make time for family fun a priority. If the children are sabotaging family activities so that they are more stressful than fun, try more one-on-one time instead. Don't become discouraged. This difficult phase will pass once the children adapt to their new roles.

Alert!

There are bound to be many things your adopted child misses, if only the way the sun shone through the part in the curtains in the morning. Allowing him to continue some of his previous routines will ease his adjustment. Just having his customary brand of bread and toothpaste will help.

Changing Roles

The presence of a new child topples the traditional pecking order. Until your natural children become comfortable with their new roles, there will probably be times when they try to hold on to their old ones. Common tactics are to engage in competitive struggles with their adoptive sibling. It can be hard to admit that bringing a new youngster into the family has complicated your children's lives. Nevertheless, it is important to acknowledge the reality that things are different now. If you try to deny the truth, your natural children will probably work harder to convince you of how tough they have it. Handling complaints with compassion can help deter youngsters from expressing their displeasure by harassing the newcomer. Acknowledge that change is hard and that it will take awhile to get used to having a new sibling. Reassure your natural children that they remain special to you, and emphasize the importance of giving themselves time to adjust. Be firm in communicating that the adopted child is staying and must be treated with kindness and compassion.

Onlies and Firstborns

Instead of being the king of the castle, an only child must share his domain and learn to consider another youngster's needs and feelings. Avoid criticizing him for being impolite when he is simply doing what he has always done. Instead, explain the need to do certain things differently. Acknowledge him when he remembers not to interrupt the newcomer, to ask permission before touching his personal possessions, to ask his opinion about which television program to watch, to spend shorter periods in the bathroom, and so forth.

When a firstborn child acquires an older sibling, the change in roles is equally dramatic. The firstborn may have to relinquish some special privileges. Small things that seem insignificant to you may have had important benefits of which you weren't aware. Going to bed fifteen minutes later than their siblings provides many firstborns with their only chance for a few minutes of uninterrupted parent/child time each day. The firstborn will no longer be the first one in the family to do all kinds of things children consider important: cross the street without holding a parent's hand, ride a bike in the street, wear makeup, wear high heels, attend high school, drive a car, go out on a date, and so forth. Although the firstborn child may have at times resented being called upon to look after younger siblings, being placed in a position of responsibility and authority also confers status and importance. Being trusted by parents and looked up to by a younger sibling engenders feelings of importance and competence and boosts self-esteem. A firstborn loses an important part of his identity when he acquires an older adoptive sibling. Having to submit to the authority of another child can feel like an insult. One solution is to put both of the older children in charge of the younger ones. Another is to ask the adoptive child to help the youngster who has traditionally been in change. In that way, the child who used to be the oldest reaps the benefits of a helper without being displaced.

Other Sibling Roles

The youngest child has to adjust to losing a lot of the special considerations and attention to which he is accustomed. Whether the baby of the family is twelve months or twelve years old, parents and older siblings tend to be more charmed by the accomplishments of the youngest child. Parents tend to be more protective of the baby during sibling battles. Family members exclaim over a three-year-old child's ability to hop on one foot or count to ten when he is the youngest family member. Such accomplishments lose their power to impress when a twelve-month-old adopted baby is wowing everyone by taking his first step or saying his first word.

Acquiring an adoptive sibling of the same sex can be difficult for an only girl or an only boy and can result in a loss of identity. If the females in the family left it to their dad and brother to mow the lawn, wash the car, and pursue other "guy" activities, their special father/son relationship ends when a new boy arrives on the scene. As you are going out of your way to make a new adopted child feel welcome, be sensitive to your other children. Try to ease them out of their old roles gradually.

Essential

When children lose an important part of their personal identity, they are likely to respond with anger, depression, or resentment. To help them through this difficult time, provide lots of reassurance that you love them. Spend one-on-one time rather than making every endeavor a family activity.

Adopting a Baby

The arrival of an adopted infant creates some of the same excitement and anxiety for your natural children as the birth of a biological sibling. There is likely to be a honeymoon period while they are getting acquainted with the new arrival. Soon, however, the reality sets in of what it means to have to share parents' time and attention with a baby. At that point, your natural children will probably exhibit some problem behaviors. The youngest child, who was used to being the baby, may work to recapture his role by acting like a helpless, needy infant. This can be frustrating if you expect him to behave in a more mature fashion and serve as a big brother to the new baby. See Chapter 3 for suggestions for handling regression.

Many people think that adopted newborns readily adjust to new caregivers, but that is not necessarily the case. Sounds penetrate the womb, so babies become familiar with their parents' voices and many household noises before they are born. An adopted newborn is suddenly placed in an environment that is completely unfamiliar. There may be excessive irritability and prolonged periods of unexplained crying, according to Lois Ruskai Melina in *Raising Adopted Children*. The stress may take a toll. Adopted infants are more likely to develop somatic problems, such as digestive ailments and chronic infections, including ear infections, bronchitis, and influenza.

If a baby is several months old when adopted, he is old enough to have developed an attachment to his prior caregiver. The separation may trigger some sadness or even a bout of depression. Symptoms of infant depression include apathy, lethargy, disinterest in food or play, and difficulties sleeping. You may find yourself walking the baby half the night to try to calm him. During the day, you may need to make extra trips to the pediatrician, administer medications, and spend a lot of time ministering to a baby that is ill or unhappy. Your natural children will probably be upset that you are too busy to be as emotionally responsive and attentive as before the adopted baby arrived. Allowing them to express their negative feelings verbally may help them to discharge some of their tension. By talking about their unhappiness, they are less likely to act out in order to get their message across. Let them know their discomfort is understandable, and reassure them that the situation will get easier when the baby settles down, you are less exhausted, and everyone adjusts.

 Essential

Help your older children take pride in caring for an adopted infant sibling by helping them focus on the baby. Instead of cooing at the infant, "Don't you feel better now that your diaper is changed," say, "Don't you feel better wearing the clean diaper your big brother brought for you?"

Adopting Sibling Groups

If you have a large family and adopt two or more children, there may not be a dramatic increase in your workload. But if you have only one or two children, adopting a sibling group turns your small family into a large one overnight. A large family brings special joys and difficulties. Your natural children have more companions. They learn to relate to youngsters from different backgrounds with differing values. The adopted children reap the rewards of having a stable, loving family without having to be separated from their siblings.

You can expect that members of an adopted sibling group will be very bonded to one another. Besides having grown up together, they have endured many traumatic losses. It is normal for them to cling to one another until they feel secure and comfortable in their new home. If they have been living in separate foster homes before joining your family, they will need time to reestablish their relationships before they invest in new ones. Rather than trying to force them to spend less time with one another and more time socializing with other family members, allow them to proceed at their own pace.

It is common for one child in an adopted sibling group, typically the oldest, to have served as a surrogate parent to the rest. For youngsters growing up in abusive or neglectful homes, this dynamic seems to be the rule rather than the exception. Such "parentified" children commonly resist having adoptive parents assume authority for their siblings. If you try to take over, the younger siblings may feel a tug of loyalties if their parentified sibling insists on continuing to serve as their primary caretaker. Unless you are careful, power struggles can readily develop over who is best suited to care for the children and who can properly attend to their needs and make decisions regarding their welfare. It is important to remember that a youngster who has dedicated his life to nurturing and protecting his siblings derives his sense of personal worth from his role as the surrogate parent. Like the middle-aged housewife facing an empty nest, a youngster may become seriously depressed when the responsibilities that provided his reason for being are taken away. See Chapter 18 for suggestions about how to help a parentified youngster let go of his role and develop a new identity.

Adopted siblings will always have a common history and special memories that no one else can fully appreciate. Similarly, you and your natural children have a past that the adopted children do not share. It is important to respect one another's prior relationships and unique backgrounds. With that said, do not encourage the idea that the biological bonds are more important than the adoptive relationships or vice versa. Affirm the importance of the adopted siblings' shared experiences by helping them to continue some of their important traditions. If a picnic in the park on Independence Day was very special to them, consider incorporating their tradition into your family's Independence Day celebrations. Create some new traditions to help your family develop a new identity. The same goes for important routines. If the adopted children are accustomed to a cup of tea with breakfast, do what you can to accommodate them. Flexibility is the name of the game.

Alert!

Over time, your adopted children should come to feel as much a part of the family as your natural children. Although the youngsters are not always going to sing together in harmony, they should come to appreciate and enjoy one another's unique tunes!

An adopted child and one of your natural children may develop a special relationship. Some parents are uncomfortable with these groupings, believing that the family should be better integrated. But it is normal for children to like certain siblings better than others. There is no need for concern unless the groups are at odds or are actively excluding one another. Emphasize that even though they may be closer to some of their brothers and sisters than others, it is important for everyone to get along.

Famous Adoptees

The list of adopted and foster children reads like a who's who list of the world's greats. Here is a small sampling of those who made it big, taken from the gargantuan list of foster and adopted children posted at *www.dil.aber.ac.uk/dils/Research/RFocus9/staf_rrf.htm.* Share the list with youngsters who entered your heart without having spent time residing inside your body. It may inspire them to know that although their past was different from that of most children, there is no end to what they might accomplish in the future. They may make their mark on the American landscape or take their place in the annals of history.

- Mark Acre, athlete
- Edward Franklin Albee, playwright
- Maya Angelou, writer
- Ann-Margret, actress
- Josephine Antoine, opera singer
- Louis Armstrong, musician
- John James Audubon, naturalist
- Oksana Baiul, ice skater
- Josephine Baker, entertainer
- Tallulah Bankhead, actress
- Michael Bay, director
- James Asheton Bayard, politician
- Ingrid Bergman, actress
- Bojangles, entertainer
- Daniel Boone, soldier and explorer
- William Bradford, political leader
- James Brown, musician
- Richard Burton, actor
- Truman Capote, author
- George Washington Carver, chemist and educator
- Rosemary Casals, sportswoman
- Nat King Cole, musician
- Patricia Cornwell, novelist
- Crazy Horse, war chief
- Faith Daniels, television journalist
- James Dean, actor
- Katherine DeMille, actress
- Adrian Dodson, boxer
- Frederick Douglass, diplomat
- Clarissa Pinkola Estés, psychoanalyst and author
- Antwone Quenton Fisher, screenwriter

- Ella Fitzgerald, jazz singer
- Gerald R. Ford, U.S. president
- Newt Gingrich, politician
- Sam Goldwyn, film producer
- Alexander Hamilton, statesman
- Ice-T, rap artist and actor
- Jesse Louis Jackson, civil rights leader and politician
- Stonewall Jackson, soldier
- Steven Paul Jobs, microcomputer pioneer
- Eartha Kitt, actress and singer
- Art Linkletter, broadcaster
- Malcolm X, civil rights activist and religious leader
- Steve McQueen, actor
- Herman Melville, novelist
- James A. Michener, author
- Marilyn Monroe, actress
- Eddie Murphy, comedian and actor
- Willie Nelson, singer
- Jack Nicholson, actor
- Jim Palmer, athlete and baseball commentator
- David J. Pelzer, writer and speaker
- Edgar Allan Poe, author
- Elvis Presley, Jr., singer
- Priscilla Ann Presley, actress
- Nancy Davis Reagan, U.S. first lady
- Eleanor Roosevelt, U.S. first lady
- Babe Ruth, athlete
- Sacagawea, guide and interpreter
- Buffy Sainte-Marie, musician and actress
- Dan Savage, journalist
- George Scott, boxer
- William Tecumseh Sherman, general
- Joseph F. Smith, religious leader
- Robyn Smith, sportswoman
- Julia Sudbury, academic

- Mike Tyson, athlete
- C. J. Walker, entrepreneur and philanthropist
- Ruth K. Westheimer (Dr. Ruth), sexologist and television personality
- Elie Wiesel, humanitarian and author
- Flip Wilson, comedian
- Oprah Winfrey, television personality and actress

CHAPTER 17

Losing a Sibling

Even when siblings are not especially close, a long separation can precipitate a grief reaction. When siblings move out to begin lives of their own, they commonly suffer bouts of homesickness for the brothers and sisters they left behind, and the younger children mourn their absence. Having a sibling leave to go to detention, prison, or a rehabilitation center presents special challenges. Even when siblings haven't been especially close, a sibling death is a major trauma. At a time when your own grief is all-consuming, the surviving children need help from other adults.

When a Sibling Dies

John's story is typical of what the surviving siblings endure as they cope with the death of a brother or sister.

> The first time my sister Annie got sick, I was five. I remember visiting her at the hospital several times. It was frightening to see her so quiet and weak. When she finally came home, she had to stay in bed and couldn't play with me anymore. Mom had to spend a lot of time taking care of her, and I had to be quiet so as not to disturb her. Dad didn't want to wrestle or play as in the past. When he sent me off to bed, he would say, "Don't forget to pray for Annie, Son." When I turned six, Annie was back in the hospital again. I had my birthday party in her hospital room. After we ate the cake Mom had baked, the nurses told us we had

to leave. We didn't get to play the games Mom and I had planned. I felt mad at Annie for ruining my party. The next morning, Mom said, "I don't think Annie is coming home again. The doctor says the medicine isn't working." Then she went to her bedroom and shut the door.

After Annie's funeral, Mom spent most of her time in her bedroom. She was too tired to play, cook, or do much of anything else. My father started working long hours. When he was home, he moved like a silent shadow through the house. He cooked dinners and took care of me, but he hardly looked at me. I decided that Annie had been the favorite and thought my parents would have been better off if I had died instead of her. I remembered that I had been mad at Annie for messing up my birthday party the last time I saw her and believed that her death was my fault. During second and third grade, I was afraid to go to school. I kept imagining that my parents had been in a car accident or had been killed by burglars. I didn't realize until I got into therapy as an adult that many of my problems stemmed from unresolved grief. I think kids should automatically be sent for counseling when a brother or sister dies. A lot of people think that talking to kids about a death makes things worse. They hope that if they say nothing the kids will just forget about it. But kids don't forget the hole in their lives.

 **Fact**

Children do not comprehend that death is permanent until age five or six. Despite repeated explanations, younger children are likely to continue to ask when their sibling will return. When they finally grasp that their sibling is not coming back, many worry about who will disappear next.

Grief and Mourning

When a sibling dies, the siblings lose their identity as the brother or sister of that child. They usually lose their parents as well. Many parents are too immersed in mourning to be emotionally available and may even have difficulty keeping up with basic household tasks, such as cooking and cleaning. Even if a toddler or preschool child is too young to comprehend that a sibling has died, his parents' upset and emotional distance communicate that something terrible has happened. Often young children have a hard time understanding exactly what is going on. Some four- and five-year-olds who have experienced the death of another relative or of a pet can comprehend the finality of death. In general, children don't grasp the concept until age six that their sibling will not return.

Alert!

Children tend to refrain from talking about their loss with their parents for fear of upsetting them. Such youngsters may suppress their own feelings. When their parents begin to recover a year or two later, the children begin to grieve. Many then develop academic problems, become depressed, or act out.

Children do not express their upset like adults. After the death of a child, some parents think the surviving siblings are not grieving. Because children have shorter attention spans and difficulty processing such intense emotions, youngsters grieve in short bursts. Rather than prolonged bouts of crying and sadness, they are likely to appear unhappy one minute and skip happily out to play the next. When the pain becomes too great to manage, numbness may set in. Instead of having long conversations about missing their sibling, they may confine themselves to an occasional question or out-of-the-blue comment. Some children regress when the subject is raised, acting less mature and becoming more whiny, clingy, helpless, and silly. The silliness of a primary school student and the smirks of an older elementary school student or teenager are not signs that they consider the whole matter a joke. Their giddiness reflects their anxiety. Stress increases the risk of various illnesses and psychosomatic disorders, especially stomachaches and headaches. Difficulties focusing, falling grades, irritability, and defiant behavior are common grief reactions.

Siblings age twelve and older share adults' understanding of death but have fewer coping skills. Because teenagers are experiencing the emotional roller-coaster of adolescence, the waves of intense sadness, grief, and anger unleashed by a major loss can cause them to become seriously depressed. Many teenagers try to hide their grief from their peers to avoid calling attention to themselves. At home, they may struggle between wanting to be strong and independent while needing hugs, reassurance, and a shoulder on which to cry. They may need to withdraw to mourn privately as well as having a supportive network of people to whom they can talk. Like adults, teens may turn to alcohol or drugs to numb the pain, or they may engage in other self-destructive behaviors. Because teenagers tend to be impulsive, there is a risk that they will act out their feelings of sadness and hopelessness by making suicidal gestures and attempts.

Stages of Grief

Like adults, children who comprehend that death is final are likely to cycle in and out of the stages of grief identified by Kubler-Ross in her book, *On Death and Dying.*

- **Denial:** Children keep expecting their sibling to suddenly appear. They expect to come home from school and find her there.
- **Anger:** Children feel angry with their sibling for having left, with their parents for not having prevented the death, or with God for having taken their brother or sister from them.
- **Bargaining:** Children promise themselves they will be good if their sibling is restored to life; children ask God to restore their sibling's life and take them instead. They may obsess about things they wish they had done differently, as if that could have prevented the death.
- **Sadness:** Children miss their sibling and long for his return.

- **Acceptance:** Children accept the reality that their sibling is gone and move forward with life. That doesn't mean that they stop missing their sibling.

Like adults, children do not go through the stages of grief in any particular order. Rather than finishing one stage and moving on to the next, they typically cycle through the various stages again and again. Even after a child seems to have accepted a sibling's death and has begun to move forward, bouts of denial, bargaining, sadness, and anger are likely to resurface at unexpected moments. Grieving such a major loss is a lifelong process. When an adult child endures another major loss decades later, thoughts about her lost sibling may return, and some of the pain is likely to return. Few people reach a point of being able to say, "I am over it." Although the pain eventually loses its edge, the memories that endure are likely to be bittersweet.

Essential

From seeing their parents so grief-stricken and feeling neglected as they mourn a deceased sibling, some youngsters conclude that the wrong child died. They think their parents would have preferred to lose them than their sibling. Your children need a lot of reassurance of your enduring love for them.

Feelings of guilt are often a special problem for children. They tend to see themselves at the center of everything that goes on, which primes them to view any type of tragedy as arising from their own actions. Many remember a fit of temper during which they wished their sibling would disappear or go away and never come back. During arguments, many youngsters exclaim, "I wish you were dead." They may truly believe they caused their sibling to die. If they were told they needed to be quiet so as not to disturb their sibling when he was ill, they may feel that the sibling died because they were too

PARENT'S GUIDE TO RAISING SIBLINGS

noisy. Whether or not the surviving children express guilt, it is important to reassure them that they are not responsible. It may be helpful to reinforce the notion by emphasizing that most siblings get mad at each other and have moments of wishing one another gone, but few of them die. Wishing doesn't make things happen. Survivor's guilt can also be a problem for children.

Helping Siblings Mourn

Children who are grieving the loss of a sibling need a tremendous amount of emotional support. Unfortunately, they need it at a time when their devastated parents are too overwhelmed to provide them with much. In interviews, people commonly state that they never began to come to terms with the loss of a sibling until they were adults. They hadn't been allowed to attend the funeral or other services. Adults avoided the subject when they were around or gave vague answers to their questions, leading them to feel they must not talk about the subject. Some parents quickly discarded their deceased sibling's possessions and refrained from ever mentioning him again. This raised the disturbing idea among the surviving children that if they were to die, they, too, would promptly be forgotten. Moreover, having a sibling die before they were even born proved to be an enduring problem for some younger brothers and sisters. They felt they were expected to replace their dead sibling, live up to his standards, or that their parents held them at a distance to protect against the pain of another loss. Their own quandary went unrecognized or was driven underground.

Relatives and adult friends can fill in the gap and serve as invaluable sources of physical care and solace for grieving siblings. However, taboos about discussing death with children persist. Many well-intentioned people fear that allowing a youngster to talk about the loss will be overly upsetting. They respond to questions and tears by changing the subject, admonishing the child to be strong, or otherwise distracting him. Professional counseling may be the best way to ensure siblings receive the information they need to make sense of what happened and help to deal with their emotional pain.

- Siblings need to understand that the child who has died will not return. Even young children need to be told the truth in direct, concrete, simple language.
- Siblings need to know that all of their feelings are normal. Even after the worst of the grief has passed, troubling emotions will likely resurface at times.
- Siblings need to know that it is normal for them to put the entire matter out of their minds at times. This does not mean they did not love their sibling, are hard-hearted, or are unaffected.
- Siblings need to have someone available to listen when they need to talk. Find someone outside the immediate family that your child can contact.
- Siblings need to be able to escape the subject of death and loss. Find someone who can laugh and play with the surviving children when you are grieving.
- Siblings need to know they are still loved. Verbal reassurance that "I love you" is especially important at a time when you are having difficulty showing your love as you have in the past: by playing, cooking, cleaning, and reading bedtime stories.

Rituals designed to facilitate mourning help grieving siblings mourn their loss. It is important for them to attend the funeral and wake for at least part of the time. Make arrangements in advance for someone to take little ones outside for a short break or home for the duration if they disrupt the service. Special activities can provide siblings with much-needed emotional outlets. For instance, some families plant a tree to create a living memorial. Tending to the tree and sitting under it can provide the surviving siblings with a feeling of connection to the child who died. Writing letters to the absent sibling can also be beneficial. In them, children can reminisce about the good times, clear up unfinished business, describe what they are doing to maintain a sense of being connected to them, and work on saying their farewells.

It helps some siblings to create a memorial by drawing pictures or making collages of pictures cut from magazines. Children may wish to add captions to the pictures to express their feelings. For instance,

PARENT'S GUIDE TO RAISING SIBLINGS

under a photograph of a rainy day, a child might write or have a parent write, "Rain is like the tears that are falling from our eyes." A picture of a meadow on a warm summer day could be captioned, "We had many happy, sunny days with Annie." Putting together a scrapbook is another way to work through feelings while creating a memorial. A scrapbook might include such things as photographs, cards, letters, drawings, movie tickets, prayer cards, report cards, poems, fabric from a favorite shirt, or a lock of hair. Working on a memory book as a joint project can help everyone come together as a family.

 *Question?*

Doesn't talking about death cause children more pain?
Children feel pain whether or not they talk about a loss. Some children make it known they do not wish to discuss it. In general, youngsters are less likely to become depressed or to act out if they can cry and express their painful emotions directly.

Watching a sad movie can provide an outlet for children who are having difficulty expressing their sadness. As *Bambi* and *The Lion King* mourn their losses, children mourn theirs. Attending a counseling group for children who have lost a sibling can be especially beneficial. Contact a local funeral home to find out whether a group for sibling survivors exists in your area. Visiting the cemetery or holding a yearly remembrance can also help children work through their grief and understand that their sibling lives on through their memories. In time, children can come to accept death as a natural, if painful, part of the circle of life. Until then, point out that feeling better for just five minutes during the course of a single day is proof that their feelings can in fact change. They may feel better for ten minutes tomorrow. Joy will eventually return to their life, just as surely as spring follows winter and sunshine follows rain.

Sibling Suicide

Suicide is the third leading cause of death among children ages fifteen to twenty-four, and suicide among younger children has become more common in recent decades. The process of helping the surviving siblings cope with suicide is much the same as for other causes of death. In addition, you may be called upon to deal with a number of other issues that arise following such a devastating tragedy. For instance, when a child learns that a sibling has committed suicide, one of his first questions is likely to be: "What is suicide?"

It may help to explain to a preschool or primary school child that people die in different ways, such as from cancer or a heart attack, and to say: "Your brother had an illness in his mind." Older children can be told that some people are so hard-hit by depression that they lose their ability to think clearly. Some become convinced that dying is the only way to end their pain. It may help older children to know that when people are depressed the pleasure centers of the brain are affected. They experience little if any joy, and their happy memories disappear, along with their ability to imagine happier times in the future. This causes them to believe that the cloud of misery that currently engulfs them has always been there and will never go away.

For surviving siblings who are old enough to understand that their brother or sister "chose" to die, intense feelings of shock, guilt, anger, sadness, and depression are to be expected. In addition to feeling lonely for their absent sibling, it is common for the brothers and sisters to feel abandoned, rejected, betrayed, and somehow responsible. They may question whether he ever loved them, given his decision to leave. Children tend to think the world revolves around them. Accordingly, they may believe something they did or failed to do drove their sibling to commit such a desperate act. As siblings struggle to make sense of what happened, they usually go through phases of flailing about for someone else to blame. They accuse other family members for not having done more to help their sibling, or they hold their sibling's friends responsible for leading him astray or contributing to his unhappiness. Some children blame God for having permitted something so terrible to happen. Siblings who were aware of their sibling's suffering commonly feel guilty for not having alerted a parent or taken some concrete action to try to save him. The guilt can be crushing. Too often, surviving siblings end up becoming seriously depressed as well.

Alert!

Family secrets are very hurtful and virtually impossible to keep. Not telling the surviving children that their deceased sibling committed suicide is likely to end in feelings of betrayal when they learn the truth. Admonishing them not to tell anyone else cuts them off from critical support. Denying that problems exist solves nothing.

Children need to be reassured that nothing they said, did, or failed to say or do caused their sibling to make such a terrible decision. But simple reassurance is not enough for children to oust such terrible thoughts. Just like adults, youngsters need to be able to discuss why they consider themselves responsible and work through their tangled emotions. Dismissing their self-blame as foolish may stop them from expressing what is on their minds. But their silence doesn't mean the troubling thoughts are gone. Some children ask questions about the morality of taking one's own life. Comments from friends or their religious teachings propel them to ask: "Isn't it a sin to commit suicide?" Whatever your religious beliefs, it may help to explain that people commit suicide when they are so caught up in their suffering that they can't make rational decisions.

Fantasies of being reunited with a dead sister or brother lead many surviving siblings to entertain thoughts of killing themselves. They are at risk for developing suicidal ideation (thoughts about killing themselves), making suicidal gestures (attempts that are unlikely to lead to death, but sometimes do), making suicide attempts (failed efforts to kill themselves), and committing suicide.

While it is important to understand that children endure the same rush of troubling emotions as adults, it is unrealistic to expect yourself to serve as their sounding board at such a difficult time. They need to talk to someone less intensely involved. Hence, getting help for them via a group for sibling survivors or individual therapy is important. It could literally save them from following in their sibling's footsteps.

Alert!

The mixture of grief, guilt, longing to be reunited with a deceased sibling, and the impulsiveness of youth can create a lethal combination. When a sibling commits suicide, the brothers and sisters are at increased risk for making suicide attempts of their own. Get professional counseling for your child.

Your children need to be able to ask questions and share what is on their minds. If you cannot cope with such difficult conversations—and few parents can—find a professional therapist with whom they can talk. The school counselor may be able to meet with your children at school, recommend a private psychologist, or refer them to a counseling group for survivors of suicide. When one child commits suicide, all of the other students at his school are at increased risk for developing suicidal thoughts and for making suicidal gestures and attempts. Most schools have crisis teams to help members of the student body process their grief. A member of the crisis team may be able to counsel your youngster. In addition, family priests, ministers, and rabbis provide pastoral counseling. Your youngsters need to know that they will feel better in time and that you continue to love them even if you are too distraught to give them much time or attention. Impress upon them that they must let you know if they ever have thoughts about wanting to hurt themselves or die. Reassure them that no problem is so great that it cannot be solved. As long as they are alive, there is hope.

CHAPTER 18

Changing Sibling Roles

The golden boy. The troublemaker. Mama's little helper. Beware of ironclad roles! The child who identifies with his role as troublemaker is primed to move into the adult role of family black sheep. Even positive roles can be detrimental if they are too rigid. Not getting into a top-rated college can devastate the family genius. Needing to change roles because a sibling has left home or a new child has moved in is difficult. Help your children embrace flexible sibling roles so they can accommodate change in themselves and one another.

Entrenched Sibling Roles

As a child, Michael enjoyed tormenting his older sister. In the end, he may have suffered as much or more than the sibling he victimized throughout their childhoods.

I can see now how bad my half-sister had it when we were kids. But it wasn't until I attended Alcoholics Anonymous and went to counseling that I realized what I had put my sister through. Christine was actually my half-sister because she was from Mom's first marriage. Mom would say, "You're just like your father," when she was mad at Christine. I'm not sure why a lot of little things Christine did bothered me so much. It seemed like she did everything right, and I did everything wrong. Maybe I just picked on her because I could. She didn't defend herself, and Mom and Dad didn't really do anything if Christine complained.

If I kicked her, they would just say, "You know you shouldn't do that," and leave it at that. Once I shoved her, her head hit the wall, and she was unconscious for a couple of minutes. I was really scared. When Christine came to, she was hysterical. She spent an hour telling Mom all the stuff I had done to her. I thought I would probably be disowned or something. Then I heard Mom say, "You're just upset right now. You'll feel better when you calm down." I guess I shouldn't have been surprised that Christine has hardly spoken to me since she left home.

When I was in my twenties, I drank heavily. I would get belligerent toward Christine when we got together for family dinners and such, and I could see she was afraid. I stopped doing that when I sobered up years ago. As part of my Alcoholics Anonymous program, I did the step where alcoholics contact people we have hurt and take responsibility for our actions. Christine was first on my list. I wrote her a letter, but she never mentioned anything. So I don't actually know that she ever got it. When we get together at our parent's house, she is clearly uncomfortable around me. She never starts a conversation and gives short, terse answers when I try to talk to her. She's on her guard, as though I might pounce on her at any minute. My therapist said I should talk to her, and he's probably right. I haven't gotten together the courage yet. I guess she still sees me as the troublemaker.

 **Fact**

A child who bullies his siblings is likely to bully other children as well. Even if he limits himself to abusing his siblings, the pattern of violence against family members usually continues. Steady dates, spouses, and his own children often become targets. The predictable result is a criminal record and failed relationships.

Creating Sibling Roles

Like most parents, you probably tell your two-year-old to be quiet so as not to awaken the baby, even though your toddler is in the midst of a horrendous tantrum and can't even hear you. But when your toddler is sleeping and his newborn sibling is fussing, you don't tell the baby to be quiet so as not to disturb his older brother. Without realizing it, you have expectations for how siblings should relate to one another, and you teach them to behave in ways that conform to certain family roles. Most children become quite adept at playing the sibling roles they have been taught. Although many parents can't see their part in teaching their youngsters, when siblings have developed some destructive patterns of relating, parents may also have inadvertently trained them to behave that way toward one another. The good news is that by changing how you respond to them and by encouraging them to change the way they respond to one another, you can help them improve their relationship.

Often parents inadvertently assign children to play opposite roles in the family. The infant with an easygoing personality is designated a "good baby," while a more emotional baby is referred to as "fussy." If these roles become entrenched, they may progress to the "good kid" and the "troublemaker" or "troubled child" during childhood and turn into the "golden boy" and the "black sheep" or "crazy one" as adults. When one child is consistently blamed when things go wrong and rarely acknowledged when things go well, his family has probably cast him in the role of scapegoat. Children who are scapegoats at home often fulfill the same unhappy role at school and on the playground. When they are falsely accused, they manage to give the impression of being guilty, even as they protest their innocence. In *I'm OK—You're OK,* Thomas Harris describes people who seem to wear an invisible sign that says, "kick me." They make good targets for anyone who happens to be in a bad mood because they don't defend themselves. The way to help a child out of a negative or overly rigid role is to affirm him whenever he steps out of it, however briefly.

- **Affirm things the family scapegoat has done well without adding qualifiers:** "I appreciate your moving your books off the desk so your brother can use it, but if you had moved them the first time he asked you, we wouldn't have had a scene."

- **Affirm the black sheep's good grade without adding subtle digs:** "I'm glad you did so well on that assignment. It just goes to show what you can accomplish when you actually do some work."
- **Affirm a golden boy's accomplishments without adding subtle pressure:** "Such a stellar report card. If you get elected class president next year, you'll be a shoe-in for an Ivy league college."

Sibling Abuse

Professionals have only recently begun to realize that many siblings seriously harm one another. They emotionally abuse one another by bullying, threatening, coercing, and making comments designed to destroy one another's self-esteem. Years of exposure to cruel words from a brother or sister are as damaging as ongoing emotional abuse from an adult. Some parents have a hard time determining whether a sibling is being emotionally abused because they try to sort out what when on and decide whether it was really terrible or not. But parents cannot use themselves as yardsticks. They must look at how the victim was affected. A few harsh words may be deeply distressing to a highly sensitive youngster. A thick-skinned child might not be upset even though his sibling made statements that most people would consider unspeakably cruel. Physical abuse includes any type of purposeful acts which could cause injury, such as shoving, kicking, and tripping or which result in physical trauma, including bruising and bleeding. Sexual abuse involves coercing a child to participate in sexual touching or acts. Not taking action when one sibling emotionally, physically, or sexually abuses another compounds the problem and is illegal. Comforting a child who has been victimized and urging him to defend himself is not enough. Some children cannot. If they try, the violence escalates. They need a parent to protect them. You need to contain the perpetrator. But as any parent with an aggressive child knows, this is easier said than done.

 *Fact*

> When young siblings play "doctor," they may be engaging in a bit of harmless sexual exploration. But coercing a sibling to engage in sexual activities is abusive and can lead to long-term problems.

Persecutors and Victims

When parents punish aggressive children for bullying or abusing a sibling, they commonly feel misunderstood and mistreated—in a word, they feel victimized. Many plot ways to seek revenge and punish the sibling who told on them. They may secretly retaliate against their victim or continue abusing a sibling even though they are consistently caught and punished. Once the persecutor role is established, it can become part of a child's core identity. When bullies are asked during therapy sessions why they abuse their sibling, they commonly list some petty irritations or make a vague statement such as "He bothers me." Some simply say "because I'm bad" or "because I always make trouble." Often the real issue is that the siblings are living out complimentary family roles. When a parent rescues the victimized child and punishes the bully, the children temporarily switch roles. The bully feels victimized, and the victim is glad to see his adversary suffer for a change. When the punishment ends, the bully is likely to resume his role as persecutor, and his sibling again becomes the victim. Thus, they keep trading roles, but nothing ever really changes.

The challenge is to impose consequences without making a bully feel persecuted and to change how the victim relates to him. Otherwise, they may continue in their customary roles as victim and persecutor and briefly trade roles when the bully is being punished. Dealing with an aggressive child by sending him to his room, grounding him, or withholding privileges only benefits the victim by providing some pleasure on knowing that the tables have been turned and the persecutor is being made to suffer. But rejoicing in someone else's misfortune is unhealthy. Doing so makes sibling relationships worse, not better.

Question?

What is the difference between a punishment and a consequence?
A punishment is designed to hurt or humiliate; a consequence is designed to teach. Children may feel they are being punished because they dislike the consequence they have been given. But at least they have a chance to learn something positive.

There are several ways to break this destructive cycle. Imposing consequences that require a bully to make restitution to a victimized child are likely to be more effective than punishments. In this way, a bully can start learning how to fulfill his role as a good sibling. For instance, explain to the bully that when a sister is upset, a good brother does what he can to help her feel better. If he caused her upset, his duty to comfort her becomes an obligation. Consider having the bully make his sister's bed in the morning or take over some of her chores. Check to see that whatever tasks you assign are completed satisfactorily, and praise him for doing a good job of taking care of his sister. Warn his sister against gloating now that the tables have been temporarily turned and her tormentor has become her servant. Not kicking her brother when he is down is her duty as a sister. It is also an important first step toward protecting herself. If a bear was asleep, she wouldn't poke at it to see if it would react. She would avoid antagonizing it. She needs to treat an aggressive sibling with similar care and avoid antagonizing him.

Alert!

Preventing your children from abusing one another is your moral and legal responsibility. If you cannot keep them safe, call Child Protective Services for help. If you do nothing and a sibling is harmed, you can be convicted of child abuse for "failure to protect."

Siblings who are being victimized need to learn to recognize the signs that a bully is getting angry so they know when to cease and desist, let a matter of contention drop, and walk away so they can protect themselves. Help your children identify the warning signs. Perhaps their sibling fidgets, becomes sarcastic, raises his voice, stands taller, flushes slightly, breathes more rapidly, or freezes and gets a mean look in his eye. They need to remember that no issue is so important that it is worth being abused. Children who don't learn to read the warning signs and take action so they can protect themselves are at risk for being abused as adults. Some women lash out verbally at men twice their size and end up being beaten or even killed. Some men try to hold their ground and refuse to give in and end up being assaulted when their wives are irate. When an adversary has enough control to discuss a dispute without becoming violent, trying to talk the matter through makes sense. Until then, it is irrational to persist in trying to reason with someone who is irrational.

Lesson Plan for a Sister

Good Sisters...	My Sister...	Teaching Methods	My Sister's Progress
Take turns	Doesn't take turns	Tell her I'll only play if she will take turns	She agrees and lets me have one short turn
Let other people go first	Always has to be first	Let her go first sometimes and tell her it's because she is my big sister and I love her	She won't let me go first, but she gave me her doll and said, "Here's a present for my little sister"
Are considerate of others	Only thinks about herself and her friends	Praise her for letting me have a turn and tell her it's nice having a sister to play with	She looked shocked, only took a short turn, and then said I could go
Listen to their sister	Only listens to Mom	Tell Mom when my sister lets me have some turns	I told Mom, she told my sister that was very nice, and my sister looked proud

 *Question?*

My son purposely provokes my daughter. What can I do?
Parents commonly say, "Ignore him and he'll stop," but he may escalate if he is angry or wants to get her attention. His behavior may improve if your daughter suggests that they be friends, invites him to play, and teaches him how to be a good playmate.

The third step for a sibling victim is to teach her tormentor how to be a proper brother. Hopefully, parents are trying to teach him as well, but some children can get through to a difficult sibling more readily than a parent. The victimized child can start by creating a list of goals for her brother. One goal might be for him to observe the rules of good sportsmanship listed in Chapter 4 so they can enjoy playing games. Next, she needs to work out some teaching methods. It might help to create a lesson plan following the example in the previous table. She needs to accept that playing together probably won't be much fun until he learns to be a good sport. Until then, she needs to regard their games as tutoring sessions. As they play, she needs to keep her goals in mind, watch carefully for small successes, and acknowledge them. Each time her brother takes turns without a struggle, remains calm when he is losing, doesn't gloat when he is winning, and so forth, she needs to acknowledge and affirm his behavior. If losing a turn at Monopoly appears to be too much for him, she can try comforting him, change the rules and give him an extra turn, or terminate the game. Encourage her to give you regular progress reports so you can help her stay motivated through setbacks and instill a sense of pride in both children's accomplishments. The point is to teach a victimized child how to step out of the victim role by serving as her brother's relationship teacher. Meanwhile, you assist by setting and enforcing limits to deter aggressive behavior and by serving as their relationship consultant and guide. Lots of hard-core, violent criminals alienate everyone but continue to serve as loving brothers toward a sibling to whom they feel attached. Don't doubt a bully's ability to open his heart to a sibling who has opened her heart to him!

The Bad Influence

Research investigations have established that younger children are more likely to use drugs, join a gang, have sex at an early age, become pregnant, drop out of school, and/or get in trouble with the law if an older sibling does. Some older siblings encourage a younger one to follow their lead. "Join a gang, and your friends are like family," they tell younger brothers and sisters. "Drugs should be legal." "Drag racing is great. Adults just don't want kids to have fun." Some older siblings have deluded themselves into believing such things, but others have darker motives. Some alienated teens bond with a younger sibling through shared antisocial pastimes. Some teens subvert a sibling rival by leading him down a self-destructive path, like the oldest sibling in the classic *Long Day's Journey into Night*. Some antisocial teens induce a sibling to join them in overly adult or criminal activities to quell their own guilt about doing things they shouldn't.

Alert an older teen who has become involved in adult or antisocial activities that younger siblings may follow his example. Urge him to protect them by helping them learn from his mistakes. If he doesn't believe he did anything wrong, he will probably continue on the same self-destructive path and may influence younger children to do the same. Obviously, the risk is greater if they look up to him. This is the time to go for family therapy to see how your other children are dealing with the family crisis and figure out ways to help their troubled sibling. If they approve of his behavior, they may join him. You may need to consider drastic solutions to protect the younger children and help your troubled teen. Separating them physically for a time may achieve both goals. There are many options: boarding schools, military schools, residential treatment centers, rehabilitation centers, or juvenile detention centers. Sometimes the best solution is to provide a separate apartment so a young adult can live independently.

Parentified Children

Some children very much enjoy the role of "Mama's little helper." In some cases, their role becomes part of their identity to the exclusion of all else. They dedicate virtually every spare moment to assisting with household chores and serving as surrogate parents to their siblings. If parents are ineffectual or impaired by mental illness, substance abuse, or a chronic illness, a sibling may take over the responsibility for caring for them as well. Usually, the firstborn steps into the caregiver role. A son may become "the little man" when his father dies or abandons the family. More often, the role of surrogate parent seems to fall to the oldest daughter. Doing such an important job can boost a child's self-esteem. But spending one's growing-up years struggling with burdensome adult responsibilities often means there is little time for the usual childhood pastimes. Many become "parentified." They worry about other family members, even when they aren't actually taking care of them. As adults, parentified children commonly continue the same role by becoming nurses, therapists, social workers, and counselors in their professional lives and by attending to needy friends and spouses in their personal lives.

Despite being exceptionally competent at caring for others, many parentified children have little experience being nurtured. Many feel guilty about being taken care of and don't even take care of themselves. They are at risk for suffering burnout, which many professionals now call "compassion fatigue." Many parentified children spend a lot of time feeling overwhelmed and unhappy. Because their sense of self-worth stems from taking care of others, having needs of their own makes them feel worthless and bad.

All of your children are likely to be parents one day; they all need to learn to nurture children of their own. So it makes sense to involve everyone in caring for one another. If you have several children, call upon all of them to help rather than overburdening one youngster. Doing so can boost cooperation, enhance bonding, and create a stronger sense of family. Point out when a parentified child looks tried and suggest he take a break. Suggest ways to cheer himself up when he is worrying about others: take a warm bath, curl up with a book, call a friend, or go for a walk. Many parentified children are adept at assessing other people's needs but aren't in touch with their own emotions and don't know how to take care of themselves. They don't seek help even when they very much need it.

Alert!

A child with a handicapped sibling is at special risk for becoming parentified. Overwhelmed parents are likely to neglect the healthy sibling and burden him with heavy responsibilities. Be sure he has time to relax and enjoy friends. He cannot do either if he must constantly supervise an impaired sibling.

Many foster siblings have a parentified child in their midst—one child who dedicated himself to protecting the rest. A parentified foster child is likely to resent anyone else who tries to usurp his reason for being by taking charge of his siblings. He may have years of experience caring for and protecting them and not trust that foster parents will do a good job. To avoid power struggles, approach a parentified child like a coparent. Partner with him by soliciting his suggestions about how to care for his siblings. He may know which foods they like and which they cannot eat due to allergies. He may know how to comfort them when they are unhappy and know some tricks for getting them into bed at night. Discuss the best way to discipline them so as not to hurt them. Offer to take over when he looks tired or is losing patience, and you will undoubtedly find that he soon enjoys having help. If power struggles develop, acknowledge all he has done to help his siblings. Express the hope that he will take the opportunity, in this new family, to let go of the burdensome responsibilities that leave him little time to relax and play. It may help to explain that his younger siblings need to learn to be more independent. For that, they need to learn to rely on people besides him.

New Birth Order Roles

Children's position in the family changes when they acquire a stepsibling, adopted sibling, or foster sibling. Your natural children may feel they aren't as special to you anymore. As you help a new child feel welcome, your natural children may even think that they are being replaced and respond with anger, depression, or resentment. A new sibling forces all of the children into new roles. To understand how hard this is, consider what most women go through when they have their first child. Although they love their baby, adjusting to their new role as mother is extremely taxing. Consider what most professionals go through when their role at work changes because their company went through a merger or downsized. Change opens many new doors, and new roles commonly turn out to be far more rewarding than old ones. But adjusting is a challenge. To help your children through this difficult time, provide lots of reassurance that you love them. Spend one-on-one time rather than making every endeavor a family activity.

Only Children

When an only child acquires a stepsibling or foster sibling, he loses his special position as "king of the castle." He must share his domain and consider another youngster's needs and feelings at every turn. Avoid criticizing your youngster when he interrupts, fails to share, and commits other social errors. He is simply doing what he has always done. Instead of reprimanding him, explain the need to do certain things differently. Point out when he does remember not to interrupt when his new sibling is speaking, asks permission before touching his new sibling's personal possessions, solicits his opinion about which television program to watch, and so forth. As he becomes better about remembering and adjusts to his new role, life will get easier for him.

Firstborn and Lastborn Children

When a firstborn child acquires an older sibling, the change in roles is equally dramatic. The firstborn will undoubtedly have to relinquish some special privileges. Small things that seem insignificant to you may have had important benefits of which you weren't aware. For instance, having a bedtime that is fifteen minutes later than their younger siblings provides many firstborns with their only chance for a few minutes of uninterrupted parent/child time each day. On acquiring an older sibling with the same or a later bedtime, the chance to reconnoiter with parents is lost. A displaced firstborn will lose the status of being the first in the family to do all kinds of things that give him status in his younger siblings' eyes and cause parents to fuss over him and express pride: cross the street without having to hold someone's hand, ride a bike, be confirmed at church, wear makeup and high heels, attend high school, shave, drive a car, go out on a date, attend college, and so forth. Although the firstborn child may have at times resented being called upon to look after younger siblings, being placed in a position of responsibility and authority also confers status and many opportunities to take charge and make decisions. Being trusted by parents and looked up to by younger sibling engenders feelings of importance, competence, and self-worth. A firstborn loses an important part of his identity when he acquires an older sibling. Having to submit to the authority of another child can feel demeaning and insulting. One solution is to put both of the older children in charge of the younger ones. Another is to ask the new sibling to help your eldest with his younger siblings and vice versa. In that way, your child reaps the benefits of a helper without being displaced.

The youngest child has to adjust to losing a lot of the special considerations and attention he is accustomed to when a new sibling arrives. Whether the youngest in the family is twelve months or twelve years old, parents and older siblings tend to be more charmed by the accomplishments and more protective of the "baby." Family members exclaim over a three-year-old child's ability to hop on one foot or count to ten when he is the youngest. Such accomplishments lose their power to impress when a twelve-month-old is wowing everyone by taking his first step or saying his first word. Don't forget to laugh at your lastborn child's jokes and applaud his accomplishments until he is able to step out of the spotlight without feeling neglected.

The Only Girl or Only Boy

Acquiring a sibling of the same sex erases some of the special advantages of being the only girl or only boy in the family. If the females left it to their dad and brother to mow the lawn, wash the car, and pursue other "guy" activities, their time to enjoy one another's exclusive company ends when a new boy arrives on the scene. As you are going out of your way to make a new child feel welcome, be sensitive to your other children. Try to ease them out of their old roles gradually by being sure they continue to get some one-on-one time to preserve your special father/son, father/daughter, mother/son, or mother/daughter relationship.

CHAPTER 19

Special Needs Siblings

C hildren typically have some intense, conflicting emotions about growing up with a special needs sibling: love, worry, compassion, empathy, and loyalty, as well as frustration, embarrassment, anger, and guilt. In the battle for attention from their exhausted parents, some children act out. Some admit defeat and withdraw. Some children embrace their parents' cause and work alongside of them as helpmates and surrogate caregivers. Late in life, adult children usually become primary caregivers. It's not surprising that the siblings of a special needs child have some special needs of their own.

Tangled Emotions

Echoes of Frank's story are heard again and again during interviews with the siblings of handicapped children.

> *I was three when my sister Francie was born, but I didn't actually find out what was wrong with her until I was ten. When I was little, all I knew was that she had to have a lot of surgeries. I kept expecting her to get well soon, like Mom said she would. I still remember the day I gave up hope things would ever change. I was seven years old. We had planned to go to the museum. But Francie got sick, and we had to cancel. When I started to cry, Mom said it was no big deal; we'd go some other time. Mom sounded so nonchalant that I*

just lost it. I started sobbing and yelling, "Francie ruins everything! I wish she'd never been born!" The minute the words were out of my mouth, I felt horrible. I knew Francie couldn't help being sick. But everything always revolved around her. Sometimes I wished I were sick so Mom and Dad would pay attention to me.

Francie stayed pretty healthy after her third heart surgery, but as soon as she was well, her mental retardation became a big issue. Mom was determined for Francie to learn to read and learn enough about life so she wouldn't end up in an institution. Mom tutored her after school every day and on weekends. I had to teach Francie things. I spent months teaching her how to put on her socks. Sometimes it all felt like too much. I wanted to yell, "Face facts, Mom! Francie is never going to read or be normal! But at least I could have a halfway normal life if you could think about something else for two minutes." I hated myself for feeling that way. I have always loved Francie. She is the kindest, gentlest person I know.

The hardest part was having Francie with me wherever I went. I lost a lot of friends because of her. I hated having to sit with Francie on the school bus. One day I told her to stay put, and I went to the back to sit with my friends so I could be with them but could still keep an eye on her. More kids got on at each stop, but no one would sit by Francie. I wanted to scream at them all. Francie kept turning around and giving me these pleading looks, and I felt like a traitor. I hated that people treated her like some kind of freak, and I hated that Francie looked and acted like one. Sometimes I fantasized that Mom and Dad would give up and just stick her in an institution. I hated myself for such thoughts. Now my parents are getting older, and I expect Francie will move in with me in the next couple of years. It will be hard on my wife and kids, but going to an institution would devastate Francie. I would never let that happen.

 **Essential**

> If a special needs child is so demanding that you can't spare ten minutes a day for one-on-one time with your other youngsters, carve out five uninterrupted minutes for them. Remain emotionally present and engaged so they have a chance to connect with you in a meaningful way.

Life Lessons for Siblings

If you are devoting a lot of energy to a special needs child, you probably won't have time to overindulge your other youngsters. This can have some character-building benefits.

- When you require your other children to put their own wishes and desires on hold while you attend to their special needs sibling, they learn to tolerate frustration and delay gratification.
- When you call on your other children to help with household chores because you are busy with their special needs sibling, they develop self-discipline and learn basic home management skills.
- When you give your other children the responsibility of watching over their special needs sibling and keeping him out of harm's way, they learn to size up situations, make thoughtful decisions, and behave responsibly.
- Because you really need your other children's help and consider their assistance valuable and important, their self-worth is affirmed, which boosts healthy self-esteem.
- Because your other children see their special needs sibling's challenges and struggles, they develop compassion for people with mental and physical disabilities.

When you are reeling from the demands of a special needs child, it is easy to feel guilty about being unable to give your other children as much time as they would like, especially if they complain. It is important to remember that some jealousy and resentment are to be expected whenever a child wants your attention and you are otherwise occupied. Even if you were at your child's beck and call twenty-three hours and fifty-five minutes per day, he can still be expected to lodge noisy objections when you ask him to entertain himself while you disappear into the bathroom or try to conduct a five-minute telephone conversation. That being said, be sure that you do spend time with your other children each day and that you are fully engaged when you do. They need attention, too, and giving it can provide a much-needed break from other worries. How much attention they need depends on the child's personality and age. There is no objective way to know whether siblings are being emotionally neglected. If they are, some disturbed family dynamics are likely to develop. They can be easy for overwhelmed parents to miss, so it is important to remain alert for signs of trouble.

Disturbed Family Dynamics

Even a healthy child with a difficult temperament can usurp so much time and energy that the entire family revolves around him. If you have a youngster with a chronic illness or a serious mental or physical disability, your workload and worries are likely to be extremely taxing. Trips to diagnosticians, doctors, and assorted therapists can make it hard or impossible to settle into a predictable daily routine, which would provide your other children with some much-needed structure and security. Even if you can afford to hire assistant caregivers and chauffeurs to help care for your other youngsters, your concerns about the health and development of a special needs child can easily become all-consuming. This can cause you to neglect his siblings. It is likely that children who act out, withdraw, or behave like little adults need more time and attention.

Sibling Acting Out

Some children find that the only way to get the attention of a busy, overwhelmed parent is to act out. It can be hard for parents to understand that a youngster would prefer being yelled at or even being punished to being ignored and forgotten. But for most children, that is the case. As long as they are misbehaving or having academic problems, their parents express concern and get involved in trying to help them. This reassures them that their parents really do care. When the youngsters are not creating scenes and misbehaving, their parents seem to forget they are alive. If children feel resentful because a sibling is being lavished with so much attention, by tormenting him they can punish him as well as their parents. Beware of punishing your children when they misbehave since this reinforces their tendency to seek attention by misbehaving. Instead, simply describe the problem and the solution—for example, "You made your brother cry. It looks like you need help controlling yourself"—and send your child to time-out. The recommended guidelines are one minute in time-out for each year, so that a four-year-old spends four minutes in time-out and a ten-year-old spends ten minutes. Afterward, provide a simple instruction, such as "You can come out of your room now. You are not to tease your brother." Then help him find a positive activity. If you are still busy with his sibling, look for a way to give your other child some attention, too. Perhaps you can invite him to play nearby so you can talk to him while you work.

Alert!

When your children are playing nicely or doing as they're told, do you hesitate to say anything so as not to have to deal with them? But do you reliably get involved when they are arguing or misbehaving? If so, you are teaching them to act out to get attention.

Sibling Withdrawal

Other children respond to a difficult sibling and overwhelmed parents by withdrawing into a protective shell. They spend exorbitant amounts of time holed up in their bedrooms. During elementary and high school, some find surrogate families. They take to hanging out at the home of a special friend, relative, or neighbor. But for others, the pattern of withdrawal becomes a lifelong pattern. If your special needs child is very disruptive and makes it impossible for your other children to play in the center of the house, beware of suggesting they play in their rooms. This encourages them to withdraw. If other family members can't converse without constant interruptions, it is critical to find a way to stave them off for at least one short period of time each day. Figuring out how to wrangle some time alone may not be easy. If you can hire a teenager to come over for thirty minutes per day, perhaps you can take your other children for a walk around the block. Stagger the bedtimes so you and your other children can spend time together in the morning, before your special needs child awakens. During the time you carve out for your other children, let them bring up problems they are having with their sibling if they wish, but avoid bringing them up yourself. Otherwise, if you spend all of the time discussing their special needs sibling, it will be as if he is still with you. None of you will get a break.

Overburdened Siblings

One way to care for your special needs child and interact with his siblings at the same time is to encourage your other children to work alongside you. But beware of overburdening them. In some households, toddlers happily run to fetch a diaper and do other small chores when their parents need help. As children mature, toddlers are assigned increasingly taxing chores. By age eight or nine, they participate as equals in the never-ending stream of household duties. They begin by keeping their eye on their sibling for a few minutes at age two while their parent steps into the bathroom. By middle school, they assume major caregiving responsibilities. Such children may end up serving as their parents' confidantes as well. The danger is that by being so focused on taking care of their parents and siblings children may come to base their entire identity on caring for others. Such parentified children are likely to continue their childhood pattern into adulthood by marrying someone who is an alcoholic or unstable and devoting themselves to their needy spouse. For helping parentified children, see Chapter 18.

Nurturing Your Other Children

When a child is putting the finishing touches on a tall tower of blocks he has spent an hour constructing and an older sibling suddenly walks over and knocks them down, most parents reprimand the perpetrator and comfort the victim. "That's not nice," they say. "You need to apologize to your brother." But when the perpetrator is retarded, autistic, or has another mental disorder, exhausted parents may press the victimized child to accept being harassed without complaint. "It's not your brother's fault. He didn't mean to upset you. He doesn't understand what he's doing. He just wants to play with you and doesn't know how," they may explain. They may try to solve the problem by suggesting the healthy sibling find another toy. While your other children may in fact need help understanding why a special needs sibling has behaved so inappropriately, it is unreasonable to expect them to be saints and destructive to encourage them to be martyrs. Nor is it healthy for them to have to suppress their feelings about being victimized and tormented.

 *Fact*

Children with a special needs brother or sister receive less parental attention, compassion, and understanding than youngsters without such a difficult sibling. Yet, because their homes tend to be more stressful, they are likely to need more emotional support.

Some parents actually teach the siblings that they must accept being slapped, kicked, punched, and put up with having their possessions destroyed by a special needs brother or sister who "doesn't know any better" and "can't help himself." Beware of blaming the victim by saying things such as "How many times do I have to tell you? If you don't want your brother to break your toys, you shouldn't leave them where he can get hold of them!" Although it is understandable that you will at times expect siblings of a handicapped youngster to behave in a more mature fashion than is reasonable, it is unreasonable to expect them to behave like adults. Having to be constantly on their guard may be a necessity, but children in this situation deserve compassion, not reprimands. They need help to ward off unprovoked attacks.

A better approach is to comfort the victim, who deserves understanding and compassion as much as his handicapped sibling. It might mean a lot to a sibling to hear you say, "I'm so sorry that your brother destroyed your tower! I can't even punish him because he wouldn't understand what he did wrong." Then, try to find a solution to prevent future problems. Can he play with his blocks in a playpen so he can be in the living room with the rest of the family and not have to worry about having his creations destroyed? Can he play with his toys while his sibling naps or is at school so that he won't be harassed? Even if you don't come up with any workable solutions, simply discussing some possibilities communicates that his need to be protected is real and important. To that end, you might say, "We need to figure out a way to keep your brother from getting hold of your toys when you are playing with them. I can try to keep him with me in the kitchen while you build towers, but if he runs out before I can catch him, he might knock them down. Do you have any suggestions?"

Alert!

> It can be hard for children to understand why a sibling with a subtle problem, such as a learning disability, is lavished with attention while they are ignored. Some children in this situation conclude their parent prefers their sibling. Problems with competition and rivalry increase.

One autistic boy delighted in pulling his sister's hair. He seemed to enjoy her shouts and the frenzy as her parents raced to her side and tried to pry off his fingers while she screamed and sobbed. Finally, her parents suggested she respond in kind by pulling her brother's hair. He immediately screamed and let her go. That one painful lesson was enough; he never again pulled his sister's hair. Similarly, some biters have been cured of biting when their victims bite them back; some hitters have been cured of hitting when their victims hit them back. This could only be a solution for a meek sibling who can also benefit from learning that there are exceptional circumstances in which it is all right for him to try to protect himself from physical harm. Allowing an aggressive child to fight a sibling will create more problems. Biting, pulling hair, and hitting are dangerous in any case. Such last-resort measures should be very, very carefully supervised to ensure no one is injured. Even lion cubs swipe at one another when certain behavioral lines are crossed, but they back off at the first yelp so as not to injure one another. These must not be considered everyday solutions for humans, and suggesting or even condoning these behaviors could be considered child abuse and carry serious legal consequences.

If you do use such extreme measures, don't confuse the lesson by proceeding to comfort the perpetrator-turned-victim. Instead, reinforce the lesson by comforting the sibling who was attacked first.

Information Gaps and Overloads

Children need information about their sibling's disability, but exactly how much they can tolerate depends on their personalities. Too many parents make decisions about what to share and what not to reveal based on their own needs to discharge tension by talking or by avoiding troubling subjects. They use their children as confidantes and burden them with more information than they can comfortably handle, or they say nothing because they cannot admit the seriousness of their special needs child's condition or because discussing it is too painful. Some parents justify not discussing a sibling's problems because they want their other children to focus on his strengths, not his limitations.

They fear that acknowledging his handicaps, deficits, and problems will become self-fulfilling prophecies. Although this sounds sensible enough, you don't help your other children by keeping them in the dark about their sibling's problems. Imagine a six-year-old daughter asking for help putting on her shoes and being told she is a big girl and needs to put them on herself, even as the mother stoops to help her ten-year-old put on his shoes. Unless the daughter has been told that her brother is mentally retarded and cannot handle such chores himself, she may conclude that her mother simply favors the brother.

Minimizing the seriousness of a sibling's condition can be equally detrimental. Some parents explain that a sibling is delayed and needs extra help to catch up. They don't add that he has Down syndrome and will never be able to lead a normal life. As a consequence, the other children keep waiting for their sibling to become normal. Some parents explain that an autistic sibling overreacts, but not that he can't control his violent outbursts. They explain that a chronically ill sibling has a problem with his kidneys, but not that he undergoes dialysis while the other children are at school. Some parents say that a sibling has problems with his vision, but not that an operation has been scheduled which might prevent him from going blind. When children aren't given enough details to grasp what is happening, they may imagine the worst or think that nothing is being done to help him.

 Essential

> Some children prefer not to know too many details about their sibling's condition. They feel upset by discussions of serious problems they can do nothing about. Offer to answer your child's questions, be truthful when you respond, but avoid giving more information than your child can benefit from hearing.

Too many siblings suffer needlessly because they don't understand why their sibling acts as he does or why their parent is so solicitous of him. They fill in the information gap with far-fetched fantasies about what is wrong. Some youngsters fear that they will catch their sibling's epilepsy, cancer, or cystic fibrosis, even though these conditions are not contagious. After witnessing the shocking deterioration of an autistic sibling, some children have spent years terrified that they might suddenly lose their own mental faculties. They need to be told important aspects of their sibling's disorder so they understand that it develops during the first few years of life. Many children blame themselves for their sibling's problems, thinking his mental or physical condition is due to their own ungenerous thoughts or hurtful actions. Seeing their parent's anxiety and solicitousness of a schizophrenic child can lead the siblings to conclude that he is going to keel over and die at any moment, even though he is perfectly healthy. They may believe their dying sibling has a minor ailment, and his death comes as a traumatic shock. They spend years feeling guilty because they never said goodbye, apologized for some small misdeed, or told him they loved him.

Too often, children learn about their sibling's condition when a peer sneers, "Your brother isn't delayed; he's retarded and won't ever catch up. Everybody knows that." Your child should not have to hear tragic news from someone outside the family. One girl was told by her cousin, "My mom said kids with your brother's problem never ever get well; they just get sicker and sicker and then die." Children from past generations have been able to access massive amounts of information through overheard telephone conversations, late night parental discussions, and journals. Now little computer experts also access logs of online chats, folders of deleted e-mail messages, and histories of their parents' visits to Web sites to find out what is going on. If you think you are protecting your children by not giving them the facts, you are probably wrong!

Sibling Social Relationships

Besides needing to know the truth so that they can understand what is going on at home, your children need to figure out what to say when friends and total strangers ask questions, stare, and make comments. Many youngsters are caught between their love for and loyalty toward their sibling and embarrassment about being seen with a sibling who draws so much curious attention. Tweens and young teens tend to be hypersensitive about not fitting in, and having a special needs sibling can be a humiliation for them. They don't understand that people see their sibling as separate and believe that judgments about a handi-capped sibling will reflect on them. Some children don't want their friends to see them with their handicapped sibling for fear of being ostracized and shunned. Yet despite their embarrassment, they may be fiercely protective and ready to fight anyone who makes a dispar-aging comment or even asks a simple, curiosity-driven question about their sibling. Role-playing with a parent can help youngsters explore different ways to respond. One child couldn't stand for adults to gawk at his paraplegic brother. He played himself, and his parent pretended to gawk at the child's brother. As they experimented with what the child would like to say and what he could say without being too disre-spectful, he came up with a solution he loved. He communicated his displeasure and helped his brother feel less self-conscious by saying loudly, "Pretend you don't notice they are staring at you. They don't mean to be rude. They're handicapped by their terrible manners."

Question?

How can counseling help my other children?
Talking to a counselor can help them work through some of their negative feelings, learn better coping skills, and develop a more loving attitude toward a special needs sibling. Hence, your special needs child stands to benefit from their gains.

Youngsters need to be able to discuss their feelings about their sib-ling, his condition, and the effect of his problems on their lives. Doing so can lessen their stress and problems with acting out. If you cannot tolerate hearing your children express their negative emotions so they can process them, ask a trusted relative or friend to serve as a sounding board. Take them to see a psychologist or counselor. Workshops designed for youngsters with a special needs sibling can be especially helpful. "Sibshops" give children a chance to connect with others who share their worries, problems, dilemmas, and concerns. See ✐*www. thearc.com* to find a Sibshop near you, or organize one yourself. The book *Sibshops,* which is listed in Appendix A: Resources for Parents, contains all the information you need to start and run a program.

Expectations for Siblings

Most children are able to adjust to having a stricter set of rules and firmer consequences than their special needs sibling. They can understand why they are being reprimanded for talking during a movie, even as their sibling with Tourette's syndrome continues shouting and cursing. But it is important to guard against expecting too much from your other children. A child who is noticeably different draws a lot of attention, and some parents feel a bit ashamed of their "defective" child. Being seen with two misbehaving youngsters feels overly humiliating; so they are overly strict with their other youngster, demanding perfect behavior at all times. Outings become exercises in ill will and frustration or grim obedience. Some parents pressure the siblings of a learning disabled child to be perfect students, as if hoping to make up for the sibling's poor grades. Your other children can end up feeling like failures if they cannot achieve accordingly to your overblown expectations.

 *Essential*

Beware of using a handicapped child as a yardstick for assessing the capabilities of your other youngsters. Parents with a mentally retarded child tend to regard their other youngsters as brighter and more capable than they are.

Beware of comparing your children. Your two-year-old is apt to seem like a genius because he is already walking and talking, and a mentally handicapped sibling didn't start doing either until he was four. But your two-year-old may actually be a bit slower than average. He might benefit from special help to keep his development on track. It is also important to avoid burdening your other children with too many expectations. Some parents deal with the disappointing reality that their handicapped child is never going to attend college, continue in the family business, or produce grandchildren by pouring all of their hopes and dreams into their other children or worse—into their only other child. Many youngsters in this situation rebel or sever relationships with parents who refuse to accept their goals. Some children dedicate their lives to living their parent's dreams and end up feeling unfulfilled and unhappy.

Help for Troubled Siblings

Some agencies train workers and offer low-cost or even no-cost respite services to parents of special needs children. A respite may be even more important for your other children than for you. Many summer camps provide unique opportunities for children with specific problems, such as learning disabilities, retardation, and diabetes, to have fun and connect with youngsters who share similar struggles. The American Camping Association maintains a searchable database to locate a camp by location or area of interest. You can also use the search terms "camp" and your child's disability, such as "cystic fibrosis" or "Down syndrome," to find a camp via the Internet. Other parents who have a child with the same problem are also good bets for babysitting help. The best way to meet some is to join a relevant organization. To find one, search the name of your child's disability, the word "organization," and perhaps the name of your state.

CHAPTER 20

Healing Adult Sibling Relationships

By the time siblings are grown, their patterns of relating are entrenched. Yet as children change, they need their relationships to change as well. To move forward, they may have to relinquish their customary roles and resolve some childhood issues. A rift can develop if one child refuses to change. Fortunately, the call of family is strong, and most siblings eventually reconcile. As the central tie that binds your children to one another, don't underestimate your ability to help them pick up the strands of their tattered relationship and knit a better one.

The Child Inside

Destructive family dynamics can keep children caught in negative sibling relationships. Many children are less tolerant of being mistreated by their siblings after they have been on their own for a time. This was the case for Krystin.

> After being away at college, I started having problems getting along with my brother and sister. I enjoy them one-on-one, but when the three of us are together, I often end up feeling attacked. I end up feeling defensive. I have a master's degree in business and make a six-figure income as a vice president of a corporation. When I go back home, I am no longer Krystin. I'm Krysty to my parents, and my brother and sister call me by my childhood nickname, Crusty. They treat me like

the awkward little space cadet they knew way back when, and I end up shrinking into the shadows and feeling pretty miserable. Hardly a holiday goes by when they don't make some reference to an incident that happened when I was nine going on ten. Mom asked me what I wanted for my birthday. I said I wanted some mules. I meant that I wanted fancy slippers, a pair of mules, but I said I wanted mules. Everyone of course thought that was hysterically funny. We weren't allowed to call one another stupid, but my brother got the message across by braying like a mule anytime I said something he considered uncool. If I said something that sounded strange, my sister would say, "Crusty is probably talking about those mules she wanted for her birthday." That was twenty years ago, but the family joke lives on.

When I'm opening a birthday present, someone in my family inevitably says, "Sorry it's only a sweater, Crusty. I know you really wanted a mule." Everyone roars. Mom used to tell me to ignore people who teased me and they'd quit, but my brother and sister never let up. I think they continue to bring up the mule joke out of jealousy. They're really saying, "Others may think you're a hotshot, but we know you're just a silly little girl." If I were more self-confident, maybe I would be able to laugh with them. But I'm basically insecure, and for that I have my brother and sister to thank. If they were trying to make me feel like an idiot, they succeeded. Sometimes I drink before going there for dinner, and I drink while I'm there. I know why they call alcohol "liquid courage." But then if I speak up, they have an excuse to ignore me. "Don't mind Crusty," they say. "She's a bit drunk."

Alert!

Why is a son so adept at pushing his sister's buttons? Probably because he helped install them! If your son knows her hot buttons, he needs to stop pushing them. Purposely upsetting someone is cruel.

Adult Sibling Conflicts

Competitive struggles often intensify when one child fulfills his parents' dreams. If a sibling decides not to marry or have children, he may nevertheless feel jealous of the child who gave you the grandchildren for which you longed. Similarly, the child who isn't fulfilling his parent's expectations by working in a high-status job may feel jealous of a sibling who is. Children want to please themselves, and they need to if they are to feel satisfied with their lives. But they don't want to disappoint their parents. You can lessen competitiveness by affirming and honoring your children's decisions. Let them know that although they didn't go the route you had hoped, you are pleased that they have taken control of their lives and made good choices. If they are making bad ones, express concern about what they are doing to themselves. Comparing them to more successful siblings is as damaging as when they were young.

If your adult children squabble, you probably feel as concerned about their relationships as ever. If you don't, perhaps you should. The call of family may be strong, but many children decide to ignore it. They decide the pain just isn't worth it. Because adult children are less dependent on their parents and siblings, they are likely to be less tolerant of disrespectful treatment. "Total strangers treat me better," many adults say. But it is one thing to want to be treated like an adult and another to act like one. When a sibling snipes, interrupts, or engages in other noxious behaviors, he is probably just behaving as he always has. If a child lets you know he is upset about inconsiderate treatment, suggest that he discuss the problem with his sibling. But the solution is to avoid taking the bait. Many people focus on the need for others to change instead of recognizing that they need to change. When their feelings are hurt, they need to say, "That hurts my feelings," rather than escalating hostilities by responding with a similarly contentious comment. Help your child by role-playing new ways to respond in order to build a more satisfying relationship.

As children launch careers and families, many become aware of personal issues that are holding them back. Many come to realize that a sibling was a principal player in creating their complexes and insecurities. They may conclude that their poor self-esteem is the result of a sibling's constant criticism. Perhaps their substance abuse problem started when a sibling introduced them to alcohol or drugs. Although the problem is now theirs alone and they must find a way to conquer it, many children decide that a destructive relationship needs to change. Adult children may appear to be overreacting when they object to being interrupted or made fun of at the dinner table or when they are encouraged to have a glass of wine with dinner. But they are probably reacting strongly because the issue is important to them. They want to create a healthier, more satisfying relationship. Encourage siblings to take one another's requests for more considerate treatment seriously. Encourage upset siblings to bring up issues when they can be given proper consideration. Creating a scene as Dad is carving the turkey on Thanksgiving is not the proper time. Yet, it might be better to set dinner aside and retire to the living room for a serious discussion. Many families find it all too easy to ignore problems that really need to be addressed.

 Essential

Respectful treatment is as important for adult sibling as for youngsters. The difference is that youngsters who felt mistreated can't leave the nest. As adults they can, and many do. To keep your family together, address and help siblings resolve their conflicts. Don't sweep problems under the rug.

Reliving the Past

Never is the power of family as evident as when grown children return home after they have lived on their own for a time. Some adults are not very self-aware and do not realize that they revert to their old behaviors when they are back with their families. But those who are more self-aware are often amazed to discover that they act much as they did during childhood. Whether they have continued to have regular contact with their parents and siblings or have just returned after a decade-long absence may not make a difference. Even though the setting is different, the faces of the key players are transformed by wrinkles and sags, and the cast has expanded to include in-laws, nieces, and nephews, old roles are hard to shed.

Despite making a concerted effort to play a different part in the family drama, many adult siblings find themselves forgetting the new lines they rehearsed and were determined to deliver. Soon they are mouthing the ones they memorized years or even decades earlier. As a consequence, some adult siblings have little enthusiasm for family gatherings. Some dread them, and some avoid them altogether even though they very much want to go. They love their siblings and want to be close, but they cannot bear to have their siblings treat them like a ten-year-old instead of a full-fledged adult. Worse, they can't bear feeling and acting like a juvenile.

Scientists are making progress in understanding why so many adult siblings revert to their former old roles and behave like children when they are together. The familiar settings, faces, and words activate neural pathways in the brain, triggering memories of the past. The emotions associated with the memories are located in an area of the brain called the amygdala. When the amygdala is triggered, it responds immediately. The frontal lobes, which are responsible for rational thought, planning, and judgment, are also activated. But they take longer to size up the situation and formulate an appropriate response. This had survival value for our ancestors. When they encountered danger, a neural pathway was triggered so they could respond instantly. They might freeze, fight, or flee before they could even pinpoint the danger and make a conscious decision about what to do. Abused children commonly raise their hands to protect their heads whenever there is an unexpected sound or movement, even though no one is present who might hurt them. Painful memories also trigger siblings to react as they did in the past. They freeze by going blank, feel the urge to argue, or feel inclined to flee, even though there is no current danger.

 **Fact**

> A sibling's familiar words or gesture reactivates old memories, caus-
> ing adult children to reexperience past events as if they were hap-
> pening in the present. A traumatized sibling may not yell or cry, but
> the feelings evoked may nevertheless be very unpleasant.

Changing Family Dynamics

When one part of a machine undergoes a small change, the entire
system is affected and doesn't work as well or as efficiently. If the
change is large, the machine breaks down and ceases to function. To get it working again, the faulty part must be replaced, or
other components must be adjusted to accommodate its absence.
Therapist Virginia Satir applied the concepts developed by systems
analysts to human systems. She noted that when one family member starts to change the others are thrown off balance. The family
doesn't function as well as in the past. But human systems can heal
themselves. When a change occurs, family members react by trying
to eliminate it so they can function normally. This is true even if the
changes are positive. For instance, the family described at the beginning of this chapter had a set pattern for producing good times. The
siblings made jokes about their sister, their parents laughed, and the
sister grinned and tried to bear it. When she began objecting to jokes
made at her expense, the other family members tried to adjust to
eliminate the change and preserve the status quo. "You're overreacting," the father said. "Lighten up," the mother protested. The sister
drank to try to eliminate the change in herself. She hoped her mellow
mood would enable her to tolerate the fun poked at her. That plan
backfired because the alcohol lessened her inhibitions; she had a fit
when her siblings teased her. But this change proved an easier adjustment for her family. "Don't mind her," they said when their daughter
made a scene. "She's had too much to drink." The family could continue much as they had before.

Satir pointed out that unlike machines, which no longer function when one part stops working altogether, human systems can change. But then everyone else must also change. If a child refuses to accept being the butt of jokes as in the past, the siblings must find other ways to start the good times rolling so the family can have fun. That sounds simple enough, but if joking at someone else's expense served other important functions as well, the project of changing becomes very challenging. Perhaps jokes that characterize one adult child as a silly little girl perpetuate the family myth that a sibling is the golden boy who is destined for success. (See Chapter 18 for more information on sibling roles.) In that case, family members must find another way to keep the myth intact. Otherwise, they must change how they view him. That could be painful. It might also challenge other values and cherished beliefs. Perhaps the myth was driven by the idea that a man should work and women should stay home and raise children. If so, changing this belief could strain the parents' relationship if they had a traditional marriage. Small changes in a living system often set other changes in motion, which set off still more. That the end results can be dramatic and unpredictable is a basic tenet of chaos theory—an apt and fitting name. Many alienated children actually help to preserve the family system by leaving rather than pushing for a change. With the squeaky wheel gone, everyone feels sad, but they are able to carry on much as they did before.

Alert!

Family therapists who use a systems approach help individual members find ways to get their needs met while helping the family as a whole get its needs met. If a family rift threatens, look for a licensed marriage and family therapist (LMFT).

Changing roles defined by birth order is especially hard. When one child changes, the other children must change accordingly. This may mean they need to revise some basic aspects of their personalities. (See Chapter 11 for more information on birth order.) A common problem is that the youngest tires of being treated like the inconsequential baby, or older children become frustrated because he won't get serious and continues having tantrums. The oldest child often tires of being the responsible one who must make all of the decisions and follow up to see that things get done correctly. Others tire of the firstborn's perfectionism and insistence that everything be done his way. The middle children may tire of having to constantly serve as the peacemakers when family members are at odds, while their own opinions and beliefs are discounted. The others tire of dealing with a maverick who challenges their values and doesn't conform.

The Family Business

Birth order issues commonly cause problems when siblings try to work together in a family business. Sometimes the problem is that they tire of their customary roles and try to change them. Sometimes it's because birth order has helped to form the children's personalities, and they step into roles in the business that are inconsistent with their natures. The family puts a middle child or the lastborn in charge because of his special skills and expertise, but the eldest child can only function as a leader. A middle child toppled the empire of one of the biggest family businesses in the world when he insisted on a role consistent with his personality, according to the article "Sib Styles of the Rich and Famous," which appeared on *Psychology Today*'s Web site. The four Bass brothers of Fort Worth, Texas began having difficulties when one of the middle sons, in typical maverick middle-child fashion, wanted his share of the family assets so he could run his own business in his own way. Not surprisingly, the eldest brother was in charge. In typical firstborn fashion, he was apparently determined to continue as leader. His brother's request was denied. In typical middle-child fashion, the sibling negotiated a solution and signed on to work in the business their father had built from his oil-based fortune. But his maverick personality remained a problem, and tensions quickly heated up. The brothers limped along for eleven years before the middle brother put his foot down. By then, the sibling relationships had deteriorated to the point that each of the four brothers took a share of the $4 billion fortune and went their separate ways. A decade later they continued to work in the same family skyscraper and live in nearby mansions but were rarely seen in the same room. Had the middle son been allowed to be himself at the outset, perhaps the family could have preserved the bulk of its fortune and their relationships. But for that to have happened, the firstborn would have had to relinquish some control. Could the family have survived such a change, or might it have hastened their split? There is no way to know.

It is important to consider personality, birth order, and sibling dynamics when starting a family business or adding your children to your company's payroll. But no matter how good your initial decisions, your children will change as the years go by and they continue to mature. Because small individual changes will reverberate through both your business and your family, the natural response is for siblings to try to keep one another from changing. With so much at stake both personally and financially, it may seem sensible to try to hold the chaos in check. But in the end, for both families and businesses to function, they must accomodate the needs of the people involved. In addition to weekly staff meetings to tend to the details of the business, hold weekly family meetings to attend to the details of your family, as described in Chapter 5. If the staff meetings bog down, call in a business consultant. If the family meeting bogs down, call in a family psychologist.

Alert!

Family businesses routinely employ accountants and lawyers to help siblings handle financial and legal matters. Siblings' need for a therapist to help them handle their relationships is often more pressing. Infighting causes many family businesses to flounder or fail.

Adult Sibling No-nos

Trying to control recalcitrant children by threatening punishments and meting out consequences commonly backfires when the siblings are young. When they are adults, about all you can do is threaten to cut off your child financially or exclude him from family get-togethers. Siding with one sibling against another is more likely to escalate problems than solve them, just as when they were young. (See Chapter 7 for more information on sibling spats.) However, you don't help your children by being a silent observer as they battle, and you do need to help them get along. Although they need to be respectful of you, don't solve their problems by pleading for mercy ("This will be the death of me") or putting them on guilt trips ("All I want is for my children to get along"). Let your children know that it is to everyone's benefit to be close. But just as when they were young, telling them to be close doesn't teach them how.

Beware of trying to solve problems by carrying messages back and forth. When they were young, you might have taken the accused aside and said, "Don't tease your brother anymore. It hurts his feelings." But even adult siblings go behind their parents' backs and say things such as "I heard you've been whining to Mom." If a child finds out that you betrayed his confidences, he may lose trust and stop confiding in you; so your relationship is harmed as well.

 **Question?**

My son hurt his sister's feelings. Can I discuss it with him?
Be careful not to betray her confidence. Tell your daughter that you want to talk to your son about the matter. If she objects, she may need to work it out on her own.

If a child confides in you about a problem he is having with his siblings but won't allow you to discuss it with them, there are still some things you can do. Accept that he is upset even if you think he is "making a mountain out of a molehill." By belittling him for being overly sensitive, you uphold his sibling's right to hurt him. Instead, try to empathize with him. You can also help him empathize with his sibling by sharing your impressions of why he might have done something hurtful. But beware of criticizing your other children in the process. Even adults behave like children as often as not. If you say, "I think your siblings are jealous," he may turn around and say, "Mom says you're just jealous." Be tactful so that your words don't come back to haunt you. Instead, you might say, "I think your siblings see how successful you are, and they sometimes wish they had made different choices. I wish they wouldn't compare themselves to you."

Improving Adult Relationships

It may be beneficial to share the positive comments your children have made about one another. If competitive squabbles are causing hard feelings, it can help to say, "Your brother told me he really admires you for having such a fine wife and lovely children." If you think a conflict stems from a simple misunderstanding, you might give your views on the matter, but be careful to convey your own impressions to avoid sounding accusatory. "To me, it sounded very harsh and critical when you said your brother should solve his financial problems by getting out and finding a decent paying job. He loves what he does. I think his problem is more complicated than you made it sound." Even if it seems that two siblings are purposely being unkind to a third, you could be wrong. They may tease him to try to lighten his mood and help him feel better and not realize they are hurting him. Teasing can also be a way of saying, "We know you're not beaten—you're a man and can still take a little kidding." But if their efforts to cheer and strengthen their sibling are backfiring, they need a new strategy.

The first step to getting warring adult siblings onto a positive track is to urge them to treat one another with empathy, respect, and compassion, just as you do with little children. When you confront an adult child, you may encounter some very childish responses. As you ask one child to treat another in a more considerate manner, remember that the child you are confronting needs to be treated with respect as well. Be ready to respond with tact, and avoid backing your child into a corner.

- **"I didn't do anything."** If your child is unaware of having done or said anything to hurt his sibling, give some specific examples of comments or actions that have disturbed you. Avoid accusatory statements. Instead of saying, "You always cut him off when he tries to speak," talk about yourself: "I am uncomfortable when your brother is interrupted and doesn't get to finish what he was saying."

- **"He started it."** Express regret that your child also feels that he has been hurt by his sibling. Suggest that he discuss the matter with his brother. Emphasize your hope that in the meantime your child will not escalate tensions by succumbing to the temptation to be sarcastic, interrupt, or be otherwise disrespectful to avenge the insults.

- **"You're making a big deal out of nothing. I was just kidding."** Beware of responding by trying to prove that your child's behavior toward his sibling was uncalled for or hurtful. Building a case for your position by listing the many hurtful things your child has said and done may impair your own relationship with your child. Letting him know that his sibling has complained reinforces the notion that you are taking sides. Simply state that whether or not you are making a big deal out of nothing that you are uncomfortable with remarks that strike you as unkind. Ask your child to be considerate of you.

- **"He's too sensitive."** You can probably agree and admit that this is exactly why you are concerned: His sibling is too sensitive to handle certain comments and topics of conversation. Ask your child to avoid doing and saying potentially upsetting things. If his sibling is sensitive about many subjects, figuring out how to avoid them could be difficult, but ask your child to give it his best shot.

- **"You always take his side."** Ask what you are doing to give that impression, apologize for hurting his feelings, promise to try to avoid doing so in the future, and let him know the things about him you find special. Many adult children are as jealous of their parents' affection as when they were younger. Reassurance of your love and approval may lessen their desire to compete, so they stop trying to make themselves look good at one another's expense.

- **"Everything I do is wrong."** This type of passive-aggressive remark may be designed to punish you for having broached an uncomfortable subject. Nevertheless, the underlying feeling of being unable to please you may be very real. Either way, some serious ego-stroking may be in order. Once your child is reassured that you appreciate him, he may be more considerate of his sibling.

Truces and Treaties

Crises have been defined as opportunities in disguise, and this seems to be especially true for adult siblings. Just as youngsters commonly react by putting their differences on hold and uniting (see Chapter 9), alienated adult siblings usually reach across the decades and emotional divides when a family member is in serious trouble. The intimacy that develops as they give and receive support during a divorce, medical problem, financial difficulty, career setback, or legal entanglement brings them together. The question is what happens when the crisis ends. Sometimes newly reunited siblings discover that time has brought some changes that make them better relationship material. They are more personally secure, so they are less critical and judgmental. Their deeper appreciation for family causes them to handle one another with more care. (See Chapter 4.) Past disputes may have been put in their proper perspective. They may not even be able to remember the issue that lead to a rift. However, many siblings need to revisit the past to clear up old grudges so they can move forward. Like other negative emotions, grudges serve a protective function. Remembering how one has been hurt by a sibling in the past reminds people that they could be hurt again. An explanation as to why cruel words were said or damaging actions were taken may be required, along with an apology.

A Legacy for Adult Siblings

Too often, squabbles ensue as siblings try to fathom the wishes of a parent who is dying or deceased. In the absence of clear instructions, children proceed based on what they would want for themselves. It is understandable that life-and-death issues create vicious sibling struggles and permanent rifts. Such arguments can turn into nasty court battles that divest the estate of its assets and children of the benefits of one another's support. Communicating a desire to be taken off life support when you are ailing or explaining how you want your estate divided during a deathbed chat invites confusion. Let your children know of your wishes in advance. Set aside time for some serious conversations to allay their concerns and smooth ruffled feathers well in advance. Back up your wishes with a legal living will. Living wills are free and are available on request from most hospitals. Splurge on an attorney to have your binding last will and testament properly drawn up and filed. Label your silver, china, and special mementoes so everyone knows who is meant to inherit what, as well as when. Some children swoop in after their mother dies, strip the house, and leave the sibling who has been living there with a barren house.

Alert!

If you don't want to risk upsetting your children by telling them how your estate is to be divided, get a will that will stand up in court. Leave personal letters explaining your decisions to deter them from challenging the will.

Sometimes greed is the overriding factor as children-turned-vultures descend to pick over their parent's estate. But often the unsavory battles are driven by other painful emotions. The adult child who never felt close to his parent wants mementoes that help him feel close. The child who only felt loved when he was given money or material goods needs tangible proof of the parental love that he can't feel any other way. Wealthier children may expect the estate to be divided evenly and may be upset when they receive less. The child who was counting on an inheritance to sustain him in his old age may sue when everything goes to the family business, which is controlled by a sibling. In addition to making arrangements for the division of your estate, it is important to communicate your reasons.

Siblings are major providers of care to one another during old age. By doing what you can to prevent dissention, you help ensure your children's well-being after you are gone. Just as people tend to focus on the legal and financial aspects of a family business and neglect the relationship issues, parents tend to do the same when creating wills. In addition to the financial and legal instructions for your estate, consider leaving instructions about how to improve their relationship. Express the wish that alienated children will reconcile and continue to nurture one another. In the end, a loving family is the greatest inheritance of all.

Resources for Parents

Bank, Stephen P., and Michael D. Kahn. *The Sibling Bond*. New York: Basic Books, 1997.

Bennett, William J. *The Children's Book of Heroes*. New York, NY: 1997.

Bennett, William J. *The Children's Treasury of Virtues*. New York, NY: 1995.

Bradford, Sarah. *America's Queen: The Life of Jacqueline Kennedy Onassis*. New York, NY: Penguin Books, 2000.

Brody, Gene. *Sibling Relationships: Their Causes and Consequences*. Norwood, NJ: Ablex. 1996.

Cartmell, Todd. *Keep the Siblings, Lose the Rivalry*. Grand Rapids, MI: Zondervan Publishers, 2003.
Tips for parenting siblings based on Christian principles.

Conley, Dalton. *The Pecking Order: Which Siblings Succeed and Why*. New York: Pantheon Books, 2004.

Dunn, Judy. *From One Child to Two*. New York: Fawcett Columbine, 1995.
Includes many useful ideas about how to prepare your toddler or preschool child for the arrival of a new baby. However, the suggestions for handling sibling relationships after the baby arrives are more likely to provoke conflict than to reduce it.

Dunn, Judy, and Robert Plomin. *Separate Lives: Why Siblings Are So Different*. New York: HarperCollins Publishers, 1990.
Analyzes research investigations on sibling differences and similarities.

Eldridge, Sherrie. *Twenty Things Adopted Kids Wish Their Adoptive Parents Knew*. New York, NY: Dell Publishing, 1999.
Describes adopted children's unspoken concerns and shows adoptive parents how to help children cope with their feelings of fear, abandonment, and shame.

Goldenthal, Peter. *Why Can't We Get Along? Healing Adult Sibling Relationships*. New York: John Wiley and Sons, 2002.
Advice for overcoming the past, breaking sibling stalemates, and mending rifts.

Harris, Thomas A. *I'm OK—You're OK*, New York, NY: Avon Books, 1967.

Keck, Gregory, and Regina Kupecky. *Adopting the Hurt Child: Hope for Families with Special-Needs Kids*. Colorado Springs, CO: Pinon Press, 1998.
Suggestions for helping adoptive children overcome their past hurts and adjust to a stable, loving family.

Keirsey, David and Bates, Marilyn. *Please Understand Me*. Del Mar, CA: Prometheus Nemesis Book Company, 1978.
Unravel the mystery of personality by learning about temperament typing.

Kubler-Ross, Elisabeth. *On Death and Dying.* New York: Scribner, 1997.
Learn to recognize the stages of grief after the loss of a loved one.

Leman, Kevin. *The Birth Order Book: Why You Are the Way You Are.* New York: Dell Publishing Company, 1985.

Levitt, Jo Ann, Marjory Levitt, and Joel Levitt. *Sibling Revelry: 8 Steps to Successful Adult Sibling Relationships.* New York: Dell Publishing, 2001.

Lorenz, Lynn. *The Multiples Manual: Preparing and Caring for Twins or Triplets.* Justmultiples.com, LLC publication, 2004.

Marta, Suzy Yehl. *Healing the Hurt, Restoring the Hope.* New York: St. Martin's Press, 2003.
A book for parents guiding children and teens through divorce, death, and crisis.

Mayle, Peter. *Where Did I Come From?* Secaucus, NJ: Carol Publishing, 2000.

McHugh, Mary. *Special Siblings: Growing Up with Someone with a Disability,* rev. ed. Baltimore, MD: Brookes Publishing Company, 2002.

Meyer, Donald J., and Patricia F. Vadasy. *Sibshops: Workshops for Siblings of Children with Special Needs.* Fredericksburg, VA: Paul H. Brookes Publishing Company, 1994.
Information for starting and running a sibshop.

Randolph, Theresa A. *How to Go On Living When Someone You Love Dies.* Lexington, MA: Lexington Books, 1988.
An insightful book on loss and survival.

Ruskai Melina, Lois. *Raising Adopted Children.* New York: HarperCollins Publishers, 1998.
Addresses the most pressing adoption issues of today and provides practical, reassuring advice for parents and professionals.

Safer, Jeanne. *The Normal One: Life with a Difficult or Damaged Sibling.* New York: Dell Publishing, 2002.

Samalin, Nancy. *Loving Each One Best: A Caring and Practical Approach to Raising Siblings.* New York: Bantam Books, 1997.
Standard advice for lessening competition, rivalry, and arguments.

Sandmaier, Marian. *Original Kin: The Search for Connection among Adult Sisters and Brothers.* New York: Penguin Group, 1995.

Schlaerth, Katherine. *Raising a Large Family.* New York: Macmillan Publishing Company, 1991.
Advice for parents with three or more children.

Schulz, Charles. *Siblings (Should Never Be in the Same Family).* New York: HarperCollins Publishers, 1997.
The famous cartoonist captures the essence of sibling squabbles as Lucy and Linus play out their roles of know-it-all older sister and pesky little brother.

Sifford, Darrell. *The Only Child: Being One, Loving One, Understanding One, Raising One.* New York, NY: Harper & Row, 1989.

Shimberg, Elaine Fantle. *Blending Families: A Guide for Parents, Stepparents, Grandparents and Everyone Building a Successful New Family.* New York: Berkley, 1999.

Siegel, Bryna, and Stuart Silverstein. *What About Me? Growing Up with a Developmentally Disabled Sibling.* Cambridge, MA: Perseus Publishing, 1994.

Sonna, Linda. *Early-Start Potty Training*. New York: McGraw Hill, 2005.
Learn how to potty train infants, babies, toddlers, and older children who are having trouble progressing.

Sonna, Linda. *The Everything Tween Book*. Avon, MA: Adams Media Corporation, 2003.

Tannen, Deborah. *You Just Don't Understand: Women and Men in Conversation*. New York, NY: HarperCollins Publishers, 2001.

Todd, Marvin D. *Linked for Life: How Siblings Affect Our Lives*. New York: Citadel Press, 2001.
A look at sibling relationships across the life span.

U.S. Department of Health and Human Services. *How Many Children Were Adopted in 2000 and 2001?* Washington, DC: National Adoption Information Clearinghouse, 2004.

U.S. Department of Health and Human Services. *The AFCARS Report: Preliminary FY 2001 Estimates as of 2003*. Washington, DC: 2003.

Welsh, Martha. *Holding Time: How to Eliminate Conflict, Temper Tantrums, and Sibling Rivalry and Raise Happy, Loving, and Successful Children*. New York: Simon and Schuster, 1988.
Useful techniques for parents who want to deal more effectively with typical child-rearing and sibling problems.

White, Carolyn. *The Seven Common Sins of Parenting an Only Child*. San Francisco, CA: Jossey-Bass, 2004.
Expert advice on parenting only children.

Wiehe, Vernon R. *What Parents Need to Know About Sibling Abuse*. Springville, UT: Bonneville Books, 2002.

Organizations

Adult Sibling Grief.com

For help coping with the loss of an adult sibling.

www.adultsiblinggrief.com

American Adoption Congress

PO Box 52730, Washington, DC 20015

www.americanadoptioncongress.org

ARC's Sibling Support Project

For siblings of special needs children

www.thearc.org/siblingsupport

Big Brothers/Big Sisters Organization

230 North 13th St., Philadelphia, PA 19107

www.bbbsa.org

(215) 567-7000

National Foster Parents Association

7512 Stanich Ave. #6, Gig Harbor, WA 98335

(800) 557-5238

National Organization of Mothers of Twins Clubs, Inc.

www.nomotc.org

North American Council on Adoptable Children
970 Raymond Avenue, St. Paul, MN 55114
(651) 644-3036

Stepfamily Association of America
✐*www.saafamilies.org*
(800) 735-0329

The Compassionate Friends
An organization to assist bereaved siblings and other family members following the death of a child of any age.
✐*www.compassionatefriends.org*
(877) 969-0010

Index

A

Abuse, sibling roles and, 228–229, 230

Acting out, by siblings of special needs child, 242–243

Activities, letting siblings find own favorite, 109–110, 112–114, 119–120

Adoption, 197–211
of baby, 205–206
discussing with natural children, 197–200
family roles and, 203–205, 236–238
favoritism and, 66
of group of siblings, 206–208
list of famous adoptees, 208–211
preparing for, 200–202

Adult siblings, 253–267
childhood roles of, 253–256
family business and, 260–261
family dynamics and, 256–260
inheritance and, 266–267
parents' remarriage and, 162–163
parents' roles and, 262–263
ways to improve relationships among, 263–264

Age of children
favoritism and, 69–70
resolving disputes and, 82–83

Aggression
channeling of, 47
entertainment and, 45
punishment and, 93
toward baby, 30, 32–33, 35, 37
see also Fighting

America's Queen: The Life of Jacqueline Kennedy Onassis (Bradford), 119

Anger
empathy and, 23–24
teaching to handle appropriately, 18–19
see also Aggression

Antisocial behavior, 8

Apologies, for teasing, 87, 90–91, 93

Arguing, 101–102

Austin, Tracy and John, 116

B

Babies
adoption of, 205–206
aggression toward, 30, 32–33, 35, 37

Babies—*coninued*
    jealousy of, 35–35
    as playmates, 36
    preparing sibling for, 29–32
    preschoolers and, 36–39
    from remarriage, 167
Bank, L., 7, 8
Bank, Stephen O., 9
Bass brothers, 260–261
Bates, Marilyn, 68
Bennett, William, 45
Bickering, *see* Arguing; Fighting
Big Brothers/Big Sisters
    of America, 150
Birth order, 125–137
    adult roles and, 259–260
    family business and, 260–261
    firstborn child, 128–130
    intellectual stimulation and, 6
    lastborn child, 135–137
    middle children, 130–134
    personality and, 125–128
Birth Order Book, The
    (Leman), 130, 132
Bonding
    of multiples, 191–193
    with stepchildren, 165–166
Boys
    of elementary school
        age, 47–48
    emotional intelligence
        and, 17–18
    stepparents and, 165
Bradford, Sarah, 119

Brain functions, adult
    siblings' behavior
    patterns and, 257–258
Brontë sisters, 112
Bullying, 226, 229–233
Burraston, B., 8
Business enterprise, 260–261

C

Campbell, Joseph, 164
Car, handling arguments
    in, 102, 105–106
Carter, Billy, 117
Children's Book of Heroes,
    The (Bennett), 45
Children's Treasury of Virtues,
    The (Bennett), 45
China, 141–142
Collectivist worldview, 175–177
Comparisons, favoritism
    and, 65–67
Compassion, teaching of, 25–26
Compatibility, myth
    of need for, 1–2
Competition
    cooperation versus, 97–102
    at elementary school age, 48
    games and, 100–102
    multiples and, 191
    myth of benefits of, 9–11
    with siblings who
        excel, 109–117
    with superstar
        siblings, 117–123
    see also Favoritism

Conley, Dalton, 177
Connery, Sean, 117
Consequences, different
    from punishment, 230
Cooperation
    competition versus, 97–102
    games and, 106–107
    team-building and trust
        and, 102–106
Counseling
    for adult family, 259, 261
    after death, 218, 220
    after suicide, 223
    favoritism and, 68–69
    for siblings of special
        needs child, 250–251
Crises, cooperation
    during, 97–99

D

Darwin, Charles, xiv
Death, of sibling, 213–223
    emotional toll on
        family of, 213–216
    mourning and, 218–220
    stages of grief, 216–218
    by suicide, 221–223
Depression
    after suicide, 221
    symptoms of, in infants,
        206
Disabilities, *see* Special
    needs children
Divorce, *see* Stepfamilies
Douglas, Eric and Michael, 119

Downey, Douglas, 148
Dunn, Judy, 3–4, 190

E

Elementary-school age
    children, 45–48
Emotional abuse, 228
Emotional intelligence, 17–20
Empathy, teaching of, 21–24
*Everything Tween
    Book, The*, 181
Exchange student
    programs, 150
"Excuse me," teaching
    use of, 20–21

F

Fairness, 70–72
Family-centered values
    handling fighting with, 78–83
    large families and, 173–177
    lessons of, 81–82
"Family court," inappropriate
    for resolving quarrels, 74–77
Family meetings, 51–61
    benefits of, 52–54
    creative problem-
        solving in, 58–60
    having fun at, 61
    making decisions in, 60–61
    methods of running, 55–58
    preparing for, 54–55
    for stepfamilies, 161–162
Faultfinding, 101

Favoritism, 63–72
  age of children and, 69–70
  comparisons and, 65–67
  individuality and, 71–72
  personality and, 67–69
  stepchildren and, 166
  taking sides and, 21, 38, 262, 265
Feelings, list of children's important, 17–18
Fighting, 73–83
  handling with family-centered values, 78–83
  handling with "family court," 74–77
  handling with family meeting, 51–61
  in large families, 180
  see also Aggression
Firstborn children
  adoption and, 203–204
  change of role in family, 236–237
  overindulgence of, 144–145
  parenting of, 128–130
Foreign exchange student programs, 150
Foster children, 151–154
  family roles and, 236–238
  parentified child and, 235
Fraternal twins, 186
Freud, Sigmund, xiii, 5, 32
From One Child to Two (Dunn), 190

G

Galton, Francis, 3–4
Games
  competitive, 100–102
  cooperative, 106–107
Genes, myth of behavior determined by, 3–5
Gifts, for baby's sibling, 33–34
Girls
  as bossy sisters, 46
  of elementary school age, 45–47
  emotional intelligence and, 17–18
Goodship, Daphne, 187
Grief, stages of, 216–218
Groups of siblings, adopting of, 206–208

H

Handicapped children, *see* Special needs children
Harris, Thomas, 227
Herbert, Barbara, 187
Heredity, myth of behavior determined by, 3–5
Hilary and Jackie (film), 114

I

I'm OK—You're Okay (Harris), 227
"I'm sorry," teaching use of, 20–21
Identical twins, 186–187

Individualistic worldview,
    173–175, 176
Individuality
    acknowledging of, 71–72
    favoritism and, 71–72
Inheritances, 266–267
Intellectual stimulation, 6

J

Jackson Five, 111–112
Jealousy
    of baby, 32–35
    of special needs sibling, 242
Joking
    about adult siblings,
        253–254, 258–259
    teasing versus, 88–89

K

Kahn, Michael D., 9
Keirsey, David, 68
Kennedy family, 111
Kidman, Antonia and
    Nicole, 117
Kindness, random acts of, 26–27
Kubler-Ross, Elizabeth, 216

L

Large families, 169–182
    advantages of, 169–172
    disadvantages of, 177–178
    family-centered values
        and, 173–177
    tips for raising, 178–182

Lastborn children
    change of role in family,
        236–237
    in large families, 178
    parenting of, 135–137
Leadership skills, 46–47
Leman, Kevin, 130, 132
*Linked for Life: How Our Siblings
    Affect Our Lives* (Todd), xv
Living wills, 266
Lorenz, Lynn, 194

M

Manipulation, emotional,
    73–74, 77
Materialism, fighting
    and, 73–78, 80–82
Mayle, Peter, 31
McCartney, Paul, 115
McEnroe, John, 115–116
Melina, Lois Ruskai, 205
Mentors, as surrogate
    siblings, 150
Middle children, 130–134, 178
Minor children, remarriage
    and, 160–162
Mission statement,
    for family, 105
Mothers of Multiples
    Society, 190
Mourning, *see* Death, of sibling
Multiples, *see* Twins
    and multiples
Multiples Manual, The
    (Lorenz), 194

My Flesh and Blood (film), 202
Myths, about siblings, 1–13

N

National Organization of
Mothers of Twins, 190

O

Onassis, Jacqueline
Kennedy, 119
On Death and Dying
(Kubler-Ross), 216
Only Child, The
(Sifford), 142–143
Only Child Magazine, 141, 143
Only children, 139–155
adoption and, 203–204
change of role in
family, 236, 238
increasing number of
families with, 141–142
list of famous, 154–155
misconceptions
about, 142–145
myth of siblings
unimportance to,
5–8
parental expectations
and, 147–148
social skills and, 148–150
surrogate siblings for,
149–154
tips for raising, 145–147

P

Parentified children,
234–235, 244–245
Parents, as role models, 15–17
Patterson, G. R., 7
*Pecking Order, Which
Siblings Succeed and
Why, The* (Conley), 177
Persecutor role, 229–233
Personality
birth order and, 125–137
favoritism and, 67–69
Physical abuse, 228
"Please," teaching use of, 20–21
Please Understand Me
(Keirsey and Bates), 68
Plomin, Robert, 3–4
Potty training, 31
Preschoolers
baby and, 36–39, 43–45
family meeting and, 59
Privileges
fairness and, 70–71
family-centered values
and, 80–83
Problem-solving skills, 95
Psychologists, xiv–xv.
See also Counseling
Punishment, different from
consequences, 230

R

Radziwill, Lee, 119
Raising Adopted Children
(Melina), 205

Raising a Large Family (Schlaerth), xv, 173
Random acts of kindness, 26–27
Regression, of toddler, 34–35
Relationships, nurturing of good, 15–27
  by boosting emotional intelligence, 17–20
  with parents as role models, 15–17
  with random acts of kindness, 26–27
  by teaching compassion, 25–26
  by teaching empathy, 21–24
  by teaching respect, 20–21
Relatives, favoritism of, 68
Remarriage, *see* Stepfamilies
Respect, teaching of, 20–21
Respite, for family of special needs child, 252
Responsibilities, for children fairness and, 70–71
  family-centered values and, 80–83
  myth of harm of, 11–13
Rituals, shared family identity and, 103
Rivalry, myth of innate, 8–9. *See also* Competition; Favoritism
Roberts, Eric and Julia, 114–115
Role models, parents as, 15–17
Roles, of siblings, 225–238
  abuse and, 228–229, 230
  bad influences and, 233

birth order and, 236–238
children in parents' roles, 234–235
creation of, 226–228
how to handle, 229–233
Rules, importance to children, 94

S

Salvanes, Kjell, 6
Satir, Virginia, 258–259
Schlaerth, Katherine, xv, 173
Science of Good and Evil: Why People Cheat, Gossip, Share, and Follow the Golden Rule (Shermer), xv, 9–10
Self-image
  competition and, 100–101
  large families and, 172
  teasing and, 85–87
Separate Lives: Why Siblings Are So Different (Dunn and Plomin), 3–4, 67
Seven Common Sins of Parenting an Only Child, The (White), 141
Sexual abuse, 228–229
Sharing, 38–39
Shermer, Michael, xv, 9–10
Sibling Bond, The (Bank and Kahn), 9
Sibling Relationships: Their Causes and Consequences (Patterson and Bank), 7

Siblings, myths about, 1–13
Siblings Day Foundation, 103
Sibshops, 251
Siding with one child,
    see Favoritism
Sifford, Darrell, 142–143
Skpe.com, 171
Smith, Kirsten, 143
Social stimulation, 7
Special needs children, 239–252
    character-building
        benefits of, 241–242
    effect on family
        dynamics, 242–245
    emotional toll on
        family of, 239–241
    expectations of siblings
        of, 251–252
    helping siblings know what
        to say about, 249–251
    nurturing siblings of,
        245–247
    parentified children
        and, 235, 244–245
    respite for family of, 252
    what to tell siblings
        about, 247–249
Spirituality, 44–45
Squabbles, see Fighting
Stepfamilies, 157–167
    divorce and remarriage
        issues and, 157–163
    family roles and, 236–238
    new baby in, 167
    new family identity
        and, 163–167

Suicide, of sibling, 221–223
Superstar siblings
    competition with, 117–120
    list of famous, 120–123
Surrogate siblings, 149–154
Sweet, Corrine, 114
Symbols, shared family
    identity and, 103

T

Talking stick, 58
Tannen, Deborah, 46–47
Tattling, 94–95
Team-building, 102–103
Teasing, 85–94
    adult siblings and, 263
    differs from joking, 88–89
    self-image and, 85–87
    ways to handle, 89–94
Teenagers, 48–50
Telephone calls, 171
Time-outs, for teasing, 89–90
Todd, Marvin D., xv
Toddlers
    clashes with babies and
        preschoolers, 36–39
    jealousy of, 32–34
    preparing for new
        baby, 30–32
    regression by, 34–35
Triplets, 186
Trust, building, 104–106
Twins and multiples, 183–196
    biology of, 186–187
    competition and, 191

increasing number of, 185
list of notable parents
    of twins, 196
list of notable twins, 195–196
preparing for, 187–191
psychological and identity
    development of, 191–195
treating as individuals, 72

V

Values, *see* Family-
    centered values
Victim role, 229–233

W

*Where Did I Come
    From?* (Mayle), 31
White, Carolyn, 141, 143
Williams, Serena and
    Venus, 115–116
Withdrawal, by siblings of
    special needs child, 243–244
Wright, Orville and Wilbur, 114

Y

You Just Don't Understand
    (Tannen), 46–47
Young adults, 43, 50

THE EVERYTHING®
PARENT'S GUIDES SERIES

The Everything® Parent's Guide to
Raising a Successful Child

ISBN: 1-59337-043-1

The Everything® Parent's Guide to
Children with Autism

ISBN: 1-59337-041-5

The Everything® Parent's Guide to
Children with Bipolar Disorder

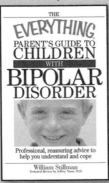

ISBN: 1-59337-446-1

The Everything® Parent's Guide to
Children with Dyslexia

ISBN: 1-59337-135-7

Expert Advice for Parents in Need of Answers

All titles are trade paperback, 6" x 9", $14.95

The Everything® Parent's Guide to Children with Asperger's Syndrome

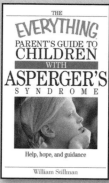

ISBN: 1-59337-153-5

The Everything® Parent's Guide to Tantrums

ISBN: 1-59337-321-X

The Everything® Parent's Guide to the Overweight Child

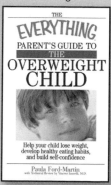

ISBN: 1-59337-311-2

The Everything® Parent's Guide to Children with ADD/ADHD

ISBN: 1-59337-308-2

Available wherever books are sold.
Or call 1-800-289-0963 or visit us at *www.everything.com*

The Everything® Parent's Guide to
Positive Discipline

ISBN: 1-58062-978-4

The Everything® Parent's Guide to
the Strong-Willed Child

ISBN: 1-59337-381-3

The Everything® Parent's Guide to
Raising Siblings

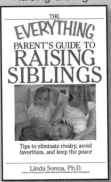

ISBN: 1-59337-537-9

The Everything® Parent's Guide to
Children and Divorce

ISBN: 1-59337-418-6

The Everything® Parent's Guide to
Raising Boys

ISBN: 1-59337-587-5

Available wherever books are sold.
Or call 1-800-289-0963 or visit us at www.everything.com